HEY, MAC, WHERE YA BEEN?

Also by HENRY BERRY

Semper Fi, Mac
Make the Kaiser Dance
A Baseball Century
The Boston Red Sox

HEY, MAC, WHERE YA BEEN?

LIVING MEMORIES OF THE U.S. MARINES IN THE KOREAN WAR

HENRY BERRY

ST. MARTIN'S PRESS
New York

Editor: Jared Kieling

LIBRARY OF CONGRESS
Library of Congress Cataloging-in-Publication Data

Berry, Henry.
  Hey, Mac, where ya been? / by Henry Berry.
    p.   cm.
  ISBN 0-312-01772-3 : $22.95
  1. Korean War, 1950-1953—Personal narratives, American.
2. Veterans—United States—Interviews.   3. Interviews—United
States.   I. Title.
DS921.6.B44 1988
951.9'042—dc19   87-36705
                                                                      CIP

First Edition

10 9 8 7 6 5 4 3 2 1

This book is dedicated to my long-suffering wife, Diana. She is not only the center of my house, but a superb typist and an ardent editor. She is also my severest critic, which makes her invaluable. Without her sunny disposition and willingness to "turn to" I would not have completed *Hey, Mac, Where Ya Been?*

Contents

Acknowledgments

As in my previous books, *Make the Kaiser Dance* and *Semper Fi, Mac*, I could have never produced *Hey, Mac, Where Ya Been?* without the Korean war veterans who freely shared their memories of that conflict. This book is not a formal history of that war; it is a collection of the personal memories of some of the men who fought the war. All but six of these men were United States Marines. Three of the others were members of the U.S. Navy, while the remaining three were members of the U.S. Army.

Here is a list of the men who helped me immensely. I thank them profusely.

Matt Akers, John Babyak, Floyd Baker, William Barber, Alpha Bowser, James Brady, Morgan Brainard, Robert Bryant, Dick Burke, John Burke, John Cassidy, Bud Cain, Saul Cavallaro, Bill Churchman, Larry Close, Bart Delashment, Joe DeMarco, Emil Dlwgash, Dudley Donnelly, Ross Dwyer, Gordon Gayle, Lou Gorman, Arden Grover, Bob Hall, Ernie Hargett, John Hitt, Jerry Hotchkiss, Bob Houston, Paul Ilyinsky, Victor Krulak, Hank Litvin, Paul Martin, Ed McCabe, Joe McDermott, Rudy Miller, Bob Mosher, Dick Munro, Raymond Murray, Dick Newman, F. Brooke Nihart, Jack Orth, Pat Patterson, John Petromzio, Harold Roise, John Saddic, Joe Saluzzi, Peter Santella, Lemuel Shepherd, Edwin Simmons, Austin Stack, Bob Smith, William Thrash, Tom Troy, Ted Williams, Ray Wilson, Chuck Woodson, George Ziegler

Additional thanks go to all the people who helped me locate these men throughout the country. As I had personal knowledge of only three of these veterans when I started the book, I practically had to start from scratch. It was not easy.

Above all, I am grateful to everyone connected with the Marine Corps Museum in Washington, D.C. The jobs done at the Museum by Brigadier General Edward Simmons (USMC-ret.) and Colonel Brooke Nihart (USMC-ret.) were outstanding. Anyone who is interested in Marine Corps history, particularly if they wore the green skivvies, owes himself a visit to the Museum.

Darien, Connecticut
January, 1988

Hey, Mac,

Where Ya Been?

It was just a chance meeting with a former Marine in Buffalo, New York. His name was McCarthy. I cannot recall his first name, but I clearly remember what was on his mind.

"Jeez," he said, "I went into the Corps in late 1950, spent several months in the States, and was sent to Korea. I was on the lines about three months when I was hit in both legs by mortar fire. I ended up spending almost a year in the U.S. Naval Hospital at St. Albans, New York, after which I received a medical discharge. Then I returned to Buffalo, where I spent some time trying to figure out what to do with the rest of my life.

"Well, I was walking down Delaware Avenue in Buffalo when I ran into a friend of my dad's. He'd known my father since they were kids together. I remember going to Buffalo Bisons ball games with my dad, this guy, and his son.

"Anyway, the fellow comes over to me, sticks out his hand, and says, 'Hey, Mac, Where Ya Been?'

"The sonofabitch didn't even know I'd been fighting a war!"

Introduction

It was mid-June, 1984. The bookstores were busily ringing up last-minute Fathers' Day purchases. I was quite busy at a one-day book-signing chore at a Waldenbooks store in a Stamford, Connecticut, mall. The book I was promoting was *Semper Fi, Mac: Living Memories of the U.S. Marines in World War II*.

A man approached me, proudly claiming that he had been a Marine, but in Korea, not in World War II. He wanted to know how I felt about his war.

"Hey, mate," he said, "when ya going to do a book on Korea? All we got is 'M*A*S*H,' ya know, the TV show where the guy dresses up like a broad. Oh, it isn't a bad show, lotta laughs, but there was a hell of a lot more to Korea than 'M*A*S*H,' you know what I mean?"

Indeed I did. I'd heard the same thing from other Korean veterans all over the country who were also unhappy about their lot.

First they'd tell me how they didn't mind not having a parade when they came home, and how they weren't greatly upset at their country's forgetting about them so fast. What seemed to be bothering them was very colorfully described by two former Marines who joined me later that afternoon.

"Look," one said, "we don't mind those Vietnam vets squawking. God knows they've been abused, but what about us? At least they built a wall for them down in Washington."

"Yeah," said the other man, "they didn't even build an outhouse for us!"

"That's right. And those guys from 'Nam never froze their nuts off in thirty-degrees-below-zero weather, with the wind cutting through you like a knife."

"You better believe it, and they didn't have a million fuckin' Chinamen coming at 'em either."

On and on they went, talking a mile a minute as they described Inchon, Seoul, and the Chosin. Both of these men had gone to Korea in 1950—one was with the Brigade at Pusan and the other had landed at Inchon—and had come back early in '51. It was not that they were bitter, but they most certainly questioned their place in history, or lack of it.

At any rate, they had persuaded me to write a book on the Marine veterans of the Korean War.

I had recently seen an announcement in *Leatherneck* magazine about a reunion in Washington, D.C., of a group called the Chosin, an organization of former Marines who had been in North Korea when the Chinese entered Truman's "police action" with a vengeance. It seemed an ideal place to start interviewing, and it was.

Over the next three years I visited with some sixty Korean War veterans. The bulk of these men were from the line companies: riflemen, cannoneers, forward observers, machine gunners, mortarmen, radiomen, tankers, and naval corpsmen.

Five of these men served with the 1st Marine Air Wing in Korea, while another was a naval doctor at the Chosin Reservoir.

One of these men was awarded the Congressional Medal of Honor, and four others earned the Navy Cross. There were three Silver Stars among my participants, and five Bronze Stars. One of my Marine pilots was shot down and spent some two years as a prisoner of the Reds. There were twenty-four Purple Hearts among those men. Three of these Marines were hit three times each.

One thing I strove to accomplish, and at which I feel I succeeded, was coverage of the Marines in Korea after MacArthur was fired. This period is even less known to the American public than the first part of the war.

As my interviews continued, I noticed similarities to two of my earlier books, *Make the Kaiser Dance* and *Semper Fi, Mac,* but I also noticed differences.

The experience of combat does not change. As I assume it was with George Washington's troops, there is always the utter confusion of battle and that little slice of hell that each man experiences. The overall strategies of a fight are for the history books. A frightened twenty-year-old Marine's efforts to stay alive and do the best job he can was what was of utmost importance to these men.

Then there were references to the Marines who did not come back. Why did one shell only wound the man I'd be talking to, and blow the head off his buddy? This seems to loom larger and larger in the minds of combat veterans as they grow older.

The differences from other conflicts seem to be in the nature of the war. These differences became more pronounced after China entered the war.

In 1918 it was simple—beat the German Army and go home. It was the same way in the Pacific with the Japanese in World War II. But what do you tell a man on the lines when he knows there is no chance of winning the war? There was no thought of losing it, but they surely were not going to get the Communists to surrender, either.

It then became a case of putting your year in and getting home in one piece. There was no antiwar talk from any of these men, and certainly no pro-communist feeling. Many of these Marines alluded to the fact that they would just as soon not have been in Korea, but there was little bitterness about it.

One problem that I ran into was the possibility of creating the illusion that the 1st Marine Division and the 1st Marine Air Wing fought the war alone.

This is not so.

Because this is a book concerned with Marine Korean War veterans, it is the Marines' war I am writing about. This does not mean that I am in any way slighting the hundreds of thousands of other American soldiers who fought in Korea. I salute them. They walked in the same moccasins as the Marines.

Finally, there was one more reason why I wanted to do this book. A few years ago, while I was watching "M*A*S*H" on television, my younger daughter came in with two of her twenty-year-old friends. I asked them if they knew what program I was watching.

"Sure," one said, "'M*A*S*H.'"

"Where is it taking place?"

"Vietnam," she answered.

They call Korea "the forgotten war."

They're right.

Between the Wars

In the summer of 1945, the American people were worn thin. A decade of dreary Depression, followed by the long, drawn-out struggle with the Axis Powers, had left the country exhausted.

True, the World War II days had seen full employment, but a normal life is impossible when a nation's sons are spread around the world, many of them facing extreme danger.

Then came Hiroshima, and a tremendous sigh of relief was heard from coast to coast. The invasion of Japan that was scheduled for November of 1945 was scrapped. Perhaps only those who had actually fought the Japanese really knew what a catastrophe had been averted. A nation that was still being governed by medieval militarists would not have been conquered easily. American servicemen who had gone to Japan at the war's end belittle the theory that Japan was finished.

"We went in near Kyushu," one told me. "They had enough artillery there to destroy the entire invasion force. That business of the Japanese Army being all through is nonsense. That war could have gone on for years."

He was probably right. At any event, the invasion would undoubtedly have been the costliest bloodletting in American history.

But this had all gone by the boards. The war that had cost America more than 400,000 lives was history. "Lucky Strike Green" had gone to war and was not coming back, but millions of American servicemen were, and they could not come home quickly enough to satisfy the American people.

There was a film in 1946 entitled *Adventure*. Its slogan was "Ga-

5

ble's Back and Garson's Got Him." It pretty much sums up the feelings of the American people. They wanted to forget war as quickly as possible and get on with their lives.

But was this to be possible? The ink was barely dry on the document signed in Tokyo Bay when it became obvious that coexisting with the Soviets on this planet was to be no piece of cake. The agreements made by Stalin at Yalta seemed to be more and more those of a flimflam man.

On March 5, 1946, Winston Churchill received an honorary degree from Westminster College in Fulton, Missouri. His commencement address was vintage Churchill.

"Beware," he said, "time may be short. From Stettin in the Baltic to Trieste in the Adriatic, an Iron Curtain has descended across the continent."

Thus, the man who, above all, symbolized the opposition to Adolf Hitler was now warning the free world against the tyranny of Communism.

Also on the dais when Churchill spoke was the President of the United States. Truman took Churchill very seriously indeed. The next year, when his Secretary of State, George Marshall, suggested the United States give tremendous aid to the remaining democracies in Europe, he backed Marshall to the hilt. This was the beginning of the eminently successful Marshall Plan.

Then, when Queen Frederika of Greece asked Marshall to send her a top combat general to aid her country in its civil war with the Communists, once again he agreed. Marshall sent her General James A. Van Fleet, who was later to lead the 8th Army in Korea longer than any other general. Van Fleet is justifiably proud that Greece was able to defeat the Communists without the help of a single American rifleman.

Another test of Truman's resolve came in June 1948. This was when the Soviets attempted to starve their World War II Allies out of Berlin. Located in the heart of East Germany, Berlin had been divided up among its occupying powers, Russia, France, England, and the United States.

The Soviet game plan was to control all land traffic going to and from the city. The hoped-for result was that the British, French, and Americans would move out of Berlin and leave it to the Russians.

The Allies countered with what aviation experts have called a technical miracle. They created the Berlin Airlift. This meant supplying Berlin by daily flights into the city. From June 1948 until September 1949, British and American airplanes brought 2 million tons of supplies into Berlin. This was too much for the Soviets. They gave up by May 1949.

When the voters went to the polls in November of 1948, if they wanted to see proof of Truman's ability to stand up to the Communists, all they had to do was look at Berlin. The blockade was going full blast then, but the airlift was making the Russians look sillier every day. Communist power in Europe went only as far as wherever the Red Army was in control. The Marshall Plan was in full swing. The threat of a Europe dominated by the Kremlin seemed dead.

Halfway around the world, in Asia, things were different. Although the United States had poured in millions of dollars to boost Chiang Kai-shek and his Nationalist Chinese forces, it had all gone for naught. The Generalissimo's government was rotten to the core. The only way the Nationalist government could be saved would involve a full-scale invasion of China. As the next few years would show, even this might not have worked. Anyway, it was never seriously considered.

In the meantime, prosperity in the United States was booming. In 1948, employment had reached an all-time high; 61,296,000 Americans were working. Harry Truman won his stunning victory over Thomas Dewey. Dorothy Parker had called Dewey "the little man on the top of the wedding cake," and this probably cost Dewey a million votes. The year 1949 saw a nasty little dip in the economy, but America was truly the richest nation in the world. Things were expected to get better in 1950, and they did.

The magic of television had arrived. By January of 1950, there were 4 million sets in the United States. If you didn't own one, you could always go to any halfway decent bar, drink a few drafts, and watch a ball game. Baseball was good on TV, but football was better. The National Football League, for years a distant second to the college game, was to be the main recipient of television's largesse. In effect, the magic screen made the NFL.

Hollywood would be hurt by the growing success of the TV craze, but not fatally. It was, however, to change.

During the third week of June 1950, two films were playing on Broadway that were of entirely different styles. One, *Father of the*

Bride, was the traditional family fare, featuring a young actress whose beauty was spellbindingly pure. Her name was Elizabeth Taylor.

The second was entitled *The Asphalt Jungle.* It was a hard-nosed tale of crime and greed. The film was partially stolen by another young actress, playing the part of a waitress. Hers was not a starring role, but her ability to walk across the screen was something not easily forgotten. In the case of Taylor, it was her face you remembered. In the waitress's case, it was her backside. Her name was Marilyn Monroe. More and more films would be made emphasizing the derriere, and fewer family-type movies.

Such things as Hollywood and television play a big part in a country's culture, but there is, of course, a great deal more. The music of 1950 was still the sound of the Big Bands, Bing Crosby, and Frank Sinatra, but a new style was just over the horizon. It was called rock 'n' roll, and it was to make the youth of America forget all the other music in the land.

Some changes in the social structure were just beginning. Women were tired of getting a college degree and ending up as some man's secretary. Blacks felt the same way. The only white-collar job they could land was in a company's mailroom. And if they lived in the South, they'd go to and from work in the back of a bus. All this would change, but in 1950 the feminist and civil rights movements were just starting.

However, all was not progress. One of the most devastating scourges in American history had raised its ugly head. By 1950, organized crime had realized there was a fortune to be made in narcotics. The drug problem would not reach epidemic proportions until the next decade, but it was growing fast.

There was one thing, however, that was not to change. To the large majority of the American people, *communism* was a dirty word. People who may have thought Karl Marx was one of Groucho's brothers, and had no idea what communism was all about, did know that they didn't like it. When Joseph R. McCarthy, the junior senator from Wisconsin, waved a piece of paper at an audience in Wheeling, West Virginia, the crowd cheered. The paper was purported to list the names of fifty-seven card-carrying Communists in the U.S. State Department. It was as phony as the World War II combat record that "Tailgunner Joe" used to help him get elected to the Senate.

McCarthy's days of power were short. By 1954 he was finished. And three years later he was dead. History has not been kind to this man, and indeed it should not be. It should not be forgotten, though, that on the eve of the Korean War, he was both extremely popular and powerful.

McCarthy started his infamous crusade in February 1950. At that time the American people knew little about the time bomb ticking in Korea, a very large peninsula jutting out into the Sea of Japan.

Politically, Korea is an impossibility, the Poland of Asia. To its west stands China and to its east Japan. On its northeasternmost border it practically meets the Soviet Union. All three of these giants have played a part in the lives of the Korean people.

During World War II it was a possession of Japan. The fall of the Japanese Empire found Korea split in two. North of the 38th Parallel it was controlled by the Soviets; south of the Parallel it was under the jurisdiction of the United States.

While the United States was following its World War II policy of "Europe first" in the late 1940s, conditions in Korea were deteriorating greatly. Both the Soviet Union and the United States were building up armies, one in the north, the other in the south. The Russians were doing a far better job. When the Russians pulled their combat forces out of North Korea in January 1949, they left a far better equipped and larger army than that of the South.

In June of 1949 the United States followed suit, leaving only a small advisory group behind. About a year later, when Brigadier General William Roberts, the CO of the advisory group, left for home, he talked with an editor from *Time* magazine. In this interview he spoke in glowing terms of the South Korean Army: "They can handle anything the North throws at them."

This was a strange statement, since he knew they had no tanks, little artillery, no 4.2 mortars, no recoilless rifles, and not a single combat aircraft. The NKPA had more than a hundred Russian T-34 tanks. The South Koreans had nothing that could stop them.

Why had this been allowed to happen? The reason was mainly that the U.S. State Department did not trust Syngman Rhee, the president of South Korea. They were well aware that Rhee was determined to unite all of Korea at any cost. Why give him the means to accomplish this? The Russians had no such restraints.

At any rate, on January 12, 1950, Dean Acheson spoke to the

National Press Club in Washington, D.C. The thrust of his talk was that, given the victory of Mao Tse-tung in China, just where was the American line of influence in the Pacific? In other words, what would the United States defend militarily from Communist aggression? The answer was the Pacific from the Aleutians to the Philippines. Japan, of course, would be defended under any circumstances. There was no mention of South Korea.

Acheson's speech did not cause much of a stir in the United States initially, but one can assume that Kim Il Sung, North Korea's premier, took it very seriously. If the U.S. military did not get involved, his army could annihilate Rhee's force in a month.

The Week of June 18, 1950

While the half-decade since the end of World War II may have seen many changes in the United States, it had also been quite settling. The Soviets may have had the A-bomb by 1950, but the U.S. would soon have a much more powerful hydrogen bomb. China had fallen to the Reds, but Truman had stood up to the Russians in Europe and all was right with the world.

Inflation had arrived, making the need to increase social security benefits a necessity. The government could handle it. Washington had announced that prosperity was "at the highest point in history." If you had to pay $27.75 for a Palm Beach suit or fifteen dollars for imported British shoes, *you* could handle it.

The newspapers stated that the Soviet Union had held out a hand to any Latin American country that wanted to throw out colonialists. What they meant was if they wanted to go Communist, Moscow would help them. What was going on? Hadn't they ever heard of the Monroe Doctrine? Let them just try it.

Red China, with the blessing of the Secretary General, was applying for membership in the United Nations. Great Britain was listening, but not Harry Truman. This was a congressional election year. The China bloc was still smarting over the Red's victory. If the United States backed their entrance into the UN, there would be hell to pay.

On June 22, President Truman opened the new Baltimore airport. It was a thing of beauty, featuring an abundance of the new streamlined equipment that symbolized the second half of the twentieth century. The country was on a roll. The coming years looked as if they were to be great ones to be an American. Truman dedicated the new airport to what he knew was in the hearts of the people—peace.

Three days later, Kim threw his Russian tanks and his excellent army across the South Korean border. The peace that America wanted so badly to keep went by the boards.

The Battle
of Washington

This means the existence of the Marine Corps for the next
five hundred years.

—Secretary of the Navy
James Forrestal to Lieutenant
General Holland M. Smith, upon
witnessing the raising of the flag on
Mount Suribachi

The days between the end of World War II and the beginning of
Harry Truman's "police action" in Korea were days of great challenge
for the United States Marine Corps. To wit, powerful elements, both
in government and in the military, were out to do the Corps in.

Actually, it started before the big bombs were dropped on
Japan. General George Marshall presented a plan to several American military leaders that called for the Army to take care of ground
warfare, a unified Air Force to handle the air, and the Navy to take
care of the sea. The Marine Corps was not mentioned.

This was the same George Marshall who had said in 1943, "Before this war started I had never heard of amphibious landings, now I
hear little else."

Next came the plan by McNarney, a lieutenant general in the
U.S. Army. It differed somewhat from Marshall's plan, but in es-
sence said the same thing. Once again, the Corps was not mentioned. When asked where the Marine Corps fit into his structure,
McNarney hedged: "That's a detail of organization I don't think I
care to comment on at this point."

The 42,000-plus casualties that were to be suffered by the Corps
on Iwo Jima and Okinawa were still to come, and already the Army
was trying to relegate the Marines to a minor role or get rid of them
completely.

When the war did end, the Army went full tilt in an attempt to
realign the military structure of the United States.

There is a lieutenant general USMC (retired) living in San Diego who was involved in this struggle to keep the Corps afloat. His splendid book, *First to Fight,* carries a detailed description of this hassle. His name is Victor Krulak. He shared some of these memories with me when I visited him on the West Coast.

"Well, I don't know about General Bradley," he said, "but I'm quite sure Eisenhower was after us. Most of the Army brass looked at us as a constant affront to their role. They resented the fact that— according to their thinking, anyway—we furnished the Navy with its own private little army.

"One case in point that really irked the Army generals was the amphibious landings. We really rubbed their noses in it when it came to this part of warfare.

"As a matter of fact, in late 1942, I, along with three other Marine officers, Bob Bare, Rex Stillwell, and Roy Hunt, [was] sent to Schofield Barracks in Hawaii to teach amphibious landing to the Army's 25th Infantry Division. It was then under the command of a professional Army officer, Major General Joseph Collins.

"Well, Collins showed us nothing but cooperation and courtesy while we were working with his troops. But just as we were about to return to the States, he left us with an ominous statement:

"'Gentlemen,' he said, 'I'd like to thank you for your help. But we're never going to let this happen again. We should not have to go to the Marine Corps with hat in hand to learn something we should already know. Amphibious landing should be part of our job.'

"From then on I was too busy with the war to worry about Collins. I commanded the 2nd Marine Parachute Regiment in the Pacific, was wounded at Choiseul, a small island near Bougainville, and was returned to the States.

"After my recuperation I was ordered to Guadalcanal, where I joined the 6th Marine Division. I participated in the Okinawa campaign and, when the war ended, went to Tsingtao, China, with the 6th. Then, in late '45, I was ordered back to Quantico, Virginia.

"Back in the States, I was soon informed by Brigadier General Thomas* of the delicate position the Corps was in. The budget crunch was on. All services were being cut drastically. Army generals like Ei-

---

*Later, in 1951, then Major General Gerald C. Thomas was to command the 1st Marine Division in Korea.

senhower were begrudging every dime the Corps would get. They felt the money was being spent to duplicate what the Army was already doing.

"Well, Thomas then set me up in Quantico with then Colonel Merrill Twining. Our job was to 'roll the spitballs' for General Vanderbilt [Marine Commandant] to use in his struggle with the Army.

"Of course, there were others involved. Jim Murray, Jim Hittle, DeWolfe Schatzel, and E. H. Hurst, all lieutenant colonels, come to mind.

"Above all, there was Brigadier General Merritt Edson, the Medal of Honor winner from Guadalcanal. Mike put his career on the line by more or less leading our group. He finally retired from the Corps so he could speak out freely. His testimony before various committees was brilliant. The hero of Bloody Ridge's last service to his Corps may have been his finest.

"Anyway, on July 25, 1947, President Truman signed the National Security Act into law. The part I liked best was the part our little group had put together. Here it is:

"'*The Marine Corps shall be organized, trained and equipped to provide fleet marine forces of combined arms, together with supporting air components, for service with the fleet in the seizure or defense of advanced naval bases and for the conduct of such land operations as may be essential to the prosecution of a naval campaign.*'

"We had not won the war, but we had held our own, so far anyway."

General Krulak is right. The struggle would continue for years. Another Marine officer who was involved in the Corps's battle for survival during this period was Gordon Gayle. I visited with Gordon, now a retired brigadier general, in Washington, D.C. Gayle, of course, knows Krulak. Retired Marine Corps generals have their own little club.

"So you talked with Victor Krulak about our troubles with the Army between the wars. And, by the way, did you know his nickname is Brute? Picked it up at the Naval Academy. He was a coxswain and a hard-nosed one. That's Brute, hard-nosed and *right!*

"Well, there were lots of us involved, one way or another, in our struggle. We'd been cut from 500,000 troops (peak) down to 70,000. I think one of the reasons we were able to win out eventually was the way we were able to get our story across to the American people and government.

"Take Edson, Red Mike, the old Raider. He wrote an article for *Collier's* magazine, stating what the Marine Corps was all about. *Collier's* had a huge circulation forty years ago.

"And Bob Sherrod, he'd been a correspondent with the 2nd Marine Division on Tarawa. Bob was a top editor at *The Saturday Evening Post*. He joined in the struggle.

"Then we had our reserves. Many of them were in important positions both in government and in the private sector.

"Senator Paul Douglas from Illinois had been with the 1st Division in the Pacific. And Leverett Saltonstall from Massachusetts. Saltonstall wasn't a Marine, but his son had been killed on Peleliu, serving with the 1st Marine Division. He wasn't about to be against the Corps.

"Oh, don't let me forget Andy Geer. He was a reserve officer, later called up for Korea and he went. Andy had great connections with the Ritter news chain out in the Midwest.

"My point is, it was extremely important to get our message out to the American people. It took a great deal of effort, but I think we did it."

The Truman Letter

With all the man-hours the Corps and its supporters put into the struggle, it was Harry Truman's temper that ended up giving the Corps a tremendous boost.

The President, an old doughboy, from Battery D of the 35th Army Division, did not particularly care for the Corps. The Marines had served magnificently in 1918 France. They had, however, only one-half of a division (the 2nd Army) in combat against the Germans. Most of the AEF felt the Corps received considerably more publicity then they deserved. They resented it.

Anyway, after the Korean War broke out, the President began receiving a lot of heat about the unprepared state of the U.S. Army. When he received a letter from Gordon McDonough, a California congressman, praising the job the 1st Marine Brigade had done at the Naktong River, Harry blew his top. He wrote McDonough one of his sharply worded replies.

"For your information," he wrote, "the Marine Corps is the Navy's police force, and as long as I am President, that is what it will remain. They have a propaganda machine that is almost equal to Stalin's."

McDonough immediately realized what he had in hand. He read the letter into the *Congressional Record*. This put it in the public domain. Truman had not yet decided whether he would run for another term in '52. He knew that if he didn't do something fast, he would lose the Marine Corps vote.

At the same time that all this was going on, the Marine Corps League was holding a convention in Washington, D.C. After much debate, and against the advice of most of his staff, Truman decided to address the convention. No one ever accused "little ole Harry" of not having guts.

The League, in turn, was on its best behavior. Truman spoke in glowing terms of the job the Corps was doing in Korea, and apologized profusely for his choice of words in his letter to McDonough. The League then voted unanimously to accept the President's apology.

In the meantime the Marines had become very much a vital part of the Korean War. They would remain as such until the end. As Marine General Holland M. Smith once said, "There's room for everyone."

And there was. But if many senior Army generals had had their way in the late 1940s, there would have been no Inchon landing—or not by the Marines, anyway.

America Goes
to War

The war came upon the American scene with hardly a ripple. Any statements that were made were usually quizzical or negative.

"Korea, where the hell is Korea?" or "Korea, what's that, a kind of VD?" were comments one would hear.

There were, of course, the ardent anticommunists, and they were plentiful. From them you would hear, "Goddamn those pinkos, why do they have to stir things up?" or "Those Reds have been a pain in the ass long enough. Why don't we drop some of those big eggs on them and be done with it?"

But there was no war hysteria, just a feeling of contempt toward the Russians for letting it happen—that is, if one thought about it at all.

Perhaps this was because of the way the war developed. The minute we heard the news about Pearl Harbor, we knew America was at war. It was not that way on June 25, 1950. All most Americans knew was that the North Koreans had attacked the South Koreans. What was Truman going to do about it? They did not have to wait long to find out.

After his dedication of the Baltimore airport, Truman had left for a weekend at his home in Independence, Missouri. When Dean Acheson called to inform him of the invasion, his first thought was for the security of the American civilians in South Korea. He immediately ordered U.S. military aircraft to cover their evacuation. They ran into Russian-made Yak fighter planes and quickly shot them down. Perhaps this gave Truman a false sense of security concerning what he faced. If so, he was sadly mistaken.

In the meantime, the Security Council of the United Nations had called for an emergency session at 2:00 P.M. Sunday, June 25 (New York time). This book is not in any way a political history of the Korean War; nevertheless, the absence of the Soviet Union at this meeting is mystifying. Surely they knew what was going to be discussed. Holding a veto power, they knew they could stop any action the UN might take. Why, then, did they allow it to become a United Nations war?

At any rate, the North Koreans went through the defending troops just as the Nazi Panzers had gone through the Lowlands in 1940. The UN called for a halt to their aggression, but the North Korean premier, Kim Il Sung, paid no attention to it.

Seoul, the capital of South Korea, fell on June 28. The South Korean Army was fast reaching the point of total uselessness. On June 30, Truman did what he had to do—he committed the U.S. Army to the struggle. Five days later a U.S. Army lieutenant colonel named Brad Smith and his 1st Battalion of the 21st Infantry faced the enemy. They were about to find out how well the North Korean troops could fight.

Smith's outfit was part of the 24th Division. It would be followed in Korea by such divisions as the 1st Cavalry and the 25th Infantry. The 1st Cavalry was, of course, not a cavalry unit at all, but it contained the old 7th Regiment of Custer fame, and it clung to its archaic name as only the military is wont to do. Like the 24th, the 1st had come from occupational duty in Japan, while the 25th had come from Okinawa and Japan.

Indeed, these divisions seem to have gone to war with the spirit of Custer's old outfit. Indians or gooks, what was the difference? If they showed the flag, surely the Reds would turn tail and run. They were in for a shock.

Most of the American equipment was old World War II material. Howitzer shells were either duds or they'd bounce off the M-24 tanks. The Americans had no antitank mines. Their communication equipment was faulty. Many of these soldiers were to pay with their lives for the military budget-cutting that had gone on during the second half of the 1940s.

Bart DeLashmet was a second lieutenant with the 29th U.S. Infantry on Okinawa. His unit was sent to Korea in mid-July, where it joined the 35th Infantry of the 25th Division. He was in almost constant combat with the Reds until the first part of October.

"You had to feel sorry for our troops," Bart remembers. "Most of them were eighteen-, nineteen-year-old kids who had been lured into the Army by the recruiting theme, 'Join the Army and Get an Education.'

"Education, hell! They ended up on Okinawa, where they did nothing but guard duty. Not only did they not get an education, they hadn't even learned how to soldier. They had to learn that in the Pusan Perimeter, and they had to learn it the hard way.

"The troops in Japan were in just as bad shape. Soft living does not make tough soldiers."

As the American troops landed in Korea, they became part of the 8th U.S. Army of Korea (EUSAK). It was under the command of a Texan named Walton Walker, one of Patton's tank commanders in World War II.

General Walker, whom Patton had called "one tough sonofabitch," had a very difficult task. As new American troops arrived, he'd immediately send them into combat. It did no good. The North Koreans kept coming.

The commanding officer of Walker's 24th Division, Major General Bill Dean, did a tremendous job with what he had, but ended up spending most of the war in a prison camp. Dean ultimately received the Congressional Medal of Honor for general action.

Town after town fell to the Communists, but as more American equipment and men arrived, the harder it became for the North Koreans to advance. Aided greatly by their complete air superiority, the untested Americans were turning into an army. They had to make a stand somewhere, and they did just that at a place called the Pusan Perimeter in the southeastern corner of South Korea.

And it was there that the Marines entered the war and were quickly given the word by Walker: *there would be no Dunkirk.*

The following short synopsis of what the Marines did in Korea will probably be of help to many readers as they continue into the heart of the book—the interviews with the men who were there.

The Marines and
Harry Truman's War

The start of the Korean War caught the Marine Corps completely by surprise. Cut back since the end of World War II to 70,000 troops, its main struggle had been to survive. The last thing on the minds of those at Marine headquarters in Washington was a shooting war, but when it came, they recognized it for what it was—a chance to show the government once again why America had a Marine Corps.

If few others in high places had remembered what the Corps stood for, General Douglas MacArthur was one who was well aware of its value.

From the onset of hostilities, MacArthur had been planning an amphibious landing behind the North Korean lines. This would then allow him to crush the NKPA between that force and General Walker's troops in the South. He would insist on having a Marine division for this assault, but before he could do this, he realized the value of keeping Walker's army intact. When he asked for a Marine brigade to join the retreating 8th Army, the Corps jumped at the chance.

"It was essential that we get involved," says former Marine Commandant General Lemuel Shepherd. "The logical place to get him the nucleus of a battalion was from the 5th Marines, one of the oldest regiments in the Corps. We knew it was under strength, as were all our units. But we also knew it was loaded with veteran Marines."

So, working as quickly as possible, the Corps put together a brigade of Marines and sent it to Pusan, a coastal area in southeastern Korea. A perimeter was being set up there that would hold back the NKPA, while MacArthur would strike on the northwestern coast of South Korea.

Along with the 5th, the 1st Battalion of the 11th Marines (Artillery) was in the Brigade, as were several other supporting units. Of great importance was the fact that the Marine Air Corps would be involved. Not only did these fliers perform magnificently in close ground support, but they aided greatly in creating a Marine presence in combat. This was to continue throughout the war.

All told, the Brigade totaled some 6,500 troops. When they landed on August 2, they were immediately sent to the front.

For the next six weeks the Brigade was to be in and out of combat. Along with the rest of the 8th Army, the Marines had to endure harshly oppressive hot weather. It is ironic that in August the 5th Marines were to suffer from the stifling heat, but by the end of November the numbing cold would almost destroy them.

Hal Roise, CO of the 5th's 2nd Battalion, talked to me constantly of a particularly difficult ridge battle where his troops suffered many casualties. He couldn't remember the name of the place, which is understandable. It was called simply "No Name Ridge."

Probably the toughest fights the Marines had at the Pusan Perimeter were their two encounters at the Naktong River, the dominant feature of the area. In the first one they had stopped the Reds cold and driven them back across the river. Then they had been withdrawn to regroup and get ready for MacArthur's amphibious landing.

A week or so later the North Koreans had struck again, driving out the Army unit that had been left there. Back to the Naktong the Brigade went, and once again stopped the enemy. When they were withdrawn the second time, they quickly boarded ship so that they could join up with the rest of the 1st Marine Division, which would meet them near Inchon. In one of the most outstanding accomplishments of the Korean War, a Marine division had been put together to give MacArthur his amphibious landing. It was under the command of Major General Oliver Smith, a Marine whose days in the Corps dated back to 1917. Smith was a tall, scholarly man whose looks belied his steely composure.

The Brigade had been in existence for a little over two months. The Marine Corps, not always overly modest, has built the Brigade's importance up to mythical proportions. To say they saved the day at Pusan is not quite true. But it is definitely true that it was a very good thing they arrived.

Inchon and Seoul

Inchon was truly MacArthur's last stroke of genius. He seems to have been the only high-ranking military officer who truly believed in it. Yet he stood fast. His amphibious assault on Inchon would occur on September 15, and the heart of his invading force would be composed of the 1st Marine Division.

The major stumbling block to his plan was the Joint Chiefs of Staff. Their chairman, Omar Bradley, had little use for the Marines—he once called them "fancy Dans"—and he didn't like the idea of an Inchon invasion in the first place. But there is as much company politics in the military as in General Motors, and no one felt strong enough to challenge the great MacArthur.

However, one thing came through loud and clear. The plan was definitely a crapshoot. If it worked, MacArthur's forces could fight their way through to Seoul. With Walker's 8th Army coming up from the south and MacArthur's troops (actually under the tactical command of U.S. Army General Ned Almond) coming down from Seoul, they would have the NKPA between a rock and a hard place. If it failed, both the great general and the Marine Corps would be in deep trouble.

It ended up working magnificently well. The 5th Marines left Pusan and came around the horn of Korea to join the American armada heading for Inchon. The 1st Marines came directly from Japan, as did the 1st Division's supporting units. Another regiment, the South Korean Marines, would be held in reserve. These Korean Marines were to spend most of the war as a fourth infantry regiment with the 1st Marine Division.

The invasion started out with the early-morning tide. There is an island in Inchon harbor called Wolmi-do. The 3rd Battalion, 5th Marines, was to capture it, since in enemy hands Wolmi-do would allow the North Koreans to rake the Marines as they went in. Carrier-based planes and naval gunfire pulverized the island before the 2nd Battalion landed. It was easily taken.

The 1st Marines and the rest of the 5th went ashore at 1730 hours. Although many of the men with whom I visited told me of several foul-ups, the overall picture was one of total success. It was the type of victory that MacArthur was striving for—one with very light casualties. The movement toward Seoul was to be different.

The next morning, September 16, the Marines started inland, the 5th toward Kimpo Airfield and the 1st toward Yongdungp'o. By this time the NKPA was fully alerted and the fighting became very heavy. Once again the carrier planes played an immense role in support of the Marine infantry, as did the 11th Marines, the division's artillery. By September 20, the 5th had taken Kimpo. One of the outstanding airfields in Asia, it was immediately put into service.

Both the 1st and the 5th had crossed the Han River by September 24, but were meeting fierce resistance on the outskirts of Seoul.

In the meantime, Homer Litzenberg's 7th Marines had landed at Inchon on September 21. They were soon on the outskirts of Seoul, where they joined the fight.

On September 26, General Almond declared the city secure and stated that the enemy was in retreat. This was considered ridiculous by the Marines who were still engaged in hotly contested battle with the North Koreans. There were to be three more days of bitter fighting before Seoul could be considered recaptured.

In roughly two weeks' time, MacArthur's plan had succeeded. General Walker's 8th Army had broken out of the Pusan area and was racing toward a junction with Almond's 10th Corps. A badly battered NKPA was headed north. What could easily be the last major amphibious campaign in history was over.

The Chosin

After the fall of Seoul, the 1st Marine Division returned to Inchon. There they boarded ship, went back down the west coast of Korea, and came up the east coast to Wonsan in North Korea. They were about to embark on one of the truly epic campaigns in Marine Corps history, a campaign that at one time raised the possibility of the annihilation of an entire Marine Corps division.

The overall plan called for the division to proceed from Wonsan farther up the coast to Hungnam. From there they would move north to the Chosin Reservoir, some seventy miles away. Then they would go northeast to the Yalu River, where they would meet up with Walker's 8th Army, also proceeding north, some eighty miles west of the Marines. Their march to Yudam-ni, on the west side of the center of the Chosin, was to take place over one road called the Main Supply Route, or simply MSR.

They started out on November 2 with the 7th Marines as the vanguard regiment, followed by the 5th. The 1st Marines were to bring up the rear. The division was to be strung out like a huge snake on the single road.

South of Sudong the 7th ran into a large concentration of Chinese troops. At first Litzenberg's regiment did not know who they were.

"They seemed better organized," remembers Bob Smith, C/1/7, "and we weren't figuring to meet any North Korean soldiers in the area. We soon realized they must be Chinese."

The 7th had not suffered the sort of casualties that the 1st and 5th had around Seoul, and were close to being at full strength. The battle was no skirmish; there were far too many Chinese to call it that. Then, as suddenly as they appeared, the Chinese seemed to evaporate. Owing to the several hundred casualties they had inflicted on the Chinese, the 7th thought they had won a victory. What had probably happened was that the Chinese had used their own men to test the strength of the Marines. Unfortunately, they had a surplus of troops and could easily afford to lose some.

There is also the possibility that Red China was sending the Marines a message, telling them to get out of North Korea, but if that is what it was, it went unheeded. The whole column kept moving.

By the time the 7th reached Koto-ri, at the top of a huge plateau, they ran into a new enemy—the weather. This incredible cold will be described by several Marines later in this book. One had to be there to realize how horrendous it was.

Cold or no cold, the Marines kept moving. As the 7th passed Hagaru-ri, the 5th Marines under Ray Murray started to pull ahead of them. It was the 5th that was slated to lead the column to the Yalu.

During the day of November 27, very serious combat broke out with what seemed to be an increasing number of Chinese soldiers.

Both the 5th and 7th Marines were involved. But it was the early-morning hours of November 28 when all hell broke loose between Yudam-ni and Hagaru-ri. The Chinese seemed to be everywhere. The exact number of Chinese involved will never be known, but most estimates range from 100,000 to 120,000. The frozen nightmare had begun.

For the next few days the situation remained static. Finally the word came from 10th Corps headquarters. The 1st Marine Division was to backtrack to Hungnam. The long trek was to start.

The movement from Yudam-ni to Hagaru-ri was unbelievably bad, and from Hagaru-ri to Koto-ri it wasn't much easier. At Koto-ri they met up with most of the 1st Marines, who'd been fighting their own war with the Chinese while the 5th and 7th were coming down from Yudam-ni.

They still had about fifty miles to go, and the Chinese were still there. But the closer they got to Hungnam, the easier it would become.

One of the reasons for this easing off was the physical condition of the Chinese. They were just as vulnerable to the thirty-degrees-below-zero weather as the Americans. And they did not have nearly enough medical supplies for their troops.

The constant pounding from the American pilots was another reason for the failure of the Chinese to achieve their goal of annihilating the Marines' 1st Division, and their lack of heavy guns was still another.

Whatever the reasons for the Marines' successful retreat, the point is they did get to Hungnam and they got there with the division intact—tired and frozen, but intact. They were quickly evacuated to Pusan to rest and receive replacements.

The war had now taken a new turn. Though the Marines knew the withdrawal had been a mighty effort, they still had been forced to retreat at the will of the Chinese. Perhaps not many of them knew that Churchill had said after Dunkirk, "You don't win wars with evacuations," but they all knew it was true.

1951

On December 18, Lieutenant General Walton Walker had been killed in a jeep accident. Only the 5th Marines had fought under Walker, but in January the entire 1st Division was put under the command of Walker's successor, General Matthew B. Ridgway. The 10th Corps was no longer an independent force reporting directly to MacArthur.

At the beginning of 1951 the 1st Division was recuperating around Masan, where the Brigade had done such a great job five months earlier. They even had a chance for some touch football games and beer. Chesty Puller wasn't kidding when he said something to the effect that the folks back home should forget about the ice cream and Mom's apple pie for the Marines. "Give 'em beer," he was alleged to have said. The troops loved Chesty.

As a matter of fact, it was in Korea that the legend of Puller reached its herculean proportions. He was the CO of the 1st Marines from its training at Camp Pendleton until February 1951. He received his fifth Navy Cross at Koto-ri, a record unmatched by any other Marine. Lieutenant General Lewis Puller has been dead for years, yet today he is as alive as ever to the young Marines.

Before the end of January the Marines were slated to take part in a huge guerrilla hunt behind the lines. It was distasteful to the troops, but it had to be done. By the middle of February they had joined a new Corps, the 9th, for Operation Killer. It never lived up to its name simply because the Chinese were now retreating.

Ridgway now went into what he considered to be the second phase of his offensive; it was to be called Operation Ripper. To the troops these names were considered strictly for the media. All they knew was that they were now in central South Korea and moving north. By the time Ripper was considered finished, the 8th Army was perilously close to the 38th Parallel; on April 4 the 7th Marines crossed it.

Then came the bombshell. On April 11, President Truman relieved MacArthur of his command. Ridgway replaced MacArthur in Japan, and General James A. Van Fleet took over the 8th Army. He was probably the best combat leader the 8th Army would have in Korea.

On April 18 the Chinese started another counteroffensive. The 8th Army retreated, but it was never a rout.

On April 24, Major General Oliver Smith was rotated back to the States. General Smith had been in command of the 1st Division since before it went into Inchon. This World War I veteran had done a magnificent job while in command of the division. He was replaced by Gerald Thomas, another World War I Marine, and one of the great Marine officers of World War II.

Over the next two months the Marines participated in some of the most intense fighting of the war. The battle casualties of the 1st Marines alone surpassed that regiment's killed and wounded at the Chosin.

At the onset of the Chinese offensive the Marines had withdrawn, always inflicting extremely heavy casualties on the enemy. Then came the counteroffensive, and once again the drive north of the 8th Army, a drive of countless firefights and hills whose names or numbers are lost in the archives of history. But by June they had crossed the 38th Parallel for the third time. The 1st Marine Air Wing, as always, played an immensely important part in this drive.

New names started to crop up, Luke the Gook's Castle and the Punchbowl. Both meant fierce combat and hundreds of Marine casualties. It was June of 1951, and the 1st Marine Division was back in North Korea. The entire 8th Army was applying excessive pressure on the Communists. The combined NKPA and CCF were in the most desperate straits they had been in since China entered the war. They then decided to put forth a request for peace talks. As it turned out, they obviously had no intention of ending the war at this time. Why, then, the peace talks?

There is no question in the mind of General Van Fleet. "They wanted time to regroup," said the general.

And so they did. It was not until September that the 1st Marine Division went back on the attack. In a nasty nine-day assault by all three Marine regiments in the middle of the month, gains were made, but nothing sensational. By September 20 the assault was called off. It was the last major Marine assault of the war.

The war of movement had now ended; the new warfare of positioning had begun.

Eventually the Marine line would extend from the Sea of Japan on the east coast for about fifteen miles westward. The Marines would hold this line until March 1952.

It was now a war of constant patrols and shelling, which brought about the introduction of the armored vest, an innovation that was to save countless lives until the end of the war. Just about every man I visited with told me of having his vest punctured with shrapnel that could have killed him if he had not been wearing the armor.

While the Marines were on this line, Major General John T. Selden relieved General Thomas as the CO of the division. Selden, also a World War I veteran, took over on January 11, 1952. In March 1952 the entire 1st Marine Division moved from the extreme right flank of the line across Korea toward Panmunjom, where the long, drawn-out peace talks were still going on.

Here the division, including the South Korean marine regiment, guarded the southward invasion route to the capital at Seoul. Since the last major CCF offensive in April 1951 had ground to a halt, they had been facing North Koreans; they now were on the line facing the Chinese. Called the Jamestown Line, it was approximately thirty-two miles long.

The war now resembled the trench warfare that had prevailed for so long in World War I. There was no thought in General Van Fleet's mind of another offensive. His orders were to hold the line until a peace settlement could be worked out.

During this time there were two major changes in the U.S. Army's high command. In June of 1952, Mark Clark replaced Ridgway as the CO of the Far East Command in Tokyo, and James Van Fleet left Korea in February of 1953. He was replaced by Maxwell Taylor. Neither one of these moves really affected the Marines to any extent.

Regardless of the peace talks, combat continued. Some of the most brutal fighting of the war occurred during the sixteen months the Marines served on the western end of the front. All the Marine rifle regiments and their supporting units would be involved.

The casualty reports tell the story. One week the 2nd Battalion of the 5th would have two killed and nine wounded. Then, at an area like Bunker Hill, the fighting would explode.

The Chinese overran the place. Then the Marines counterattacked and took it back. Back and forth the opposing forces would go. Now the weekly report would list fifty Marines killed and 162 wounded.

Most books on the Korean War merely touch on the combat after the recall of MacArthur. Not this one. Nine of the major sections are devoted to Marines who faced the enemy after April 1951. Because five of these Marines were wounded three times each, and four others once, these men suffered over 100 percent casualties. One of the three was hit three different times during a period of a few minutes. He received one Purple Heart.

Two of the others were fliers. One was shot down and captured. The other crash-landed behind American lines in a plane that was burning and had only one wheel. The shooting war definitely was not over in April 1951. As a matter of record, the United States military suffered more casualties after the Great General was recalled than it had suffered up to that time.

Development on the Jamestown Line consisted of a heavily fortified trench system. In front of this line there was a string of outposts. The distance from the trench to each outpost would vary from 200 yards to a half-mile. The threat to those in the trench would depend on the size of the Chinese attack, but to those in the outposts it was constant. According to Ross Dwyer, a retired major general who was a major in Korea, most of the Chinese activities were aimed at the outposts. It was only the major assaults that went for the trenchlines, and such attacks would normally occur only after the Communists had overrun the outpost.

The 11th Artillery was spread out behind the thirty-two miles defended by the Marines. They had 105 and 155 mm howitzers, and deadly weapons called Charlie rockets. The outpost's job was to phone back any Chinese movements. Then the artillery would open up.

The Marines in the outposts would number anywhere from five men to a platoon, depending on the sector. Some of these posts were considered so hazardous that they'd change the guard every four or five days.

This was the type of war the Marines fought on the western front. It was Russian roulette. If a man stayed there long enough, the odds were he would probably get hit, wounded but not necessarily killed. But don't tell someone who lost a limb or still eliminates through a bag that he was lucky. He might disagree with you.

On August 29, 1952, John Selden was replaced by Major General Ed Pollock, still another longtime Marine. In 1942, Lieutenant Colonel Pollock had directed the fierce fighting at the Tenaru River on Guadalcanal.

Pollock remained in command until June 1953, when Major General Randolph Pate took over. Pate arrived just in time to head the Division during the extremely rugged fighting that occurred during the closing days of the war. He would later be the Commandant of the Corps.

If you talk with some of these veterans today, they will mention such names as Carson, Reo, The Hook, Vegas, Berlin, East Berlin, Echo, or any number of other places where they lost buddies. Then they will be apt to smile.

"Christ," one veteran will say, "I'd forgotten all about that hellhole. But when I talk about it, I can remember it vividly."

"Take East Berlin," one told me. "I'm sure only those of us who were there remember it now. Come to think of it, I'm not sure they even heard about it back in the States while we were fighting, but it was one hell of a scrap. It was right toward the end of the war. I'm sure the chinks knew just when they were going to quit. They wanted all the high ground."

How right this Marine was. In June and July of 1953, the Communists really turned on the heat from one end of the line to the other. The Marines alone suffered about 2,000 casualties from July 1 until July 27 (Korean time), when the war ended. Starting with the Brigade at Pusan, the Marines had been in combat almost exactly three years. They had suffered some 31,000 casualties. It had been one hell of a "police action"!

Lemuel Shepherd

The Marines and Navy have never shone brighter than today.

—Douglas MacArthur
to Lem Shepherd aboard the
McKinley, off Inchon

Very few Marines have done more soldiering than Lem Shepherd. From Belleau Wood, where he was wounded twice, to the frozen wastelands of Korea, Shepherd personified what an American military officer should be.

I first saw Major General Shepherd in August 1945. He had just brought his 6th Marine Division to Guam after the brutalizing battle of Okinawa. I was a replacement in that division. During the five months I was to spend with the 6th Division, I never heard a word that could be considered critical about the general.

This is very unusual, because Marines can be extremely critical. They seem to spend half the day bitching about something, mainly their officers.

I next ran across the general in 1976. I was working on *Make the Kaiser Dance*. Not only did Lem spend three hours with me, discussing his days in France during World War I, but he and Mrs. Shepherd hosted a onetime PFC and his wife for dinner at the La Jolla Club in California.

Ten years later it is not the exploits of a young officer I am interested in. It is the man who was in command of all the Marines in the Pacific for the first half of the Korean War and was Corps Commandant for the second half of that conflict.

This time when I visited with the general, he had recently celebrated his ninety-first birthday. His eyesight was fading and his legs could no longer take him down the field. But when he discussed Korea, it all came back clearly.

There was one thing above all that stood out during this interview. This was the general's feeling about duty. Perhaps he expressed it best when he discussed the famous Red Sox baseball player Ted Williams.

"That man was at the top of his game," mused General Shepherd. "He was making good money and, at thirty-three years of age, probably didn't have too much longer to earn it. But his country was at war and Ted answered the call to duty."

Such a statement may seem a bit passé to many today. But, I wonder, would anyone feel such a statement was out of date if he heard the general say it? With Lem, it comes from the heart.

GENERAL LEMUEL SHEPHERD USMC
Commandant 1952–56

In May of 1950 the commanding officer of the Fleet Marine Force, Pacific, was a man named General Watson. He told General Cates [Marine Commandant] that due to ill health, he wanted to go out immediately rather than wait until later in the summer when he was scheduled to retire.

So Cates called me at Quantico. Clifford Cates and I had been close friends since we both served in France with the 4th Brigade in 1918.

"Lem," he said, "why don't you take over from Watson? I'll drive over to Quantico and personally pin your third star on your shoulders. You can then take some leave. Drive out to the Coast with your family. Take your time. Stop off at Yellowstone Park. Do some fishing. Then go out to the Coast and take a steamer to Honolulu. Things are pretty quiet out there. I'm sure Admiral [Arthur W.] Radford won't mind."

This sounded great. I told Mrs. Shepherd that we'd better pack up our gear. We then leisurely started driving for Colorado Springs. I did send a telegram to Admiral Radford, giving him my itinerary and stating when I'd be arriving in Honolulu.

We arrived at Yellowstone Park on the Sunday that the North Koreans crossed over into South Korea. Korea was not in my bailiwick. That belonged to MacArthur. I really didn't think much about it.

A week or so later, all hell had broken loose. President Truman had sent some American troops over from Japan, but nothing seemed to be able to stop the Communists. Just to be on the safe side, I sent another telegram to Radford asking if I should change my plans.

The next morning I started out for my favorite fishing spot. I'd just about reached the lake when I spotted this young fellow running toward us. He was waving what looked like a telegram. I turned to my aide, who was traveling with us.

"Jimmy," I said, "if that fellow had arrived a few minutes later, we would have been out on the lake."

Jimmy smiled.

"General," he said, "you better see what he's got."

It was a telegram, all right, and it was from Radford. There was nothing urgent about it. He did suggest that perhaps I should fly to Honolulu rather than take a steamer.

That was it. I quickly called El Toro [Marine air base, El Toro, California] and arranged for them to get a plane to Salt Lake City as quickly as possible. Then I booked passage on a clipper from San Francisco to Honolulu. Two days later I arrived in Honolulu, where I was greeted by "Brute" Krulak, who was to be my G-3, FMF PAC [Fleet Marine Force, Pacific].

"General," he said, "we received a dispatch from MacArthur's headquarters in Japan. They want us to send a Marine brigade to Pusan as quickly as possible."

"Can we do this?"

"Yes, I've checked it through. We can put together a brigade out of the 5th Marines."

The wheels were then started to get the Marines into the act.

Next I went to see Admiral Radford. I had never met the man, but he greeted me cordially.

"Good to see you, General. We have a real can of worms in Korea. I don't like the looks of it at all. Dispatches that are coming in from MacArthur's headquarters seem to be so conflicting. I want you to fly to Tokyo, see MacArthur personally, and find out what is really going on. Admiral Sprague is flying in from San Diego today. He'll go with you. I'll send you over in my plane."

So, the next morning, along with Colonel Krulak, I headed for Japan. We arrived at Tokyo at 8:00 A.M. The next day we went to

MacArthur's headquarters. The first one to greet us was General Almond, MacArthur's chief of staff.

Well, hell, I'd known Ned Almond since my VMI days. Ned was Class of '15, two years ahead of me. We walked into see General MacArthur.

Now, to go back a bit. I had been assistant division commander when the 1st Division landed on Cape Gloucester on New Britain Island in 1943. This was the only time a Marine division had served under MacArthur in World War II. I had a couple of lengthy briefing sessions with him back in '43 and he keenly remembered them.

Next he went into his days with the 42nd [Rainbow] Division in World War I. Our brigade had seen a lot of the Rainbow in France. He seemed to enjoy telling me what a great outfit we'd had in 1918. Oh, he could be a charmer when he wanted to! MacArthur was one of the few people I've known whose sense of presence was awesome.

But it was Korea we were there to discuss, and MacArthur briefed us thoroughly. He said things were bleak, but he felt General Walker could hold enough of South Korea so we could soon mount a counterattack.

By this time I was getting a bit tired. I had what I'd come for, so I told the general I'd better be getting back to Admiral Radford. MacArthur followed me out. Right next to his door he had a big map of Korea. When we reached it, he put his hand on my shoulder.

"You know, Lem," he said, "if I had that 1st Marine Division, I'd land it right here," and he pointed to Inchon. "I could then cut the North Koreans' supply line to the South."

This interested me greatly. I didn't know much about Inchon, but I surely wanted to get a Marine division into the war. When you have just a brigade, you have almost no control over it. But a full division, particularly with a Marine air wing added to it, is a different story. There was a war on and that's what the Marine Corps is for, to fight a war.

"Well, General," I answered, "if you want that division, why don't you ask for it?"

"Do you think I could get it?"

"The 1st Division is at Camp Pendleton. It is in my sphere of command. But I cannot commit it without the approval of the Joint Chiefs and the Commandant."

"I see," he said. "Why don't you sit at my desk and write a dispatch to General Cates and the Joint Chiefs and I'll sign it? I need that division."

I looked at MacArthur's desk, which was four times the size of mine, and I pictured myself writing a very delicate dispatch to Washington with MacArthur peering over my shoulder.

"General," I said, "let me go outside with Colonel Krulak and we'll write the dispatch."

I had my work cut out for me. These were the days when that fellow Louis Johnson was Secretary of Defense. He had no use for the Corps. He'd cut us down to 70,000 troops, spread all over the world. We had a 1st Division, but it was woefully understaffed. Everything had been slashed tremendously.

Well, I wrote the two dispatches and gave them to MacArthur to sign. I was taking a big gamble, though. Heaven knows where we would get the 20,000-plus men needed for the division. MacArthur wanted the landing on the fifteenth of September, a little more than two months away.

So I returned to Pearl Harbor to await word as to what had happened concerning MacArthur's dispatches. When I arrived, there was a wire waiting for me, stating that Clifford Cates was flying out to Camp Pendleton to see the Marine brigade we were rushing to Korea. This brigade consisted mainly of the 5th Marines, under the command of Ray Murray. The brigade had been put together by Eddie Craig, an old friend of mine.

I grabbed the first California flight I could get. Cates was my boss. I'd have to sell him on the idea of giving MacArthur the 1st Division. When I got to Pendleton, I quickly went to see him. At first he had his doubts.

"Lem," he said, "I don't know. I've been trying like hell to get a Marine division into NATO. In case the Russians try anything, I want us there."

"But, Clifford, we already have a hot war going on in Korea. We've got to get a division over there! If we don't, people like that nut Johnson will start on us all over again. We have to get in this war with everything we have!"

Cates was all Marine. He knew I was right.

"Well, Lem," he answered, "I'll have one hell of a fight with the Joint Chiefs. I'm not a regular member of that group, you know. General Collins won't want us there. He's never forgiven us for all the publicity we got over Guadalcanal. That's stuck in his craw. And Omar Bradley, he's never liked us."

"Cliff, you can do it. Remember, you do have MacArthur behind you. He was chief of staff when Bradley was a major, and he's the general in the field."

Well, the long and short of it was MacArthur got his division, but we had to work like the dickens to get it for him.

We grabbed Marines off ships, from Navy yards, air stations, embassies, anywhere we could get them. We even pulled an undersized regiment out of our 2nd Division. It was also mainly a paper division. Then we got the old warhorse, Lewie Puller, to head up the 1st Marine Regiment.

Cates wanted O. P. Smith to command the division. Smith was from the University of California, very quiet, very studious. He was about my age and had long service in the Corps, mostly in a staff capacity. He didn't drink, but he didn't make a big thing about it. I believe he was a Christian Scientist. Smith was at headquarters with Cates, who was convinced Smith could handle the job. As it turned out, the Commandant was right. Smith did an excellent job, particularly later on at the Chosin Reservoir. He turned out all right.

Whatever, we were working on a shoestring to get MacArthur his division. It was nip and tuck all the way. Due to the tide situation, we had to be ready by September 15 and it was practically the first of August when we got started.

We did have an ace in the hole, and that was our reserves. President Truman had called them up and they were pouring into Camp Pendleton.

Naturally we didn't want them all in the same regiment. We tried to spread them around. The logistical problem was horrendous. But somehow, by the skin of our teeth, we made our deadline. At least a quarter of the men who landed at Inchon had been truckdrivers, businessmen, schoolteachers, and what have you, six weeks before they went ashore.

And that was the *real* secret of our victory at Inchon—the way we pulled troops out of the woodwork to get MacArthur's division for Inchon.

But it seems our troubles never ended. A few days before we were to leave MacArthur's headquarters for Sasebo, where we were to board the *Mount McKinley*, a typhoon struck the Sea of Japan. This caused all kinds of havoc with our fleet.

Nevertheless, the invasion was set for September 15. Instead of flying, MacArthur figured we should drive to the *McKinley*. I rode with MacArthur and Ned Almond. We didn't get to Sasebo until nine o'clock that evening. Hell, I don't think the *McKinley* really docked. We just kinda jumped on board.

Well, we hit Inchon right on schedule. The 3rd Battalion, 5th Marines went to that area sticking out in the harbor [Wolmi-do] in the morning, while the rest of the 5th and the 1st Marines struck Inchon later in the day. The 7th Marines came in a few days later.

The landing was a pleasant surprise. The resistance was nowhere near as bad as we feared. You see, we'd become used to fighting the Japanese. That war had only been over about five years or so. The North Koreans were tough, all right, especially as we got closer to Seoul, but they weren't the Japanese. Those Nips would fight to the last man.

Later on that first day, Admiral Struble invited me and Ned Almond to take a ride into the beach in his gig and get a firsthand look at what was going on. This sounded fine to me.

As we got close to the seawall, a North Korean mortar landed near us. Then this big Marine sergeant, standing on the seawall, yelled down to us.

"Get the hell out of here, you idiots!"

"*This* is Admiral Struble's barge!" our irritated coxswain yelled back.

"I don't give a damn if it's Harry Truman's. There's mortar fire coming in and we're about to blow this wall."

I said something about Marine sergeants usually knowing what they're talking about. Then we got the hell out of there. All in all, though, the Inchon operation was perfection, very few casualties.

The drive toward Seoul was a horse of a different color. Ray Murray's 5th Marines took Kimpo Airfield, crossed the Han River, and came toward Seoul from the north. My old friend, Lewie Puller, brought his 1st Marines south of the 5th. He fought hard in that

town across the Han from Seoul, can't recall the name [Yong-
dungp'o], and on to Seoul. The 7th Marines, under Litz [Homer
Litzenberg], had joined the fight by now. By the end of September,
the campaign was over. The Marines had put together a division,
invaded Inchon, and captured Seoul, all in three months' time. I
think we did a damn good job.*

---

*While the South Korean marines and parts of the 7th U.S. Army Division
became involved, the large majority of the fighting was done by the 1st Marine
Division. From September 15 through the next three weeks, they suffered 2,430
casualties.

Al Bowser
and Inchon

Lieutenant General Alpha L. Bowser (USMCR ret.) has often been called "the brains of Inchon," and as the G-3 (intelligence officer) of the 1st Marine Division, he undoubtedly was the leading light in the logistical planning for this amphibious assault. Faced with an incredible paucity of time, Bowser (then a colonel) and his staff worked around the clock to produce the great victory on September 15, 1950. It was as close to a military miracle as was possible.

I visited with General Bowser at a reunion of the Chosin Few in Washington, D.C. He still marvels at the way things turned out.

"When the war started, I was in the FMF Pacific at Pearl Harbor," stated Bowser. "When General Smith was told he was to be given the 1st Marine Division, he called General Shepherd, who had just taken over command of all the Marines in the Pacific, and asked if I could be sent back to Pendleton to be G-3 of the 1st. Lem agreed."

Things were moving extremely fast at this time. When Bowser arrived in California, the 1st Provisional Brigade was leaving the States for Pusan. It was mid-July, and Bowser knew nothing about any Inchon landing. His job was to help turn the thousands of Marines arriving at Pendleton into the 1st Marine Division.

"I first heard of a possible landing around the first of August," continues Bowser. "General Smith told me on the QT. We didn't know where it would be, even though Inchon was one name mentioned.

"Then we got word from the Brigade at Pusan. They were in action and suffering casualties. We had to send via airlift two groups of 500 Marines to the Brigade at Pusan.

"This meant we had to give top priority to this order because if Pusan fell, there'd have to be a setback for the amphibious landing we were preparing. We had to drop everything to get those Marines airborne. Then v'e went back to our job of getting the men and the ships for the rest of the 1st Division."

When they had lined up enough "bottoms" (ships) to get the whole division to Korea, Colonel Bowser was told by General Smith to put a planning group together and fly to Tokyo.

"'Go to El Toro, get a special plane,' Smith said, 'and do it as quickly as possible.'

"So," said Colonel Bowser, "we left on August 15, stopped first at Pearl Harbor to see General Shepherd, refueled at Guam, and proceeded directly to Japan.

"Upon our arrival in Japan we were met by two Marines on MacArthur's staff. I was told that MacArthur's G-3, a General Ben Wright, wanted to see me at once. I sent my staff to the USS *Mount McKinley*, where I was to set up my command post, and headed for MacArthur's headquarters. I was ushered in to see General Wright.

"'Colonel,' he said, 'the general wanted to see you, but in his absence I can give you his message. The Inchon landing is on for September 15.'

"I was thunderstruck. I was the G-3 of a division now ordered to assault a port city about which I knew very little, and we were to do this in about four weeks."

Bowser's problems were monumental. What about the tides? He'd heard they were troublesome. The mud flats, was it possible that their amtracs would get stuck in the mud flats?

How about the seawalls? He knew they were there, but how high were they? Could the Marines be slaughtered trying to get over them? Above all, Bowser wanted to talk to someone who knew Inchon cold. He went to Army Intelligence.

"Look," he said, "your group was at Inchon for three years. Don't you have anyone who really knows this port?"

A few days later he got his answer. He chuckled when he told me about it.

"'Yes,' they told me, 'we have a warrant officer who was assistant port director.'

"'Oh, for Christ's sake,' I said, 'give me his name!'

"Well, this guy was a walking gold mine," continued Bowser. "He was more important to me than any of the Army brass.

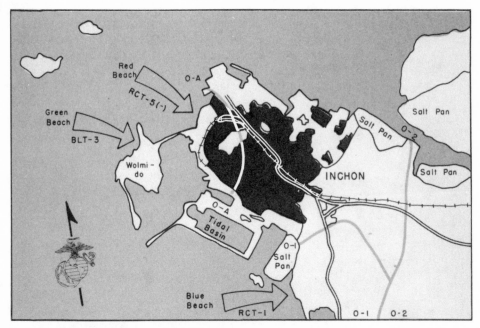

Inchon—MacArthur's last stroke of genius.

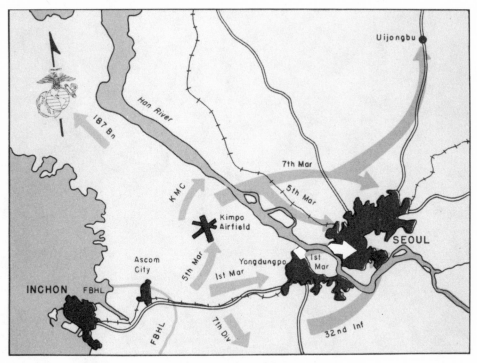

Seoul—the second part of MacArthur's great gamble.

"Next, a guy from the Far East Air Force came to me.

"'We have a new camera that can take photos at a very high speed. What pictures do you want?'

"This was great. Believe it or not, everything was falling into place.

"There was another problem. This one belonged to G-4, but we all worried about it. The 5th Marines were coming from Pusan. No problem there. But the bulk of the 1st Division was coming from the States in commercial shipping. They'd have to land in Japan on commercial ships and then transfer over to amphibious craft. Could we move these people and the tons of equipment they'd need for a landing in time for MacArthur's deadline of September 15? That they did it was another tremendous job!"

This date had to be met because of the tide situation, which presented another problem for Bowser.

"I'd made four landings in World War II: New Georgia, Bougainville, Guam, and Iwo. Every one was made early in the morning. This time the whole Division, minus the 3rd Battalion of the 5th, was going in late in the afternoon. We'd have only two and a half hours of daylight to do the job. Wow!"

In the long run, all these problems were met straight on. One way or another, Inchon was an outstanding success. And no one deserves more credit for it than Al Bowser.

Ray "Highpockets" Murray

"Don't I know you?" I asked.

"Yes sir, Colonel. My name is Leon Uris and I was in your battalion in the Pacific."

"What are you doing now, Leon?"

"I'm a cub reporter on the *San Francisco Examiner*. But what I'm really doing is writing a book on our battalion. I hope you'll enjoy it."

The above conversation took place in San Francisco in 1946. Ray Murray was just about to leave for duty in China at the time. Uris's book, *Battle Cry*, was published in 1953. One of his first autographed copies was sent to Murray.

In *Battle Cry*, all of Uris's characters are based on actual people who served in the 6th Marines during World War II. There is no doubt who Ray Murray is—he's unquestionably "Highpockets," the part so ably played by the late Van Heflin in the film.

The only difference between the two is that Murray was not killed on Saipan, just badly wounded. He went on to lead the 5th Marines from the Pusan Perimeter through the Chosin Reservoir in Korea. He was awarded the Navy Cross for bravery at the Chosin.

Following service in Vietnam during that conflict, Major General Murray retired from the Marine Corps in 1968. He now lives in Oceanside, California.

Retirement for Major General Murray is quite pleasant. He plays a great deal of highly acceptable golf with many of his former Marine Corps pals. He must thoroughly enjoy the ideal climate of Oceanside, particularly if he thinks of the abominable subzero weather of the Chosin.

LIEUTENANT COLONEL RAY MURRAY
CO, 5th Marines, 1st Marine Division

It was 1935. I was about to graduate from Texas A&M when the dean called me into his office.

"Ray," he said, "how would you like to be a Marine?"

I answered, "Well, I don't know, what actually is a Marine?"

"Oh, it's a small organization. They are expanding a bit, and I have the opportunity to recommend a few of our men for commissions. All you would have to do is pass a physical examination."

"Thank you, sir, give me a day or two to think it over."

So I went to the library and asked to see anything they had on the Marine Corps. They gave me a Marine Corps manual and a stack of papers that told of the changes in the Corps that was bigger than the manuals.

Anyway, I liked what I saw and I decided to take the physical. I'd been on the football team at college, was in excellent shape, and passed with flying colors. Next came the swearing-in.

Joe McCaney, another one of the Texas A&M graduates, who had also been selected by the dean, and myself went looking for someone to swear us in. Our orders called for either a military officer or a notary public to do the job.

We decided to go to San Antonio. We didn't see any military men; very few of them wore their uniforms in '35. We did find a notary public, I think he was a druggist, who swore us in. After it was over, I looked at McCaney.

"Joe," I said, "you may be the first Marine I've ever seen." Joe laughed.

Shortly after that we took a train for Philadelphia. We really didn't know what we were getting into. We had found out that the Marine Corps consisted of 17,000 enlisted men and 1,026 officers. It was smaller than the New York City Police Department.

Philadelphia was the basic school for officers. I spent nine months there, after which I was ordered to San Diego to play on the football team. This was the peacetime Marine Corps, and things such as a football team were taken very seriously.

For the first two years, officers were on probation. When this period was over, you took an examination. If you passed, you could not only stay in the Corps but you could get married. I passed, stayed in the Corps, got married, and nine days later kissed my bride good-bye and left for China. I spent the better part of three years there. My wife joined me for the last two years, which made things very pleasant.

I eventually joined the 6th Marines and went to Iceland with them in the summer of '41. I was a machine-gun officer. I stayed with the 6th until the invasion of Saipan in June of '44. A mortar shell put me out of action on that island shortly after I landed. It was the end of World War II combat for me.

Shortly before the Korean trouble started, I was a lieutenant colonel stationed at Camp Pendleton, where I was the executive officer of the 5th Marines. Colonel Krulak was in command of the regiment.

Around the middle of June in 1950, Krulak was transferred to Pearl Harbor, which left me in command of the 5th. Then the North Koreans crossed over and the crap hit the fan. They seemed unstoppable.

Soon the word went out for a brigade of Marines that was to be rushed to Pusan. The bulk of such a brigade had to come out of the 5th Marines. The only problem was the state of the 5th. We did have one thing in our favor—namely, the men we had were the cream of the crop.

Our three battalions were each minus one rifle company and each company was minus one platoon. We were able to scrape together the three missing platoons from troops stationed at Pendleton, but we had to sail minus the three missing companies.

We did have a reinforced artillery battalion from the 11th Marines, with both 155s and 105s. We also had a tank company, an engineering company, and some motor transport people, plus a weapons company, but all of this was understaffed. Nevertheless, we were the best that could be put together. We sailed for Korea around the middle of July. We really didn't know what in hell awaited us, but we were ready.

As we pulled in to Pusan, General Craig was waiting for us. He spotted me.

"Colonel," he yelled, "get ready to go as soon as your men are disembarked. You are going right to the front."

I knew that's what we were there for, but I was a little surprised at the rapidity of it all. But the Pusan Perimeter was all that was left of South Korea. You could go about sixty miles to the north and about half that to the west. We were badly needed to help defend what our forces still had.

Our biggest immediate problem was the heat. My God, it was hot, terribly humid, absolutely miserable. In a command post tent that was blacked out, you could hardly work over a map without sweat—not perspiration, I mean *sweat*—gushing off you. It was like a sauna bath.

Well, we started out. Our first objective was about thirty miles away. The long journey on the transport had put my men somewhat out of shape. They were dropping out like flies. We were pouring water over them, letting them rest for a while under what shade we could find. At least a third of the regiment was affected by the heat.

We managed to keep moving, though, in an attempt to break out of the Pusan Perimeter. Our first success came at a town near our objective. I can't remember its name, but we did drive the North Koreans out of the area. It must have been a mechanized unit that was facing us, because they left a mess of motorcycles, jeeps, assorted transportation of all kinds. I've often wondered why they didn't drive that stuff away, but I guess they felt they'd be sitting ducks for our air wing, which was supporting us. Some of our men had a high time driving around in Russian-made jeeps and motorcycles.

Just before we reached our objective, we were ordered to pull back. A U.S. Army artillery unit on our left had been overrun. I was to get aboard a helicopter and be flown to Army headquarters to find out what was going on.

While I was there, I was told to fly over the area where the artillery outfit had been, and drop a message telling the survivors where to reassemble. We put the message in an old 81 mm shell carton with a streamer on it.

When we reached the area, we could see the artillery pieces, but there wasn't a soul in sight. We flew in low to drop the carton when, bang, all hell broke loose. The North Koreans opened up on us with everything they had. I distinctly remember yelling to the pilot, "Take evasive action!"

My pilot must have been a good one, because he got that chopper out of there in one hell of a hurry. When we were out of range of the Commies, he started to laugh.

"Jeez, Colonel," he said to me, "if I told the manufacturer of this chopper what I just did with it, they wouldn't believe me."

I don't know what the manufacturer would have thought of it, but he scared the crap out of me.

Shortly after that, we were ordered to what we called the Naktong Bulge. A North Korean division had crossed the Naktong River and broken through our lines. We were ordered to a place called Yongsan, where we spent the night. The next day we joined the battle. It was a hell of a fight, but we did succeed in knocking the North Koreans back across the river.

After that we moved to Masan, where we were to get ready for Inchon. I didn't know much about the coming invasion, so I had to go through a great deal of briefing.

Then, suddenly, another North Korean division came crashing over the Naktong and broke through the lines at the same place they had broken through earlier. We were quickly ordered back to the front, and fought until we had once again knocked the Communists back across the river.

We were there until the night of September 6, when we were withdrawn to Pusan. I remember that date vividly because it was raining like the devil and there was mud everywhere. We were to leave for Inchon on September 12, so there wasn't much time to get ready for the big show.

And, you know, that's one of the things that has always amazed me. Normally it takes months of planning to put together a major amphibious landing. Yet I can't think of an important part of Inchon that went wrong.

Oh, I'm sure the troops had some things to bitch about. But as far as anything major, no, it went like clockwork.

This doesn't mean it wasn't hard. It was. I had a real tricky maneuver to work out. I had two battalions landing abreast in columns of companies. This meant that boats were coming from two different places to form the assault waves.

One thing that helped was the arrival of the missing companies. We had sailed from San Diego minus a rifle company in each battalion. These companies joined us shortly before we left Pusan for Inchon.

Another thing was the regiment. Most of the 5th had been together for quite some time. "Brute" Krulak was the colonel during our training at Pendleton. It was peacetime training, but Brute didn't fool around. When Krulak left for Hawaii to be Shepherd's G-3 in June of '50, we were a seasoned outfit.

We did get a break. It was real late in the afternoon when the 2nd and 3rd Battalions went in. We didn't have much daylight left. But two oil tankers had been hit by our shells and were blazing away. They lit up the whole area.

Our casualties were quite light, but each man you lose is a tragedy in itself. We lost one Marine, a 1st lieutenant named Baldomero, who ended up receiving the Medal of Honor. He was wounded in the shoulder as he was about to throw a hand grenade. He'd already pulled the pin. He yelled, "Hand grenade!" and he jumped on it, smothering the full blast with his body. "Baldy," as he was called, had been a very popular officer with the troops.

Well, a day or so after we landed, we started off for Seoul, about thirty miles away. The North Koreans were fully alerted by now, and the resistance really stiffened. As fast as we were trying to move out, we were bound to bypass many of the enemy troops but they were taken care of.

You see, part of my command was the South Korean Marine Corps, the whole bloody thing. It was just one regiment, and they weren't very well trained this early in the war. They were good fighters, though, and really disciplined. Above all, they were tough, mean as a boil. They followed us and did the mopping up. They didn't miss many of the Communists.

Anyway, I kept the 5th moving. I remember Hal Roise's 2nd Battalion ambushed a whole column of the enemy. Got them all. Hell, I don't think he lost a man.

We went through Ascom City, but it wasn't easy. It was the same at Kimpo Airfield. My regiment's job was to come at Seoul from the north side while Lewie Puller was to take his 1st Marines into the city south of us, near the suburb of Yongdungp'o. Both of us had to cross the Han River to do this.

When we reached the Han, I sent some of the recon company across to see what we'd be running into. They made a cursory examination and signaled us to come on over. I told the rest of the recon company to cross. The whole regiment was to follow. It was about ten o'clock in the evening at this time.

Then, wham, the North Koreans opened up. The recon men on the other side were lucky to get back. I figured we'd better wait until morning. I sure didn't want to lose half the 5th Marines crossing over.

Well, much to my surprise, the next morning the North Koreans had pulled out. I guess they figured we'd be moving closer to Seoul before we crossed. Instead we crossed right there with no opposition whatsoever. As we moved in toward Seoul, though, we ran into a very determined enemy.

There is one hill that stands out in my mind as symbolizing how tough it was. I even remember the number, Hill 105. I sent my 1st Battalion against it and they managed to take it.

But there was an area over on the left of 105, heavily fortified, that gave the Communists a straight field of fire into 105. My 1st Battalion had the hill, but they were catching hell on it.

The South Korean Marines had joined us by then. I sent them up against those troops on the left three or four times, but they couldn't break them.

Finally I gave the job to Hal, and his 2nd Battalion took the place, but they paid a heavy price for it.

Well, we got into Seoul and things weren't too bad for the 5th from then on. I guess Chesty's 1st Marines took the majority of the losses inside Seoul.

After we took Seoul, MacArthur was walking on water. He was seventy years of age and I think he felt he could do no wrong. He had made us part of the X Corps before we went into Inchon. Our divisional commander, a major general named Oliver Smith, reported to Ned Almond, who in turn reported directly to MacArthur. Relations between Smith and Almond were strained. It wasn't a good setup.

After Inchon, Almond became enamored of amphibious landings. With the taking of Seoul, he ordered our division back to Inchon, where we received our replacements and boarded ships. We then went down the coast of Korea and came up on the other side, ending up at Wosan in North Korea. We called it Operation Yo-yo because each day we'd get ready to go in, but the landing would be delayed because of the mines in the harbor.

On the other hand, there's an ideal corridor route between Seoul and Wosan. We could have move up that corridor, reached Wosan, and sat there. If we had, the whole story of the Korean War well might have been different.

Anyway, it wasn't to be. We finally landed at Wosan, then went up the coast to Hungnam. From there our whole division started its march into history.

Well, we started up the main supply route. The weather was brisk but quite pleasant. No one complained about it, anyway, not at first. Our orders were to go straight to Hagaru-ri, at the bottom of the Reservoir. The 7th Marines were in the lead. We would pass through them and take the lead between Hagaru-ri and Yudam-ni, which is on the left side of the Reservoir, about fourteen miles from Hagaru-ri.

Then we both would continue on a northwest angle until we joined up with the 8th Army near the Yalu. The next move, we hoped, would be to turn around and go home. The Chinese had other plans. I think it was the twenty-seventh or twenty-eighth of November when they told us what these plans were in no uncertain terms.

Hal Roise's 2nd Battalion was leading us. He ran into the roughest action we'd had so far that day with the Chinese, but that night it was a first-class fight.

It all started right after Jack Stevens's 1st Battalion came into Yudam-ni. This was the rear battalion of the 5th Marines.

My God, the Chinese were blowing their bugles and shouting up a storm. I said to myself, "Oh boy." I felt this was going to be it.

It was probably Bob Taplett's 3rd Battalion that took the brunt of the assault. [The Chinese] broke through his command tent, even killed his exec [Major John Canney]. But they were hitting us all. Three of the officers in Charlie Company [1st Battalion] went down that night, and I know many of the officers in the 2nd were also hit.

They didn't forget my headquarters. I was in my tent when machine-gun bullets started to whiz through it. They had it zeroed in. I said to Joe [Lieutenant Colonel Joseph L. Stewart], my exec, "Joe, we better get our asses out of here!"

There was no time to dig a hole. By now the weather had turned very cold and the ground was frozen. We'd had a hell of a time getting our tent pegs in the ground.

We started to run around looking for some protection, but we were running right toward a line of Marine fire.

"Don't shoot, don't shoot," I yelled, "I'm Colonel Murray."

Oh, was I proud of those guys. They stopped firing. They could see me. Our men weren't trigger-happy. Takes a good outfit to react that fast.

Well, we beat the Chinese back. They'd only hit by battalions.

If they'd hit us with everything they had that first night, I don't think we could have stopped them. We couldn't have killed them fast enough.

Well, why didn't they? Because all they had was what they could carry on their backs. Instead of getting more ammunition, they'd send in another battalion, pull the first one off the lines. We never had all of them hitting us at the same time. Thank God for that!

We spent the next two or three days up at Yudam-ni, waiting to find out what we could do. There was still no word from Almond. To keep going up toward the Yalu was suicidal. Going back was no bargain, but at least we'd have a chance.

There was one thing that did happen at this time that I'll never forget. I was sitting down looking at the skyline. I could see it all with my naked eye. First I saw a unit of Chinese. They started firing, and a few of them started dropping.

Then I put on my field glasses. Now I could clearly see some Marines who were firing back. Then I saw some Marines drop. It was like being at a movie, only those were real bullets going back and forth.

Anyway, here we were, the 5th and 7th Marines. We now were in real trouble. Homer Litzenberg, colonel of the 7th, came to me with a suggestion. I was a lieutenant colonel. Litz was my senior by rank and many years by service. I could have been commanded by him, but all he did was suggest. I've never forgotten that.

What he wanted was for us to intersperse the regiments of our troops, particularly the officers. It made a lot of sense to me.

What didn't make any sense to me, however, was what Almond was doing. Did he still think we were facing a handful of Chinese? Certainly he knew that Walker's 8th Army was catching hell from the Chinese to the west of us. I never could understand those people at Corps headquarters.

Anyway, two or three days after that first bad night, we did get the word to come back to Hungnam. It was going to be quite a trip.

We lined up the convoy with Bob Taplett's 3rd Battalion in the lead and Roise's 2nd as the rear guard. The rest of the 5th and the 7th were in between.

We didn't get very far that first day. It was snowing, and the going was very slow. There was always the pressure from the Chinese, and the road was very difficult to maneuver. It became even worse that night because we couldn't use the lights on our vehicles. But we had to keep going. It was only fourteen miles from Yudam-ni to Hagaru-ri, but they were the toughest fourteen miles in my life.

About halfway through that first night, our convoy came to an abrupt halt. I waited ten or fifteen minutes. Then I got out of my jeep to see what the hell was going on.

I walked past four or five vehicles until I got to this truck. It had stopped. The column had moved on far ahead. I couldn't see anything in front of us.

I looked in at the driver's seat. There was a black Marine slumped over the wheel and a white one slouched down in the passenger's seat. At first I thought they'd been shot. This was a favorite trick of the Chinese. Pick off our drivers to slow us down.

Hell, no, they both were sound asleep. Just plain exhausted. I roared and scared the daylights out of them. The look on that driver's face was priceless.

"Get the hell going," I said. "No one sleeps until we get to Hagaru-ri."

"Yes sir, Colonel, yes sir," they both answered, and we got going again.

That's the way it was those three days. I didn't sleep at all. But you know how it is when your adrenaline is flowing. With the consistent attacks by the Chinese, and when they weren't attacking, the threat of an attack, well, you just didn't think of sleep.

Even the cold weather was tolerable. And, God Almighty, it was cold! You hated to take your pants off to take a crap. And when you did, it was frozen stiff before you got your pants back on. That's pretty cold.

We did get to Hagaru-ri. Here we tried to catch our breath for two or three days. Then we started out on the second lap of our journey, headed for Koto-ri.

The area between Hagaru-ri and Koto-ri was rather flat and the road was a little wider than the one we'd just traveled. I don't know how long our convoy was, but we must have had hundreds of rolling stock from jeeps to tanks. My jeep hadn't even moved when the Chinese hit us from two directions. It was dark by this time and the confusion was immense.

I'd set up my CP behind a tank. Two or three hundred yards from where I was, these Chinese were coming at us in force. I sent two tanks down there in a hurry, not to use their tank guns, but to use their machine guns.

What a job they did! The next morning I looked out, and in the distance all I could see was dead Chinese. The CO of the 41st British Commandos of the Royal Marines, Doug Drysdale, was with me, as were two or three other officers. We started to walk toward the dead Chinese.

My God, for three or four hundred yards you couldn't walk without stepping on a body. Several of them had been hit with phosphorous shells and their quilted uniforms had caught fire. The poor bastards had burned to death.

Then we looked over on our right and saw this lone Chinese trying to run through this snowfield. Every Marine within range was shooting at him. Finally someone hit him and he went down. You were almost sorry to see the guy get it.

That night there was another big fight in the middle of the column. The Chinese actually broke through and were raising hell, but eventually the line was straightened out.

Well, we got to Koto-ri, where we met up with most of the 1st Marines. One battalion of the 1st had joined us further up the line.

From Koto-ri on, it became easier and easier, even though it was never a snap. I think this was due to the unbearable conditions of the Chinese troops. They had shot their bolt. By the time we got to Hungnam we were in much better shape than they were. Hell, we could have stayed at Hungnam as long as we wanted to.

One thing I did do at Hungnam was relax my rules on drinking. Some of my officers overdid it, but I figured they'd earned it.

You see, when I first went ashore on Guadalcanal in '42, we had a senior officer in the 6th Marines who didn't draw a sober breath on that island. From then on I was dead set against heavy drinkers in combat.

Oh, I wasn't a fanatic about liquor. I've consumed my share in my lifetime. You just have to use good sense. Whenever a bottle would show up, I'd have several men break out their canteen cups. I'd pour each man a shot until the bottle was gone. I'd usually have one myself. But no more than one. Combat is very serious business. You have to have a clear head.

Well, late in that winter I was sent back to the States. But to me, Korea will always be the one we let go away.

I remember back when we had taken Seoul. Then Almond moved us to Inchon so we could sail around to Wosan in North Korea. I had Stewart Alsop or his brother, can't remember which, as a guest in my mess. I've always been very frank with the press and I think they appreciated it.

Well, I told Alsop I thought we were crazy to be headed for North Korea.

"Oh no, Colonel," he answered, "we've got to unify South and North Korea."

"Mr. Alsop," I answered, "that isn't why we came here."

Matt Akers:
The Corporal
Goes to War

The outbreak of a war means different things to different people. To the senior officers it means huge logistic problems. The overall task of putting a fighting unit in the field is mind-boggling.

For the junior officers it's more of a personal problem. In peacetime, all platoons, companies, and so on are under strength. The lieutenant tries to fill up his platoon, the captain his companies. To Corporal Matt Akers, the outbreak of the war was a pain in the neck.

Akers had graduated from the very exclusive St. Marks School, outside of Boston, in 1948. At wit's end as he tried to decide what to do, Matt decided to postpone college so he could enlist in the Corps for a three-year cruise.

After the normal Parris Island stint, he was sent to Marine Corps Sea School at Portsmouth, Virginia. After completing a ten-week course, he went aboard ship.

"It was great duty," remembers Matt. "I was on a capital ship, and, believe me, there is no better duty in the Corps. I figured I'd run out my enlistment, then start college."

These plans went awry for Akers when the Korean War started. His ship was at an East Coast port when the word came to proceed posthaste to Korea.

"I was the captain's orderly when we got the word," remembers Matt. "I was also his confidant. Our captain was a great seaman, all business when we were at sea. But when we got to port, he knew how to play.

"I had hit the sack when the officer of the deck stuck a flashlight in my face. It was about 0200.

"'Akers,' he said, 'where the hell's the captain? You're the only one who knows. We have urgent orders from Washington that he must see immediately.'"

Matt was on the spot. He had driven the captain to a rendezvous out of town. It was all on the QT. If he knew his captain, and he felt he did, the old man would have consumed a good deal of Scotch by 0200. He only hoped his lady friend had been more conservative; he might need her help in sobering the captain up. At any rate he had to move fast.

"Sir," he told the OD, "I don't know exactly, but I can find the place. I'll be back as quickly as possible."

"So," said Matt, "I took off. I knew exactly where the old man was, but I didn't want to tell the OD.

"I got to the spot, and sure enough, the old man was loaded. His friend was a real classy lady, though, and we started pouring black coffee down the captain's throat. We finally brought him around some. Then, with her help, we got him into the car. Fortified with an additional thermos of black coffee, we took off.

"Of course, I'm going like a bat out of hell, so naturally we're stopped by a policeman. I'm explaining the situation to the officer, and the captain's mumbling away about going to war again. The police officer thinks it's all quite funny.

"'Take off, Marine,' he said, 'but take it easy. You don't want to get killed before you go to war.'

"We got back to the ship. I got the OD to come ashore and help me get the captain aboard. We sailed for Korea that afternoon. Our captain was all business by then, but he must have had one hell of a hangover."

Hal Roise:

The Marine's Marine

I first heard the name Hal Roise at a reunion of the Chosin Few in Washington, D.C., in the fall of 1984. From PFCs to captains, it was always the same, not the same words, but the same meaning. In the words of those who served with him, he was "the Marine's Marine."

"He's long retired," said Hank Litvin, "living, I think, down in Florida."

Litvin was only part right. Roise was indeed retired, but he was not living in Florida, he was living in Branford, Connecticut, not fifty miles from where I live.

I immediately called Colonel Roise and set up a meeting.

It seems that after twenty-seven years in the Marines, Hal had left the Corps to sell real estate in the Washington, D.C., area. The market was low, and while Hal might have been a great officer, selling was not his calling.

Then he heard from Joe Stewart, like Roise a onetime lieutenant colonel in the 5th Marines.

By this time Stewart had become an executive in the Armstrong Tire and Rubber Company, and was in a position to offer Roise a job as head of security for Armstrong. Hal accepted and spent the next thirteen years in that post.

There is a time-honored expression among Marines: "We take care of our own." So be it.

Hal is now retired, living rather comfortably on Long Island Sound, about ten miles east of New Haven.

LIEUTENANT COLONEL HAROLD ROISE
CO, 2nd Battalion, 5th Marines

No, I hold no grudge against anyone about going to Korea. Remember, Harry Truman said we were going into South Korea to chase the North Koreans back across the 38th Parallel. It was supposed to take two or three months. Then we were to go home.

But, after we had done that, why did we start heading for the North Korean–Chinese border, especially with the oncoming Korean winter? Doesn't anyone read history? Both Napoleon and Hitler broke their picks on brutal Russian winters. Why was an invasion of North Korea going to be any different?

And China. Like or dislike the Chinese Reds, they had succeeded in ridding their own country of the white man's dominant presence for the first time in God knows how many years. How did they know we were not planning a return to China? They had sent out word via India that if any white soldiers came anywhere near their border, China would enter the war.

So what did we do? We sent our troops north with a notoriously hard winter about to begin. It was suicidal, but it didn't have to be. We could have done it so differently and come out a winner. Here's how:

With the Inchon-Seoul campaign a great success, and the breakout from the Pusan deadlock, we had dealt the North Koreans one hell of a blow. We should have continued right on schedule, with the 10th Corps swinging around to Wonsan and the 8th Army capturing Pyongyang. We should have dug in, consolidated our lines, brought up the heaviest artillery we had, and set up our air power.

Then we could have sent out word to the Chinese that we would go no further. We would let it be known that if we had a firm guarantee from the North Koreans that they would stay put, we'd eventually go back across the border. After all, what the hell else did we want? That's what we went there for. We didn't go to conquer North Korea, and we certainly didn't go to fight China.

I played quarterback at the University of Idaho in 1938, and I guess that's what I'm doing, only it's now Monday-morning quarterbacking. But, damn it, you can't fight China, too many people, and we lost so many fine young men going north. It was a damn shame.

Well, I was raised in Moscow, Idaho, up near the Washington border, and graduated from college in 1939. I had taken ROTC training, so I graduated as a second lieutenant in the U.S. Army Reserves. By this time the rumblings of war were coming loud and clear from Europe. I felt we were eventually sure to fight Hitler. Don't ask me why, but I somehow felt I'd rather be a Marine officer than an Army one. So I went over to Seattle and got a commission as a Marine regular. I didn't know much about the Corps; it was a pretty small outfit then, but I was now part of it and would remain as such for the rest of my life.

By late 1941 I was stationed on the battleship *Maryland*. We didn't realize it, but we were a sitting duck on battleship row at Pearl Harbor. But, after all, who thought the Japanese would come that far to hit us?

On Saturday night, December 6, I'd been ashore at a party at the officers' club. I'd only been on the *Maryland* a short time, so I figured I'd better go back early the next morning and try and learn something about my ship. I was walking into the wardroom for some bacon and eggs when I began to hear some firing. Then a sailor came running into our quarters.

"Japs, Japs, the goddamn Japs are attacking us!" he's screaming.

By this time this loudspeaker was blaring general quarters, and people are running every which way. It was quite an introduction to combat for a young second lieutenant.

Now jump ahead eight or nine years to June 25, 1950. Once again there is a surprise attack, this time on the border between the two Koreas. What was my reaction this time? Nothing.

Hell, I can't even remember what I was doing when I heard the news. Yet it was sure as hell going to affect my life, just as much as the bombing of Pearl Harbor.

I was a lieutenant colonel by then, CO of the 2nd Battalion, 5th Marines, one of the oldest regiments in the Corps. I was a married man, the father of two children. My main job was coaching the battalion's football team—and by the way, we had a good one. The last thing in the world I wanted was another war, but then again, who ever wants a war? Only a nut.

Anyway, we soon heard that Truman was sending some soldiers

from Japan to Korea. That was it. I thought the Marines would also be going, and soon. I was right. The North Koreans had moved very fast and were knocking the hell out of everything in sight. They had to be stopped before it was too late.

So the Commandant [Clifford Cates] decided to quickly send a brigade, made up mainly of the 5th Marines, to a place called Pusan on the southeast coast of Korea. The rest of the 1st Division would follow in a month or so. MacArthur had already formulated his plans for the Inchon landing, but if we didn't hold at Pusan, things would really be fouled up.

The man put in charge of the brigade was a brigadier general named Ed Craig. He was an old-line regular and a top-notch Marine. He worked so fast that we were nicknamed the Fire Brigade, and that's what we were supposed to do, put out a fire. Before we had much time to worry about it—wham—they landed us at Pusan.

This was in early August of '50. Just a month or so before, I had been more interested in my football team than in what was happening halfway around the world, but that surely changed in a hurry. A day after we landed, we started off for the front.

From then on we were constantly being moved around from one place to another, wherever needed, and it was then that our lack of men became apparent. We left California in such a hurry that we had only two rifle companies per battalion instead of three.

Normally, you'd maneuver a battalion with two companies on the lines and your third company in reserve. This being impossible, I held one platoon from each company in reserve and fought with what I had left. I'd rotate the reserve platoon with the others according to the situation. Since I had the 2nd Battalion, my two companies were Dog and Easy. Fox Company didn't join us until we were getting ready to move on Inchon.

In the meantime there was a big hassle going on about us. Walker wanted to keep us right where we were, while MacArthur wanted us for Inchon. His plan was to use the whole 1st Marine Division for the landing. Lewie Puller and his 1st Marines had already left the States, as had the missing companies of the 5th. Litz's [Homer Litzenberg] 7th Marines were getting ready to embark from Pendleton.*

---

*The 7th Marines of the 1st Division landed at Inchon on September 21, six days after the 1st and 5th Marines.

Naturally, like it or not, Walker had to release us. We went back aboard ship and headed for the west coast of South Korea. MacArthur was going for broke. If we succeeded, the road to Seoul would be open. You might say it was MacArthur's last hurrah.

The landing itself was almost a complete surprise. Just about the only casualties my battalion suffered occurred in the weapons company and were inflicted by friendly fire. Tragedies like that always occur in a battle. They seem to be unavoidable, but are always sad. Most of my battalion had already landed when the North Koreans started to fire out at the LSTs [Landing Ship, Tank]. Our Navy fired back, and some of the shells landed among our people. All in all, though, we suffered very few casualties and were soon able to start out for the Kimpo Airfield, on the outskirts of Seoul. Kimpo had one of the best landing fields in the Orient.

The closer we got to Kimpo, the stiffer the resistance became. The second night out, we reached a point between two hills. I decided to bivouac the battalion there in the valley. Early the next morning I was about to drink my coffee when one of my men came up.

"Colonel," he said, "the gooks are coming down the road. Looks like a couple hundred of them, with six tanks."

It was a setup. We had everything we needed, 75 mm recoilless rifles, rocket launchers, and our own M-26 Pershing tanks. Above all, we had the element of surprise. Unbelievable as it sounds, they didn't know we were there. All we had to do was wait for them.

It was a misty morning. At first all we could hear was the clanking of the T-34 tanks. Then we could see them. Their infantry was talking and laughing, some were even eating breakfast. When they got close enough, I sent out the word to open fire.

My God, it was a slaughter, certainly not a pleasant sight, but war is like that. I'll tell you one thing, though. It was one hell of a cheap way to get rid of a lot of troops that would have done the same to us.

Now for the unbelievable part. Our casualties were one Marine, and I'm quite sure he was hit by friendly fire. He was hit in the leg. We evacuated him. So back to the States went a Purple Heart Marine as a big hero. More power to him.

Shortly after the ambush, we continued on our way to Kimpo. I was later told that the big man himself, Douglas MacArthur, along with Lem Shepherd, General Almond, and several other big wheels, showed up at the site. Mac was alleged to have said that all those dead North Koreans were a sight for sore eyes.

We took the airfield, which I feel was a real turning point in the campaign. Our planes were soon landing and could give us great air-to-ground support the rest of the campaign. This was tremendous because the North Koreans were now fighting us inch by inch.

But they couldn't fight those Corsairs. They'd fly in very close support of our advance. Sometimes they'd fly so close that we could see the gooks jumping into holes. We'd told the pilots not to fire because they'd be bound to hit some of us. But by constantly keeping the North Koreans in their holes, my men could run right up to them and shoot them before they knew what was happening.

It wasn't always that easy around Seoul, though. We were standing on a hill, trying to figure out what Easy Company was doing, when a shell landed right in front of me. It racked up my radioman pretty badly. He didn't die, but we had to evacuate him. A piece of shrapnel went into my arm at the same time. A corpsman bandaged the wound and I thought that was the end of it, but I was wrong.

A few days later my arm really began to bother me. I went back to the divisional hospital, where they X-rayed me. Sure enough, there was a hunk of shrapnel that had to come out. So they cut the wound open, removed the lead, and sewed it up. I went back to my command.

Well, you know Murphy's law—if anything can go wrong, it will. Some clown back at Division put down that I was badly wounded and had been evacuated. It worried the hell out of my wife.

Anyway, we never did go into the center of town. It was Puller's 1st Marines who had most of that nasty house-to-house fighting in the heart of the city. That was brutal, but Seoul was soon declared secured. MacArthur had one of those dramatic ceremonies he loved so much, and we got ready for the next step. The scuttlebutt among

the men had us going home—but there was no chance of that. There
was a lot of war left.

Sometime around the middle of October, they moved us back to
Inchon and put us aboard LSTs. We shoved off back down the west
coast, around the tip of Korea, and up the east coast until we reached
the port of Wonsan, well into North Korea.

We spent about a week there, then boarded a train for Hungnam, further up the coast. It was the beginning of the Chosin campaign. Thank God we didn't know what we were in for.

Once at Hungnam, my battalion started north, aiming for the
Chosin Reservoir. Also going up was the U.S. Army's 32nd Infantry
of the 7th Division. We'd send out a patrol each day to keep in touch
with the 32nd. The other two battalions of my regiment were also
going up.

As it turned out, one of our division's biggest problems was the
distance between our 10th Corps and Walker's 8th Army. They were
also going north, eighty or so miles away, over on our west.

MacArthur had split his command. The 7th Army Division and
our own 1st Marine Division were in the 10th Corps, headed up by
an Army lieutenant general named Ned Almond. The 3rd Army Division was in the same corps, but we didn't see much of them until
after we'd come down from the Chosin.

Almond reported directly to MacArthur, which didn't sit too
well with Walker. His 8th Army was far bigger than our 10th Corps.

Well, the next thing we knew, we were seeing more and more
signs of the Chinese Army. We were all concerned about this. I remember one young private stating what we were all thinking.

"I don't think these Chinamen are here as tourists," he said.

Fortunately for us, we had a major general in charge of the division named Oliver Smith, who was one smart Marine. He put out
the word that while our orders were to keep going, no one said how
fast we had to go. We sure as hell didn't break any speed records.

Now it was getting to be late in November. The day before
Thanksgiving, they got turkey dinners up to us. We had established
a temporary battalion headquarters in an old schoolhouse near the
Chosin. It was the last good meal we were to have for quite a while.

The next day we changed directions. We started to move over to
the west side of the Reservoir, while the 32nd kept going north on
the east side. Those poor devils got all the way to the Yalu River
before the Chinese hit them in force. They were clobbered.

Our job now was to go through the 7th Marines near Yudam-ni and to lead the march to the Yalu, where we would join up with the 8th Army.

By now, I might add, the weather had turned extremely cold. We were also greatly concerned about the Chinese. We knew there were many thousands of them in the hills, certainly enough to play hell with our column. It was just a matter of time before they hit us big; we all knew this.

Why, then, did we keep going north? Very simple. Those were our orders.

Well, we had gone about three or four miles through the 7th Marines on the night of November 27. We'd run into some roadblocks put there by the Chinese. I'd call in our bulldozers to push them aside. We went up to the top of this hill, and I figured I'd better stop the column. It was getting dark. I felt this was as good a place as any if we were going to be hit by the Chinese.

And as it turned out, this was the night the Chinese struck up and down the line. Hell, they were everywhere. We did all right, even though the Chinese managed to break through in some places.

I'd thrown in everything I had to repulse them. Everyone had a rifle—cooks, truckdrivers, clerks—I mean everyone. If you ever saw a complete battalion in combat, this was it.

Easy Company, over on my right, was under Sam Jaskilka. Sam kept calling for illuminating shells, but we had none. There was an old dilapidated house right in front of Easy's line of fire. Sam did have some tracer bullets, so he kept firing them into the old building until it caught fire. It illuminated the whole area. Easy now had a clear picture of the Chinese, and those Marines shot the hell out of them. What a job they did!

The next day I tried to take stock of my situation. I knew China was in the fight in earnest. It was a brand-new war. God knows how many Chinamen there were facing us.

One thing I knew for sure, there was no way we could keep going north, even if I wanted to. We didn't have enough men.

I think it was a day or two later that we finally got the word from Almond. We'd have to backtrack all the way to the coast.

So we started down. The whole area was full of mountains and hills, with this one route going straight down. We had to first get from Yudam-ni to Hagaru-ri, about fifteen miles down the MSR. The 7th Marines had built an airstrip there on their way up. We heard that Almond had been unhappy about their building it, but thank God they did. We would be able to airlift our wounded—yes, and our dead also—out of the mess we were in. And with the amount of Chinese we were faced with, there were going to be a lot more casualties before we got there.

Besides, the weather had become incredibly cold. I never saw anything like it in northern Idaho when I was a kid, and that area is not exactly Florida, you know. Plenty of our men were already dangerously hurt by the weather. Some of them would also have to be flown out.

Well, as we were trying to cover those fifteen miles, it became tougher and tougher. I remember we picked up some men from Fox Company of the 7th Marines. They'd been pulverized on one of the many hills the Chinese struck. Ray Davis had to take most of his 1st Battalion of the 7th back to that hill and get what was left of Fox Company out. I later heard that every officer in F/7 was either wounded or dead.

Remember, most of the time we had hills on either side of us. These hills were usually filled with Chinese. I can recall one morning, as we were starting up, looking through my field glasses and watching several hundred of these Chinese also getting ready to move. It was a particularly cold morning and they were stamping their feet, trying to get warm.

They got warm, all right. A squadron of our planes showed up out of nowhere. They opened up with bombs, machine guns, and napalm. They slaughtered those people. I was thinking only of our own survival. All it meant to me was a couple hundred less Chinese to worry about as we tried to get the hell out of there.

Shortly before we got to Hagaru-ri, we were maybe three or four miles away, I met with the other two battalion commanders in the 5th Marines, Jack Stevens of the 1st and Bob Taplett of the 3rd. One of them had a bottle of brandy and we had a drink. The three of us figured that if we could get to Hagaru-ri, our chances of getting through to the sea would be greatly increased. The next step then would be Koto-ri, another ten miles farther down the MSR. Here we had also set up a landing strip so we could evacuate more Marines. Puller's 1st Marines would join us there, which would greatly increase our force.

Well, we did get through to Hagaru-ri, where we were able to put our troops in shacks for the night. At first the Chinese seemed to get off our backs for a while. I guess they figured there was still plenty of time to finish us off when we'd be strung out again on the way down.

The next day, or maybe the day after, when my battalion was on the east side of town, they hit us again. We had a good defensive position and we threw them back with heavy casualties.

Next it was more of the hill fighting. This time we succeeded in pushing the Chinese off the place and holding it until we started down again. Each hill where we fought had a number, but I'll be damned if I can remember them. I do know that it was here that Captain Peters was hit in the leg by a phosphorus shell. I went over to the tent we had set up to see how he was coming along.

My God, what a mess! His left leg was bent way out of shape and was all aglow from the phosphorus. I didn't think he was going to live, much less not lose his leg. Our doctor, Hank Litvin, did one hell of a job on Peters.

Shotly after that night we started down the MSR once again. Now it was somewhat different, though. After Hagaru-ri, we felt we had a realistic chance of making it to Hungnam. Then when we got to Koto-ri and could evacuate more of our battle and weather casualties, we knew the Chinese couldn't stop us.

After we got closer to the coast, we started to find Chinese bodies that were frozen stiff. We were suffering gravely from the weather, but so was the enemy, probably more so. Their soldiers were tough, but they were also human. And that's one of the reasons we were able to get to Hungnam. The Chinese supply lines were dreadful.

After we got there, we took stock of what we had. The weather had hurt us more than the Chinese had. We were battered, all right, but we were still intact. Nevertheless, we were evacuated back down to Pusan in South Korea. Shortly after that, I was sent back to the States. I spent the next fifteen years at various Marine Corps posts all over the world. I retired in 1966, after twenty-seven years.

Why didn't I go for thirty?

My last post was at the Pentagon. I was the Marine Corps's representative for NATO in the nation's capital. Everyone there was gung-ho as hell about Vietnam, everyone but me.

It wasn't that I was pro–North Vietnam. But the whole thing

looked like a quagmire to me. How did we know China wasn't going to step in as they did in 1950? I just didn't think our intervening was worth the effort.

This type of thinking made me a leper as far as the big wheels at the Pentagon were concerned. So I figured I'd just get out.

I take no great satisfaction in being right about Vietnam. I just wish we hadn't gone there.

As for the Chosin, it will always be with me. I don't think you can overestimate the job the Marines did there.

Above all, I never considered surrendering and don't think any other Marine thought of it, either. Marines don't do that.

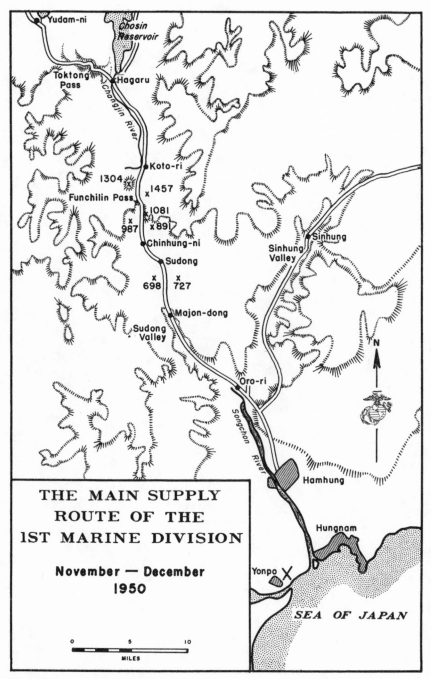

Yudam-ni

Chosin
Reservoir

Toktong
Pass

Hagaru

Changjin River

Koto-ri

1304

x 1457

Funchilin Pass

x 1081

x
987

x 891

Chinhung-ni

Sudong

x
698

x
727

Majon-dong

Sudong
Valley

Sinhung

Sinhung
Valley

Oro-ri

Songchon River

Hamhung

Hungnam

N

**THE MAIN SUPPLY
ROUTE OF THE
1ST MARINE DIVISION**

**November — December
1950**

Yonpo

SEA OF JAPAN

0   5   10

MILES

The Chosin—A Marine epic.

The Real Marine

The period between World War II and Korea was a tough one for the Marine Corps. Everything was cut to the bone, and enlistments were difficult to obtain. The Corps even instituted a policy where the recruit could spend one year of his enlistment on active duty and the next three as a reserve. These short-timers were not always popular, particularly with those who had fought in World War II.

To Sal Cavallaro they were a pain in the neck.

"I'd learned to bitch in the Pacific," said Sal, "and I thought I could beat my gums pretty good, but these guys were impossible. They hated the Corps and everything about it.

"But to tell you the truth," Sal continues, "I wasn't too happy myself then. It was 1950 and it just wasn't the same Corps I'd gone into in '43. I was stationed at the Boston Navy Yard and everything was spit and polish. Dress blues inspections, Christ, did we have inspections! We were the candy-ass Marines. Hell, I was a combat Marine, I wasn't a trained seal!"

Sal was right. He had an outstanding record as a squad leader. During the fighting on the outskirts of Seoul in the early morning of September 26, his squad was trying to stop the charge of some North Koreans by throwing hand grenades.

"'Throw 'em high, throw 'em high,' I'm yelling. 'That way they'll burst just before hitting the ground.'

"So the guys over on our left are really catching hell. They're calling for us to come over and help 'em. I yell back, 'Shut up, we're coming.'

"Then there is a flashing light and I don't wake up for four days. It was the end of the Marine Corps for me, which was just as well. I spent the next three years in and out of hospitals. They must have operated on me twenty times. I had originally planned to make a career out of the Corps, but I guess you can't expect action all the time. I couldn't take that peacetime, toy-soldier stuff."

Paul "Spider" Martin and Joe McDermott

Paul Martin is one of the very many Chosin Marines who gets very upset when he hears that the Chinese sprung a trap on the Marines in late November of 1950.

"How in the hell," says Paul, "can they call it a trap when we knew they were all over the place? Trap? Baloney!"

"Spider," says his buddy, Silver Star winner Joe McDermott, "is right. Our whole recon company knew the Chinese were there. It was just a matter of time before they were going to hit us."

Ernie Hargett, another member of the recon company, told me the same thing at the Chosin Few reunion.

"We were getting reports from our pilots, who were constantly flying up to the Yalu. They'd tell us how many headlights they'd seen on their flights. One night in late November they reported over 500, all headed for the Chosin. They sure as hell weren't going to a ski resort!"

Several other Marines have agreed. They are sick and tired of the "trap" mystique of the Chosin Reservoir. If it was a trap, the Marines certainly went into it with their eyes open.

Paul Martin and Joe McDermott are New Yorkers, Paul from Brooklyn and Joe from Manhattan. They both now work for New York banks. Joe is married and is the father of three children.

Paul has never married. He is an extremely active Marine historian. The two of them made their own history while in Korea.

CORPORAL JOSEPH MCDERMOTT
PFC PAUL MARTIN
Recon Company, 1st Marine Division

JOHN: We were both in the 1st Division's Recon Company. Our job was to work as the eyes and ears of the division. When we started out from Hungnam, we were assigned to the 7th Marines; they were leading the march up the MSR.

PAUL: Old "Blitzen Litzen," that's what we called the colonel of the 7th (Homer Litzenberg). Many of the Marines in the 7th thought he was great, but most of our guys didn't think much of him.

JOHN: Yeah, his problem was he didn't know how to use the Recon Company.

PAUL: That's right, and General Bowser had specifically told him not to foul up recon, but we all thought he did.

JOHN: All right, when we got to Hungnam, we were immediately sent in a flanking movement toward Walker's 8th Army.

PAUL: Get this, we ended up about forty miles from our division, all alone in the middle of North Korea. Litzenberg wanted to find out if there were any Communist troops that he should be concerned about as he headed north on the MSR.

JOHN: There were only 126 of us in Recon. If we had run into a large concentration of Reds, we would have ended up like General Custer at the Little Bighorn.

PAUL: We were all alone, no artillery, no communications, just our jeeps.

JOHN: Then we got word of a good-sized body of enemy troops not far away. That was enough. We headed back to Hungnam and we all heaved a sigh of relief. None of us wanted to be part of a wiped-out unit.

PAUL: The next day we started up the MSR to join the 7th Marines. This would be different. If we ran into a buzz saw, at least we wouldn't be alone.

JOHN: I can't remember which day it was, but I do recall those first two or three Chinese prisoners we nailed on our way up.

PAUL: Oh, you mean the one who infuriated Sergeant Dunn?

JOHN: You might say that. We had this Sergeant Dunn. He had been raised in China, both his parents were missionaries. When the Reds took over, they shot both of them.

So Dunn is talking to these gooks. They're telling him they're a small group of Chinese volunteers who have come to Korea to fight with their brothers in North Korea against the imperialistic invaders. You know, that line of bullshit that had been drilled into them. The sergeant is translating all this for us and laughing like hell.

Then Dunn asked them where they were from. The first one answers, and Dunn blows his top: "Ya lousy sonsofbitches, that's where my parents were murdered in cold blood."

Dunn takes his rifle butt and slams it into this gook's jaw. Christ, the jaw is dangling over at one side like it belongs to someone else. The gook would have been better off if Dunn had shot him.

PAUL: Yeah, but do you remember how the other prisoners are jabbering a mile a minute after that? They were scared shitless. Anyway, we sent the word to Division that we had some Chinese prisoners. We later heard that this information did get to Almond.

JOHN: You know what Almond said? "You Marines aren't going to let a few laundrymen stop you, are you?"

PAUL: A few laundrymen? What the hell did he know?

Well, on November 3, we get to the 7th Marines and I see all these trucks backed up. What the hell is going on? We can see some artillery shells exploding in the hills in the distance. One of our lieutenants went to the CP of the 7th Marines. When he came back, he had this funny grin on his face.

"Men," he said, "the Chinese are here."

You know how Marines are. Some of them are saying, "Big deal," others, "Well, fuck them!" I remember one guy saying, "Hey, no tickee, no washee."

But most of us are saying to ourselves, "For Christ's sake, there are a billion people in China, just how many of them are here?"

Then the lieutenant gives us the old gung-ho pep talk: "Gentlemen, this is the first contact the Chinese Communists have had outside of China. The whole world is watching us. We better give 'em a good show."

The two forward battalions are blocked off. Recon Company has
been given the job of breaking through to them. We can do it.

JOHN: Well, he made us feel ten feet tall, all right. But how in
the hell can 126 men rescue two battalions?

PAUL: Right, but what I have always gotten a kick out of was the
reaction of most of the men. Once the lieutenant said the whole
world was watching, one of our guys goes, "Wow!"

"You know what that means," he said, "it'll be in the *Omaha
Gazette*"—or whatever the hell paper he said—"that means my girl
will read all about this."

All the Marines seemed to feel the same way. It's going to be in
all the papers. Whoopee!

JOHN: We had to get out of our jeeps, leave the road, and backtrack quite a ways. Then we went around the bend, crossed this
river, and climbed up some hills. Eventually we got to a point where
we could look down and see where the Chinese had their roadblock
set up.

PAUL: We could also see the gooks moving around. They weren't
dug in. It looked as if they were waiting for the 7th Marines to try
and break the roadblock. They were quite a ways away, barely within
rifle distance.

We spread our men apart so it would look like there were
three or four times as many Marines as we actually had, maybe a
whole battalion. Then we started a steady fire down on the Chinese, a constant stream of single shots coming from all kinds of
angles.

JOHN: Oh, you should have seen the chinks. You know the old
expression "fucked up like a Chinese fire drill"? That's what it
looked like. They must have thought we were a whole regiment.
The first thing we knew, they started to pull out. The roadblock
was broken.

PAUL: The next day we got the word to get back into our jeeps
and start moving north again. We knew what we'd seen was no handful of Chinese volunteers. They may not have had any heavy equipment, but, damn it, if they had regiments, they certainly could have
had divisions, maybe even armies. We were all asking ourselves,
"Why go north?" The strategies called for us to get to the top of the
pass at Koto-ri. We went through Sudong and reached Chinhung-ni,
just south of Koto-ri. We had started to have firefights with a combi-

nation of Chinese and North Koreans at this time. Sporadic, nothing big.

JOHN: That's where we ran into the NKPA's tanks. There was a haystack over on our right. I said to our lieutenant [Donald Sharon] something about the stacks looking suspicious. We had been hearing rumors of NKPA tanks. They still had several in the field, even though we'd knocked out plenty since Inchon.

"Okay, Mac, check it out," he told me. "Remember, those Russian-made T-34s are vulnerable as hell around their periscope. You can stick a grenade in there and blow it to hell."

I latched on to Walter Cole, a PFC from Jersey, and we cautiously started to move toward the haystack. As we got closer, we could see there definitely was a gook tank there. I turned to Walter.

"Signal Sharon that we've got ourselves a gook tank here. I guess there's no one inside or they would have fired on us. I'm going to climb aboard and drop a grenade down the 'scope."

First I had to brush all the camouflage shit off, then I jumped aboard. I took the butt of my M-1 and smashed the periscope down into the tank. Then I looked into the hole to see if anyone was in there.

This was a mistake. A burp gun started blasting away, just barely missed blowing my head off. I could actually feel the breeze as the slugs went by. I quickly dropped a grenade into the opening and jumped off. Then Cole yelled over to me.

"Mac, for Christ's sake, don't you realize we're taking fire from the hills?"

So Cole and I dropped behind a boulder. As we looked out, we were amazed to see the tank has started to move and its cannon is aimed right at us.

"Holy Christ," yells Cole, "what a fucking way to go!" We both started to laugh, you know, an involuntary reaction. Remember, we're really on a high, the kind that only combat can give you. Then the tank stopped moving. Both of us jumped on board and Cole sticks another grenade down the turret. The muffled sound of a grenade going off inside a tank is really something. That was it. The tank didn't move again.

What we figured was the driver was protected by steel plating. My grenade didn't get him, but Walter's did.

I later heard that I was up for a Navy Cross which was knocked down to a Silver Star. Someone else also got a Silver Star, but not Walter Cole. If there was another Marine involved in knocking out that tank, I sure as hell don't remember him. Cole got shafted; he should have received that other Silver Star.

PAUL: There were four other gook tanks there that eventually were also knocked out. The tanks were manned by North Koreans, and I think the troops firing on us from the hills were Chinese. There was no coordination between the two. A tank can be a real powerful combat unit, but the gooks didn't know how to use them.

JOE: At any rate, the Chinese kept up the pressure on the 7th Marines for two or three more days, then they seemed to vanish. Scuttlebutt had it they were through. There was talk of a Chinese delegation going to the UN in New York City to try and get a settlement of the war.

PAUL: Well, it was all baloney. They had just been testing us. Now they'd take a breathing spell. Fortunately for us, our general officers didn't believe the chinks.

First, they kept widening the roads. Next, they started moving the heavy equipment up and, above all, built an airstrip at Hagaru-ri to evacuate the casualties.

JOE: When Almond heard this, he asked O. P. Smith, "What casualties?" That airstrip ended up saving a lot of lives.

PAUL: Another thing. General Smith invited a couple of naval officers to his quarters for a cup of coffee. He told them to keep his back door open. They returned to Hungnam and told Admiral Joy to be ready for an evacuation if it was needed. When we did come down a month or so later, Joy was ready for us.

In the meantime, the 7th Marines had taken off for Yudam-ni. We were still patrolling around Sundong and Majon-dong on the MSR. We called it the OSR—Only Supply Route.

JOE: I'll tell you something, though, there was a great feeling of anticipation. Where were the Chinese?

PAUL: I'd say the high water mark came on Thanksgiving Day. That's when we saw the photos of the 17th U.S. Infantry on the Yalu. They'd gone up there from the east side of the Chosin. The photos had several high-ranking officers, all smiles, standing on the banks of the Yalu. They were probably flown up there, had the picture taken, then flown back.

Our division got our orders from 10th Corps headquarters. We were to head for the Yalu from the west side of the Chosin. The Recon Company would establish a link with General Walker's 8th Army. This would undoubtedly mean the end of the war.

JOHN: Now for an amazing thing. Our company's jeeps were stopped at the checkpoints around Majon-dong. It had turned real cold by this time, and no vehicles were allowed to go further north without chains and plenty of antifreeze. It took almost a day before we could get all set. This meant that instead of being at Yudam-ni when the Chinese hit, Recon was headed for Koto-ri, about thirty miles south of Yudam-ni. But there was to be enough Chinese to go around, believe me.

PAUL: I think it was shortly after midnight, November 28, when the Chinese really clobbered the 5th and 7th Marines up around Hagaru-ri and Yudam-ni. We're getting all kinds of reports, but no one really knows what's going on.

JOE: One thing was certain, those fuckin' Chinamen were all around us. Koto-ri was at the top of a long mountain pass.

PAUL: There's a hell of a lot of confusion everywhere. We finally end up out of our jeeps, set up on a defensive line, southeast of Koto-ri. What we really had were outpost positions, spread quite far apart. Joe and I were at the same outpost with two other recon Marines. If the gooks were to hit us from the south, there was not much there to stop them. We looked our layout over and saw what a dangerous situation we were in. We called in to the CP. Don't know who answered, but we gave him the word.

"If they attack in this direction," we said, "there's no one here to stop them." You know what they said to us?

"*You* are there to stop them."

JOE: Holy Christ! Four men. How many could we stop? I'm manning a fifty [.50 caliber machine gun], don't even know if it works. At about 0200 I decided to fire a burst just to find out what kinda shape it was in.

I had no sooner let go when everyone in that spread-out line started firing. What a fuckin' racket, some guys are even heaving grenades.

PAUL: The moon was moving, creating shadows, that's what they were firing at. Well, we just sat there all night, alone with our thoughts. We expected to be hit by overwhelming numbers any minute.

When I was in grade school, they had a collection for the starving children in wartorn China. I gave a dollar. I kept wondering if the kid who got my buck might be with the attacking Chinese.

JOE: At about 0700 our lieutenant, Don Sharon, came around. "Men," he said, "here's the word. No more worrying about what the Chinese are going to do, they've done it. The bastards are all around us. We'll be doing nothing but fighting from here on. So just relax."

And, you know, he was right. No more wondering about getting home for Christmas or anything else except the Chinese. Believe it or not, it was a relief.

The Guy Who Was Left Behind

There is a tradition in the Marine Corps that you do not leave your dead, and above all, you do not abandon your wounded. There are times, however, when the first rule has to be violated. Hundreds of dead Marines were lashed to trucks coming down from the Reservoir or evacuated from Hagaru-ri or Koto-ri by air.

"They took up very little room on the planes," one Marine said. "We'd just pile them on top of each other."

However, many others had to be left behind. In some cases it was just impossible to get all the bodies out.

There are other cases in Korea where units were driven from a field. They'd leave with their wounded but not all their dead. In these cases there would usually be a counterattack. At this time, earnest attempts would be made to find their dead, sometimes successful, sometimes not.

Austin Stack talked of two Marines being declared missing from his unit during the guerrilla mop-up in South Korea. An extensive search was soon under way.

"We finally located them," said Stack. "They were hanging up in a barn where the North Koreans had left them. We cut them down and sent the bodies home."

As for the wounded, that was a different story. I had never met a Marine who knew of any wounded being left behind in Korea until I met Joe Saluzzi, a machine gunner with D/2/7. Joe was with the 7th when it came to the outskirts of Seoul.

"We were near Seoul," says Joe, "probably in a suburb. It was the morning of the twenty-sixth of September. We hadn't really been in combat as yet, but we were getting all these cheers from the civilians; you'd think we were heroes."

What Joe and the rest of Dog Company didn't know was that there was a unit of North Korean troops lying in ambush for them. Owing to the huge mass of cheering civilians, they couldn't send out their flanking scouts. They were sitting ducks.

The North Koreans opened up. Lieutenant Goggin went down, as did several others. Platoon Sergeant John O'Neill was killed.

"John was a real good man," said Joe. "He had a wife and children back in the States. When I saw O'Neill riddled with bullets, it was a tremendous shock.

"Then the gunner, Vernon Midkiff, got hit in the stomach. He was another fantastic Marine. I was the assistant gunner. We were trying to get the gun into action when Vernon was hit. Right after that, it was my turn.

"My God, it felt like someone had hit me in the chest with a baseball bat. The bullet had cracked one of my ribs and was painful as hell. I could hardly breathe. I was gasping for breath. I crossed myself because I thought I was dying. I remember saying to myself, 'God, please let me live. If you do, I'll go to Mass every Sunday and Holy Days of Obligation. I'll be a good Catholic till I die.' Then I mustered up all my strength and called over to Midkiff.

"'Vernon,' I said, 'how the fuck are we going to get out of this?'

"But I didn't have the breath to yell. Vernon did.

"'Corpsman, corpsman, over here,' he's yelling.

"A Marine named Smitty showed up. I think he was later killed at the Reservoir. There were two other Marines with him.

"'Joe,' he said, 'Vernon seems in real trouble. He may be dying. He's bleeding from his mouth. [Vernon survived.] We'll take him first and come back for you.' They stuck Midkiff in a poncho and took off. Then I started to drift in and out of consciousness."

At this point, Joe is not sure of many things. He thinks he saw several North Korean soldiers and he knows that he heard very heavy shellings. His company, realizing the NKPA had the area, called in artillery. Miraculously, Joe wasn't touched. The next morning he did see several Communist soldiers who had not been so fortunate. They were all dead.

"Shortly after dawn the next morning," says Joe, "I looked up to see four Korean kids grinning at me. There was an old man jabbering away to the kids. Then the kids took off.

"A little later the youngsters returned with some kind of a mat and, as gently as they could, lifted me onto it. They picked me up and started off. There must have been some NKPA snipers around because someone was shooting at us, but it didn't bother my saviors; they just kept going, finally arriving at our command post.

"The first guy I saw was Lieutenant Goggin. He'd been the first man hit, but he obviously was going to make it.

"'Thank Christ, Joe,' he said, 'we thought you were dead.'

"Then Sergeant Ralphs of my company came over, along with several others. One of them pointed out how it was impossible to get me.

"'These North Koreans were everywhere,' he said. 'It would have been plain suicide to go back for you. Then when our artillery started shelling, we figured you were a goner.'

"Our corpsman, a guy named Joe Slansky, came over and went to work on me. He did a great job. Poor Joe, he was later killed, I believe at Sudong, when the 7th first met the Chinese.

"That was the end of the war for me. I told Goggin to take care of those beautiful kids. One of them wanted to come to the hospital with me, but that was impossible. I gave him my helmet, gave another my watch. Before I was through, I had emptied out my pockets for them. I don't know what happened to the four of 'em, but I hope they've had good lives.

"Okay, now you may ask, am I bitter about being left out there? Not in the slightest. Sometimes isolated cases like mine do happen, but as a policy, Marines do not leave their wounded. If you bet on it, you're going to win ninety-nine out of a hundred times."

Eddy McCabe:
The Long Island
Flash

Eddy McCabe is one of the several Marines I interviewed who enlisted in the Marine Corps in the period between World War II and
Korea. His reason for joining the Corps was his desire to see a bit of
the world. He had no notion whatsoever of going to war.

He got his wish. As a member of the 2nd Marine Division he
traveled all over the Mediterranean, making sure he carefully re-
corded each port of call on his seabag. This made him salty, an image
that all Marines are interested in cultivating.

Eddy expected to spend Christmas of 1950 as a civilian. Instead,
he was hospitalized in Korea with a very bad case of dysentery.

He was finally discharged at the end of 1951. He then found
himself eager for an education, so he looked for a college where he
could play his favorite sport. It turned out to be Syracuse University.
When I asked Ed what his major was, he smiled.

"Lacrosse," he answered.

I interviewed this veteran of the 1st Marines at a bar he managed in New York City called The Guardsman. He maintained order
there as if he were a gunnery sergeant.

PFC EDWARD MCCABE
D Company, 2nd Battalion, 1st Marines

In 1948, Parris Island was really a little game you played with your
DI. I suspect it always was like this and always will be. His job was

to get it into the heads of seventy guys that they had to do things his way. Period. And as soon as each individual realized this, there were no problems.

Put it this way. The shithead* is a horse that the DI has got to put a saddle on. Once the boot realizes this, the better off he's going to be. You know the old expression, "There are two ways to do things, the Marine Corps way and the wrong way"? Well, you better believe it.

Of course, you always had the hard noses. All those guys did was make it hard on themselves. I quickly figured out the smart thing was to go along with this guy all the way and I'd have no problems. I was right.

Now, I'm not saying the DIs were sweethearts. Far from it. But they weren't the sadistic bastards some authors say they were. Not ours, anyway.

Several years after I got out of the Corps, *Look* magazine had an article about Parris Island. The cover of the issue had a photo of this DI with his mouth wide open, obviously chewing this kid's ass out. The boot looks utterly confused. You can even see the saliva in the DI's mouth, and one of his back teeth is missing. The DI has got on one of those World War I campaign hats and the sweat is plainly visible on both their faces. Inside the issue it says that it's the real McCoy. The photographer had taken the shot from a couple of hundred yards away. I thought it was so great I had the damn thing framed.

Christ, do you know I had this girl over to my apartment the other night; she took one look at the picture and shuddered.

"That's disgusting!" she said.

But then again, what the hell did she know!

Well, back to '48. I'm from Floral Park on Long Island. I'd been an air raid warden's runner during the big war. My mother had a brother named John Foley. He'd signed a contract with the New York Yankees before going into the service. He played some ball in Hawaii with one of the service teams, but ended up getting killed on Saipan. I think he was with the New York National Guard [27th Division, U.S. Army].

Anyway, I remember one of the letters he'd sent my mother,

---

*This term for a boot represents a change. In World War II it was "shit bird." This is progress!

shortly before he was killed, in which he'd done some bitching about the Marines. He told her not to believe everything she read about the Corps in the Pacific, that the Army was also out there, even though the Marines were getting all the press.

Nevertheless, I joined the Corps right after I graduated from high school in 1948. There might have been some times during the next four years when I regretted it, but not now. As the man once said, "There are no ex-Marines, just Marines no longer on duty."

After Parris Island, I went to Camp Lejeune. There I was put in motor transport, which is good duty. But when I heard they were putting together another group for a Med cruise, I jumped at it. There was no war going on then, and I looked at it as a great chance to see the Mediterranean area, and it was.

My unit was Dog Company, 2nd Battalion, 2nd Marines. We were put on the cruiser *Des Moines* and made landings all over the Mediterranean, Gilbraltar, France, Italy, Crete. You name it and we were there. And the liberty was sensational.

And by the way, we were labeled the Goodwill Detachment, but it was somewhat of a shock to find out that everyone didn't love us. When I was a kid, I'd seen the newsreels of Americans being cheered everywhere they went. I guess by '49 they were sick of the Yanks over there.

The cruise took about six months, then we came back to Lejeune. I'd put the names of every place we'd been on my seabag, which, of course, meant I was salty as hell. From then on I figured I'd spend the rest of my enlistment at Lejeune. I was already thinking about what I'd do after I was discharged.

Then came reality. In June of '50 I had gone home on a seventy-two-hour pass. I was sitting on the beach, trying to make a little time with this young beauty, when a friend of mine came over.

"What do you think of the North Koreans attacking the South Koreans?" he said.

I didn't know what he was talking about. Oh, I knew all about the two Koreas, all right, but I hadn't heard about the attack. Besides, the 1st Marine Division was now the West Coast division. They were supposed to take care of anything in the Pacific. Our division's responsibility was Europe and the Middle East. I went back to the important business at hand.

By the time I got back to Lejeune, things were different.

Truman had committed us to the war, all right, but no one seemed to know what was going on. It stayed like this for a week or two.

Then we got the word. We were no longer D Company, 2nd Marines. We were going to be D/2/1 and we were heading for Pendleton, posthaste. But there was no panic. We all felt that as soon as Uncle Sam and the United Nations made a show of strength, the Commies would back down. How wrong can you be? After all, Harry Truman was calling it a police action. To us that meant no big deal.

By the time we got to California, Chesty Puller had been put in command of the 1st Marines. He'd been on the beach, in charge of the Marine garrison in Hawaii. We heard he'd made a big pitch for the command. General Shepherd knew Puller was a great combat leader. No problems there. To us, Puller meant a quick victory.

We only spent a couple of weeks at Pendleton, then they put us aboard ships at San Diego. We didn't need much training. Our battalion had been together for a year or so. We weren't like some of the other groups, not our battalion. We were ready, even though a lot of the equipment we had wasn't in good shape. Most of our gear was World War II stuff. For instance, I think all our trucks were from the Second World War. There was very little we had that was brand-new.

Whatever, when we left San Diego, it was like a Hollywood production. There were three or four transports pulling out. Many of the wives and the girlfriends who had come to see us off had gotten through security and were standing dockside. They were crying and waving handkerchiefs.

Then someone started singing "Auld Lang Syne." The next thing you know, everyone was singing it. I remember when I was a young kid seeing a film called *The Four Feathers*. The same thing happened, even down to the singing of "Auld Lang Syne." The big difference was that those Brits were going out to fight natives. Well, it sure as hell wasn't Zulus we were going to fight, even though the government might have thought so. It was a well-armed, very tough bunch of North Koreans. Many of their officers had fought with the Chinese Eight Route Army against the Japanese. They knew their business.

So we sailed out. Naturally we had a few problems with some of the sailors, which I guess is par for the course, but it was a quick trip and we landed at Kobe, Japan, around the first of 'September. One of the first things I saw was a coincidence beyond belief.

We had a sergeant named Olawski, and as the ship pulled in, he spotted this Jap working on the dock. When the sergeant got ashore, the first thing he did was go over and give this Jap a big hug. The two of them are standing there, talking and laughing a mile a minute. We knew the sarge had been on one of those cruisers we lost a day or so after Pearl Harbor, and had spent the entire war as a POW. The only thing I knew about Japanese prison camps is what I'd seen at the movies. They weren't very pleasant. So, when I got a chance, I asked Olawski what the hugging was all about.

"McCabe," he said, "that guy was our favorite guard in the prison camp I was in during World War II. He'd always try to get us a little extra food, some smokes, things like that. There are Americans who are alive today because of that guy. All the Japs weren't bastards, you know."

Well, we went ashore and they marched us through the town. The Japanese weren't paying much attention to us, which seemed to annoy our battalion's CO. He stopped the march. "Men," he said, "fix bayonets!"

We did.

"Now, forward march!"

What a difference. The Japs started with their "ah, so" business, as they will. I guess there's something to say about that cold-steel routine.

By this time I was the runner for Dog Company's executive officer, a first lieutenant named Jay Thomas. I was a PFC. Most of our noncoms were World War II Marines, and promotion was real slow for those of us who had come in after the war. It was different in other battalions where you had a great many reserves.

Well, after ten days in Japan they put us aboard LSTs and we headed for Inchon. It was quite a sight to wake up one morning and look out and see what seemed to be the whole damn U.S. Navy. MacArthur wasn't fooling around. He had been just about the only one who believed in the invasion. He knew his reputation was really on the line.

We were to go in on amtracs, which were a lot different than those darn LCIs. I was always falling on my ass when we'd practice on the LCIs.

Our company commander was named Welby Cronk—how's that for a name? Strangely enough, both Cronk and Thomas were on the same amtrac going in. Being Thomas's runner, I was also on that amtrac. Dog Company would have been in real trouble if we'd taken a direct hit.

There were three amtracs in front of us, but they got bogged down with those crazy tides. We did get in. I was the first guy ashore, as my job was to make sure the rest of the company knew where we had landed. I took off right away.

This was quite an experience for me, as I'd never been in combat before. The first person I met was a Korean woman with a young child in her arms. The kid had been wounded by our shelling and was bleeding all over the place. The woman was talking a mile a minute, but I didn't understand a word she was saying. I showed her where to find our doctor. I was later told the child's wounds were all superficial and the doctor was able to patch her up. Then I took off again, trying to find our battalion.

In the meantime I was wearing a brand-new pair of boondockers that the Army had given me just before we took off from Japan. They felt a little strange, so I kept my old ones in my pack, and thank God I did.

Jeez, the minute I started running, the new brogans began to kill me. It took about three minutes for them to raise huge blisters on my feet. The next thing I know, one of my feet started to bleed like hell. I finally took off this bloody mess and put on my old ones. I'm just about to take off again when some Marines showed up. One of them took one look at my discarded shoes and turned to his buddy.

"Holy Christ," he said, "there's some guy's foot!"

"No," I yelled back, "I just got rid of a gift from the Army."

Well, I found the 2nd Battalion's headquarters, reported our position, and went back to D Company. I found out that we'd suffered just a few casualties, but one of them was our exec, Jay Thomas. He'd been hit with a bullet that had ricocheted off something and ended up going into his cheek. I understand he just spit it out. It had probably been fired by some trigger-happy Marine.

Okay. The place we had landed was called Blue Beach. As you look in at Inchon, it would be to the right of where the 5th Marines went in. We didn't have much daylight left, so we settled in for the night, which brings me to one of the biggest gripes I have about Korea.

There were these three sergeants in our company—one was a gunny—who'd been in World War II. Christ, had they ever, that's all they talked about.

"When the going gets a little rugged," they'd say, "just watch what we do. This will be nothing compared to World War II, blah, blah, blah."* They were a swift pain in the ass.

Well, these three guys dug such a hole that first night that if you fell in you'd break your leg. They fired every bullet they had, the result being a dead cow or pig, can't remember which.

Anyway, the next day we started out for Seoul, moving fast, maybe too fast. We bypassed a lot of North Koreans who ended up giving the people behind us a hell of a lot of trouble.

As we were moving, I think it was the second or third day, who shows up but the woman whom I had seen when I first landed—the one with the wounded child. Now she had a bouquet of flowers that she wanted to give the doctor. She felt that he had saved the kid's life and she wanted to show her appreciation. Can you beat that? She must have walked all the way from Inchon, maybe eight or nine miles. She was some kind of woman!

In the meantime, the North Koreans had regrouped and we were beginning to take casualties on a regular basis. One of those hit was a warrant officer named Kent. This gunner was a particularly good friend of mine. He'd already had a lot of time in the Corps and was planning to be a thirty-year man.

Well, poor Kent was riddled with shrapnel. I took one look at him and figured he was a goner. But the Korean War was the first time the Marines used helicopters. They had Kent aboard one of these choppers five minutes after he was hit, and whisked him away to a hospital ship off Inchon.

Then, about a year later, I ran into him at the Brooklyn Navy Yard. He was still in the Corps, even though he had to wear a leg brace. Hell, he was playing on the base's basketball team.

After Kent was hit, I began to get this funny feeling in my stomach. The next thing I knew, wham, the runs. And I mean I really had

---

*It never changes. In 1918 France, the doughboys were told the same thing by the men who had been on the Mexican border.

them! It was no better the next morning; I'm taking about eighteen, twenty craps a day.

By this time we'd halted near a tire factory. I had to go again, but I was getting no sympathy from my buddies.

"For Christ's sake, Eddie, stick a cork in it, will yah!" said one, while another is more realistic.

"Eddie, if you have to go, will you please move away from us. The stink around here is bad enough!"

It just happened that there was a pile of tires about a hundred yards ahead of us. I ran over to this pile and perched my ass on the rim of one of the tires. It was actually quite comfortable.

So, there I am, shitting away on the top of the pile and waving back to my buddies, who are laughing like hell, I may add.

Then, bang, the gooks opened up on us. Things are no longer funny. I started to run back to our lines, clutching my pants as I ran.

Now, do you remember those newsreels we used to see at the beginning of the football season? You know, where they always had the Notre Dame squad running between a line of tires? That's what I looked like, only I had my pants clutched in my right hand. I understand it was quite a sight. Rest assured, the rest of the guys really gave me the business when I got back.

Shortly after this, we reached the Han River. Colonel Puller came over and he's whacking each guy in the ass and wishing us well. No one knew what was going to greet us on the other side.

By now that blister I developed from the Army boondockers hurts like hell. Our corpsman noticed that I was limping.

"Hey, Eddie," he asked me, "have you been hit?"

"No, but I guess I've developed some kind of a blister." I took my boondocker off to show him.

"Christ, Eddie, that's infected. You better get back to the field hospital before you get gangrene."

I felt a little foolish going back with all these wounded guys, but there was nothing else to do with that foot.

I ended up spending about a week back before my foot healed. By the time I got back to my company, Seoul had been taken. The fighting had been real rugged for a while, with the North Koreans putting up quite a fight for the South Korean capital. They told me that our battalion had lost five corpsmen alone during one hour in

Seoul. You can't give those guys too much credit. Those Navy corps-men attached to the Corps are just as much Marines as the rest of us.

Okay. On my way back I was traveling with four other Marines, who do we run into but Colonel Puller—Christ, that guy was every-where! He asked who we were, so we told him we'd just got out of the hospital and were heading for our units.

"That's great, men," he said, "come on into my tent for a sec-ond."

So we went in and Chesty produced a bottle of Old Grand Dad bourbon.

"Take a shot for luck," he said.

We all did and were on our way.

A week or so later they sent the whole regiment back to Inchon, put us aboard LSTs, and sent us over to Wonsan, on the east coast of North Korea. We prepared for an amphibious landing under fire, but it never came.

Now, you know that they always give Marines a steak breakfast just before they land. Each morning we're expecting it, but it never came. We later found out the harbor had been mined and they were trying to clear the mines out. When we finally did go in, it was a lark. I don't think there was a shot fired.

The first day we were there, we just sat on the beach. Our 1st Battalion went south, where they ran into a hornets' nest. They were caught unaware. Some of them were even bayoneted in their sleep-ing bags. We commandeered a train and were rushed down to help them. Some of the North Koreans were still there and we did have some firefights, but it didn't amount to much. But our 1st Battalion really caught hell. If the North Koreans were a defeated army at that time, you'd never know it. It was a real professional raid. They knew what they were doing.

There was something that happened on our way back to Wonsan that shows you how screwed up you can get in war.

One of our guys turned to his buddy and started a conversation.

"Jeez," he said, "I wish I was back in Atlanta. I'd be getting ready to go out on a date."

His buddy gave him a funny look.

"On a Monday night?"

"Monday? What do you mean? It's Saturday!"

"Bullshit, it's Monday!"

The first thing you knew, they were getting ready to have a fistfight over what day it was. And you know something? The rest of us didn't know which one was right. War is truly screwy.

Well, we were on a supply train at this time. The weather had turned cold and we were beginning to freeze our asses off. Nothing like what was to come later, but cold enough.

One of the guys decided to look and see what was actually on the train, so he opened one of the boxes.

Jeez, the boxes were loaded with these beautiful gabardine coats with a fur lining. They looked like something MacArthur would wear.

So, we figured, what the hell, why should we be cold when there was something like this aboard. So, we put them on. We were probably the best-dressed Marines in Korea.

Then along came Captain Thomas.

"McCabe," he yells, "what in the hell have you got on?"

"Some new foul-weather gear, Captain. And I have your size right here."

Thomas looked it over, put it on, and walked away.

That was it. We all liked Captain Thomas.

In the meantime, the 5th and 7th Marines had already started off from Hungnam for the Reservoir. We were to go up what we started calling the MSR and join them.

At this point, everything was rather relaxed. We all thought the war was just about over. I think Thanksgiving was a little early that year. They got turkey with all the trimmings up to us. They also started giving us our foul-weather gear, but once again, so what? The scuttlebutt had us going home by Christmas, that's all we thought of.

Then came the big rumor about the Chinese. Both the 5th and the 7th had been seeing these Chinamen every day. We'd heard the 7th had run into some real combat with them earlier in November, but then the Chinks had seemed to vanish. I guess we didn't believe anything big was going to happen because we didn't want to believe it. Besides, it was getting cold, and I mean real cold!

Then they hit us, all along the line. We were near Koto-ri at this time, with the 5th and 7th about thirty miles or so ahead of us, near Yudam-ni. Puller wanted to go help them out. Our battalion was to take a convoy up to Yudam-ni. We started out, but we'd gone only a mile or so when the Chinese fire pinned us down.

Then some Air Force Mustangs showed up. And, what a job they did on the chinks. We were to see plenty of the Marine Corsairs before the campaign was over, but that first round belonged to the U.S. Air Force.

It seemed at this time that the Chinese were all around us. Whenever there'd be a heavy concentration of them, we'd usually go after them, and that's where we lost a Marine and perhaps it should never have happened. It was a tragic foul-up.

You see, the Corps has always been loaded with Polish guys. Sometimes we'd call them Stash, but it was mainly Ski. Well, one of them got hit. I helped carry him down to the airstrip we had built so we could evacuate our wounded.

Later on, when they called this guy's name at roll call, I answered, "Evacuated." That was it.

The only problem was, I had mixed the names up. I'd answered for the wrong guy. The missing Ski was never found. The whole thing has haunted me for years. He was probably dead or captured, but I wish it hadn't happened.

The airstrip I was just talking about was at Koto-ri. The Corps had put that strip up in a hurry, and it's a good thing we did. One hell of a lot of wounded Marines were evacuated over the next week or so.

And speaking of Skis, it was the same with the American Indians, only difference was we called them Chief. Every Indian I met in the Corps was Chief.

We had one in our company called Chief Obergh, don't know where the Obergh came from; he must have had some Swedish blood. He was raised on a reservation, though, and he had a face just like the guy on the old Indian nickel.

The guy was some kind of a Marine. At night he'd frequently go out with a knife and wire. He'd never talk about his sorties when he'd return, and he always returned. Most of us didn't want to know.

Another guy in Dog Company was a first lieutenant, name of Ted Culpepper. He was a real live hero. The lieutenant, you see, was somehow politically connected. Culpepper was a big name in Virginia, Ted's home state. I think there had been a Civil War battle at a place called Culpepper Courthouse.

Anyway, a few days before the Chinese hit us, Ted had got a jeep and headed back to Hungnam. Then he hitched a plane ride to

Tokyo, picked up a couple of cartons of bourbon, and returned to Hungnam.

He started up the MSR in his jeep the day the Chinese hit us. Don't ask me how, but he got through. It seems to me he might have been wounded, but he made it back.

I ended up with one of the bottles. I tried to spread it out, just taking a nip when I really needed it. It was great medicine in that fuckin' cold weather. Hell, if I'd had my way, they would have given Culpepper the bloody Medal of Honor.

Well, one way or another we did get back to Hungnam. We were pretty well used up. I was lying there half asleep, with my eyes closed. I opened them up and saw a truly amazing sight. There were fifty or so Chinese running toward us with nothing on but their sneakers. I mean, they were balls-ass naked. A bunch of MPs quickly showed up and started rounding them up.

What had happened was some Marines had corralled these chinks. When they had started to approach Hungnam, the Marines had stripped them and told them to take off. You can bet they ran like hell in that weather.

I never found out what happened to them, but I did hear that as we sailed out of Hungnam, we released many of our Chinese prisoners to fend for themselves.

Well, they soon put us aboard ship. For the first time in weeks we were given hot food. I gorged myself for hours. Then I spent the next few hours sitting on the trough we were using for a head.

You see, the diarrhea I'd picked up at Inchon was still with me. It was really dysentery. I was one sick guy. I took all my clothes off and looked in the mirror. What a sight! I looked just like I'd been released from Dachau. My arms were so skinny the ID bracelet I wore slipped off my wrist.

Anyway, the ship we were on was a civilian one. They did have a doctor on board. He took one look at me and immediately put me in the sack. By the time the ship reached Pusan, I was too weak to get up. They carried me ashore on a stretcher.

Jeez, it was embarrassing as hell. They're asking all these other guys where they were wounded. When they got to me, I weakly answered, "I wasn't hit. I got the shits."

Nobody laughed this time. They turned me over to the Army hospital as quickly as possible.

Now, can you believe this? The hospital was segregated. They had all the dogfaces in one area and the Marines and the South Koreans in another. That's where they put me, anyway, in with the gooks.

The food was good. I started to regain my strength. It took me about a week to get on my feet again. But once I did, I was itchy as hell to get back to my company.

One day I was looking out the window when I spotted these two Marines. "Are you going back to the front?" I yelled.

"Yeah!" came back.

I grabbed my rifle and what else I had, and ran over to them.

"Where you headed, soldier?" one of them asked.

I'd forgotten that the hospital had burned my Marine outfit and given me an Army uniform. I laughed.

"I'm no doggie, I'm PFC McCabe of D/2/1. Get me the hell out of here."

These guys thought this was funny as hell.

"Okay, mate," the driver said, "let's shove off." And that's how I got back to Dog Company of the 1st Marines. I was home.

It was now Christmas Eve, with 1950 about to become 1951, when I arrived. Shortly after this, Colonel Puller called the whole regiment together to give a speech.

"Men," he said, "we're all going home."

Christ, bedlam followed. The men roared for about twenty minutes.

Then Chesty finished his speech.

"That is, after we've killed a few more gooks."

Dead silence. Only Chesty could have gotten away with that one.

Then, on New Year's Eve, there was a real tragedy. We had an interpreter who was a real pain in the ass. He was either a Japanese or a Korean, can't remember which one. To us, this guy was real bad news.

We also had a very popular sergeant named Musick. He was everything a Marine should be, one of the best I'd ever known.

So, a whole crew of us, including Musick, had gone out to celebrate. We really tied one on. When we got back, this interpreter started in on us. Oh, he's telling us what a bunch of assholes we all are, his usual garbage. What we didn't know was that Musick had just gotten a letter from his wife telling him she wanted a divorce. He was in no mood to be trifled with. Anyway, this interpreter, who we all felt was not only a bastard but pretty stupid to boot, started in on Musick.

Jeez, the sarge grabbed his .45 and emptied it into the jerk. Then he calmly went to sleep.

There was hell to pay the next day. Musick was immediately put on trial. Of course he was convicted. They sent him back to the States and put him in federal prison. I don't know what happened after that, but I was later told the one person who kept track of him for years was Puller. Chesty is long dead, but I don't know about Musick.

In the spring of '51 I received my orders to return home. Just as I was about to leave, I ran into a soldier I knew from home. He'd just arrived in Korea. We shot the shit for a while, then he took off for the front.

I came home on a slow boat to China. By the time I got to Floral Park, this guy had been wounded, was flown back to the States, and was in a U.S. Army hospital. The guy had beat me home. Can you top that?

The Mountain
Comes
to Mohammed

Puller

Bud Cain, Jr., was a nineteen-year-old PFC from southern New Jersey. He was pinned down by machine-gun fire near the railroad tracks at Yongdungp'o, on the outskirts of Seoul. He was trying to figure out what to do, when an older officer showed up out of nowhere.

"How's it going, son?" he asked Bud.

Cain looked at his visitor. He immediately recognized the World War II raider cap, the pipe, and the way the old-timer had of spitting his words out of the side of his mouth. It was Chesty Puller.

"Great, Colonel, just great."

"Thataboy. Now, we're going to have some heavy duty for a while, but you can handle it. Hang in there, Marine, and good luck."

With that, Puller was gone, looking for some more of his men to talk to. Chesty has been dead for several years, and the nineteen-year-old PFC is now fifty-six years of age, but that chance meeting in 1950 remains one of his fondest memories.

The Meeting

When one is dealing with a bigger-than-life personality, such as that of General Puller, it is not always easy to separate the wheat from the chaff.

However, one thing is certain: there was a meeting between Chesty Puller and Douglas MacArthur somewhere between Inchon and Seoul.

It happened on September 18. MacArthur had been impatient to go ashore at Inchon, and what the general wanted, he got.

"The first person I want to see is Lewie Puller," he said. "He was under my command at New Britain. He's a real fighter."

So MacArthur and his entourage started out in search of Colonel Puller and the 1st Marines. They sent a message ahead, telling Puller that MacArthur wanted to decorate him with the Silver Star.

"Signal them that we're fighting our way for every foot of ground," replied Puller. "I can't leave here. If he wants to decorate me, he'll have to come up here."

When MacArthur received the message, he laughed.

"I've told you that man is a fighter. Let's go to the front and we'll find Puller." Anything like this was right up MacArthur's alley. Like Puller, Mac was absolutely fearless, and he loved the dramatics.

They found Puller atop a steep ridge. For the next two hours they toured the front, including the spot where the Marines had ambushed a North Korean column just a few hours before, destroying six North Korean tanks.

"That's just the way I like to see their tanks, blown to pieces," said MacArthur.

It is a shame that for the two hours these two flamboyant characters spent together they did not have someone like Johnson's Boswell along. Their conversation must have been priceless.

At any rate, their encounter belongs to history, along with such meetings as Grant and Sherman at Shiloh, and Pershing and Foch before the second battle of the Marne. That's the way the 1st Marines felt about it, anyway.

Hank Litvin:
The Doctor
Goes to War

Henry Litvin was a Philadelphia lad with no military interest whatsoever. He had enrolled at the University of Pennsylvania during World War II, choosing a pre-med course. He also enlisted in the U.S. Naval Reserve.

Upon his graduation he entered Penn's medical school, finishing up in 1948. This was followed by a two-year internship, also in Philadelphia.

In June 1950 he became a full-fledged doctor. Now it was time for his active tour of duty in the U.S. Navy. Henry's first post was to be Newport, Rhode Island.

When he arrived at Newport, he got the shock of his young life. He was told that he had been transferred to the 2nd Battalion, 5th Marines, out at Camp Pendleton in Oceanside, California. It was tremendously confusing to a new doctor who had not realized the Marines had no medical corps. It was all handled by the Navy, and he was now a part of it.

From Pendleton, Litvin was quickly sent to Korea, where he served with the 5th Marines at Inchon and Seoul.

But it was to be the Chosin Reservoir that would stick most in his memories.

"It was a continuing nightmare," Henry will tell you today, "until we got to Hungnam. The suffering of our division coming those seventy miles to the sea, with the Chinese on all sides of us, was horrendous."

After the war, Dr. Litvin studied psychiatry and has been a practicing psychiatrist in the Philadelphia area for several years. For his heroic work at Chosin, Litvin was awarded the Legion of Merit.

LIEUTENANT (JG) HENRY LITVIN USNR
2nd Battalion, 5th Marines, 1st Marine Division

Of course I remember the Chosin. If I live to be a hundred, I won't forget it; the incredible cold and all the damage that 30-degrees-below-zero weather can do to the body and to my efforts to help the wounded, it's all still here.

For instance, there was this young officer I had met aboard ship when we were crossing the Pacific. His name was Karl Seydel, a big, healthy bruiser who had played football at Washington State. He looked like the stereotype Marine, you know, the ones on the recruiting poster, the kind of Marine who would break down a wall for the Corps.

Yet, in reality, he was a very gentle guy. This rough-looking Marine would actually stand next to the railing of the ship and recite poetry. He was a reserve officer from Seattle. He'd also tell me all about the plans he'd made for when he'd be out of the Corps.

Well, on December 5 we'd been working on the wounded for days. I was beat down to my socks, hadn't slept for hours. Then they brought in Karl. He'd been shot in the head. One look told me he was dead. Just like that—dead. I couldn't control myself. I broke down and cried like a baby. It only lasted a few minutes, though, then I pulled myself together and went back to working on the living. But that's what it was like at the Chosin—misery and death everywhere.

Okay, let's go back about five months before the Chinese hit us. You know, they're Chinese now, but back then it was chinks, Chinamen, gooks, or worse.

Anyway, I'd graduated from medical school at the University of Pennsylvania in 1948 and had spent two years interning at Philadelphia General Hospital. When I finished this stint, I was a full-fledged doctor.

In the meantime, I'd been in the Naval Reserves at medical school with the understanding that when I finished interning I'd spend two years on active duty. So, on July 1, 1950, I was ordered to report to Newport, Rhode Island, for duty.

Boy, did this sound great, Newport in the summer! I'd never been there, but I'd been reading about it all my life. The prospect of strolling around that town in my dress whites, perhaps with a suntan, was very appealing.

Then, shortly after my arrival at Newport, I got the word that I was being transferred to the FMF. Now, what the hell was the FMF? I was in the Navy and I'd never heard of the FMF. I immediately went to see my commanding officer.

"Sir," I inquired, "what is the FMF?"

"Why, Fleet Marine Force, U.S. Marine Corps, of course," he answered.

"But, sir, I'm in the Navy, not the Marine Corps."

My CO looked at me as if I were nuts.

"Son," he said, "the Marine Corps does not have a medical corps. The Navy handles it for them."

You see, I was so unmilitary I didn't know that the Navy handled the medical part of the Marine Corps. After all, I was a doctor. My job was to save lives, not fight a war. Regardless, I was soon at Camp Pendleton, California, where I was immediately attached to the 2nd Battalion, 5th Marines. Part of the 5th had already been sent to Korea, and we were soon to follow.

Fortunately for me, there were a lot of junior officers around who seemed to get a big kick out of my unmilitary bearing. Hell, I was a Philadelphia kid, never had been camping, never been a Boy Scout or anything like that. I was a fish out of water, and did it show. There was one time when I was supposed to roll my pack. Those officers couldn't have been nicer. They showed me how to fix things, the blanket roll, everything. Then I started to put it on my back.

Now, do you realize what the impact of seventy pounds will do to you when you've never had a pack on? Hell, I fell right over on my ass. All the other officers laughed like hell. I started laughing also. It was a riot, all right, but the important things is, it never happened again.

Well, I may not have had much military experience at the time, but I was an outstanding doctor, or so I thought, as does every other doctor who has just finished his internship. Maybe the best word for it is "omnipotent," but, whatever, it is a period in every doctor's life when he feels he can do anything and save everybody. He's cocky as hell, to put it mildly.

But I was to get my comeuppance at the Reservoir, all right, and in the worst way possible. To see so many of those young Marines die without being able to help them was the most heartbreaking experience of my life.

Okay, let's center in on the Chosin. By the time we landed at Wonsan, I'd found out about the horrors of war at Inchon and at Seoul. I also knew that silver bars or no silver bars, no one else was going to dig my foxhole for me. If it was to be dug, Lieutenant Junior Grade Henry Litvin was going to dig it.

After we landed, we started moving north, heading for the Reservoir. A junior officer, particularly a doctor, has no knowledge of the grand strategy whatsoever, but the scuttlebutt had us eventually linking up with the 8th Army, who were also going north over on our west, up by the Yalu River.

Now, as we'd moved north, we kept seeing more and more signs of Chinese soldiers. In that quaint way the Marines have of talking, we were constantly hearing, "Hey, where the fuck are all these Chinamen coming from?"

Then there were several remarks about Chinese hand laundries, but the most amazing thing we heard came from a sergeant who was with the 5th Marines in China after World War II. He had some of the real young Marines half believing a physical impossibility about the privates of Chinese women. At least the kids let the sergeant think they believed him.

More and more, we thought it seemed to be getting serious. General Almond, CO of X Corps and MacArthur's headquarters in Japan, kept telling us to pay no attention to the Chinese troops.

"They're not in the war," said Almond.

"Then what in hell are they doing here?" replied the Marines.

Were we going into a trap?

We got the answer soon enough.

By this time we'd gone through a battalion of the 7th Marines up near Yudam-ni. We didn't realize it, but this was just about as far north as we were going to get.

Well, I believe the day was November 27. We'd been running into more and more Chinese roadblocks. I think it was near one of them that our battalion had our first real serious firefights with the

Reds. That night we'd set up a personnel tent where we could work on the wounded. The other doctor in our battalion, a man named Jim Sparks, and myself, plus about ten corpsmen, were in the tent doing our best when we started to hear all these damn bugles, whistles, and firing. Then this young Marine came running into the tent.

"They've broken through!" he was yelling. "The gooks have broken through our lines!"

Keep in mind it was well below zero at the time, with a chill factor that was brutal. Nobody talked about chill factors in those days, but believe me, it cut through you like a knife.

Nevertheless, this Marine was in his stocking feet. He seemed in a daze. He kept yelling for Colonel Roise; he wanted to make sure Roise knew what was going on. We tried to convince him that if Roise didn't know what was going on, he'd have to be dead.

Then came the crucial cry: "Corpsman, corpsman!" It seemed to be coming from all directions.

This brings me around to a pet peeve of mine. We all know how great the Marine is in combat. If he weren't, we would never have gotten out of the trap the Chinese had sprung on us. But what about the corpsman, the unsung hero of just about every fight the Marines have been in in their history? Just let that cry of "Corpsman!" go out, and most of the time one of them will appear.

From the time we hit Inchon (September 15) until I left the battalion in April, our medical unit had over 100 percent casualties. And most of the time I'd have to play God. I hated it. Let's say we'd get a call from Captain Sam Jaskilka, CO of Easy Company.

"Doctor Litvin," he'd say, "we're catching hell and I'm all out of corpsmen. Can you send us one?"

Then I'd have to look over at what we had left. No one ever complained. They knew what was coming and they'd look at me with stoic eyes. I'd order one to turn to. He'd mumble something like, "Yes, Doctor," or maybe, "Aye, aye, sir," grab his gear, and take off on the double. Some of the time they'd be back with a wound of their own and some of the time they'd never come back—not alive, anyway. For the rest of that night, and I guess for just about every night until we got to Hungnam, we were working on our wounded.

One case in point came from that first night's attack. I'd done all I possibly could for four wounded Marines. I reported as much to Colonel Roise.

"Colonel," I said, "unless we can get these four to a place where they can get additional treatment, they're going to die."

"Okay," he answered, "send them down in a truck as soon as you can."

Of course I sent them, but what I didn't know, and what the Colonel didn't know, was that we were already completely surrounded. The Chinese had cut the main road in two and had done it in several places. They ended up ambushing the convoy with the four wounded men, killing everyone. We came upon the burnt truck a while later. I just hope those Marines weren't alive when that truck went up.

Whatever, that incident has bothered me ever since. Could they have made it if they had come down with the main column? With the information I had in hand, I certainly made the only decision possible. But still, was I right? I guess it's just one of those things that makes war so loathsome.

You see, when you are working in a hospital, you have everything you need. But when you're out in the field, and it's so cold the blood from the wounded will actually freeze on your gloves, or, worse still, if you take your gloves off, the blood will freeze your hand to the wound, it's truly miserable.

We could do a reasonably good job on the arm and leg wounds and, of course, on the superficial body wounds. As for the frostbites on the extremities, we soon became experts on those, but it was the bad body and head wounds that broke your heart. Say a Marine takes a bullet in one of his lungs. If he was at a base hospital he had a real fighting chance, but out on a litter, with the weather so cold your spit would freeze before it hit the ground, it was very hard to save him. Hell, the blood plasma would freeze before you could get it into the guy.

We did get a blessing when we reached Hagaru-ri. The Marines had built an airstrip there, and the relief planes started to come in. It was an all-day proposition. Before they were through, they took close to 5,000 men out of there. What a job those pilots did! They saved a lot of lives and limbs.

I ended up walking all the way down. I had a jeep, but riding in it was colder than walking. I couldn't take a chance of anything freezing. Whenever we'd stop, I'd go to work. And remember, a vehicle is full of gasoline. If the gas tank got hit, it was apt to go up. This happened plenty of times.

It was things like that I had to get to know if I was going to stay alive. Fortunately, my chief corpsman had been with the Marines during World War II and he knew it all. What he did, I did. When he ducked, I ducked; when he dug a foxhole, I dug a foxhole; when he ate, I ate. All in all, it worked out damn well.

I had another senior corpsman, and even though he made all the right moves, we still lost him, while I panicked and survived.

It happened one morning on that brutal fourteen-mile stretch between Yudam-ni and Hagaru-ri. All of a sudden we started to receive a lot of small-arms and mortar fire. The corpsman jumped into a ditch and I followed suit. We were huddled there, waiting for the Marines to come and clear the hills.

Then I fell apart. I got up and ran for my jeep and dove under it. Something made me do it, don't ask me why, I don't know. I yelled over to the corpsman, "Hey, come over here, it's safe."

Oh my God, just as I yelled, the gooks riddled the ditch, shot the corpsman through and through. We would have both been dead if I hadn't run over to the jeep, yet it was a stupid thing to do.

I guess in the long run I was just lucky. Every man who came down from Yudam-ni was either hit or had his close calls. My point is, there was no such thing as a rear echelon during our march from Yudam-ni to Hungnam. The Chinese were all around us. No place was safe. Men were getting hit constantly.

One of these Marines was a career officer, Uei D. Peters, CO of Fox Company. Peters was hit near Hagaru-ri.

We had set up our tent and I was working on the wounded. It was nighttime and once again the Chinese had hit us. It was like clockwork. The planes would keep them off our backs during the daytime, to an extent anyway, but at night there he'd be, Charlie Chink, down from the mountains.

And there I'd be, with a Coleman lamp going, trying to patch someone up, set a fracture, ease their pain in any way I could, while outside we could hear the firing. It was like being at a John Wayne movie back in the States. Then a bullet would whiz through the tent and you'd know you weren't at any movie.

Well, they brought in Captain Peters and I went to work on him. Peters was a gung-ho, fiery kind of a guy—the Corps came first with him.

"Come on, Doc, patch this thing up," he's saying. "I've got to get back to my company. Those goddamn chinks are everywhere!"

Patch him up? One of his legs is on a ninety-degree angle. It was a compound fracture, without a doubt. And it's glowing. Well, what is this glowing? I had never seen anything like it before. So I turned to one of our corpsmen.

"What is that glowing?" I said.

"Oh, Doc, that's white phosphorus."

"White phosphorus? What the hell is white phosphorus? They never told us about that at medical school. What can we do about it?"

"Get the copper sulfate and keep dabbing the leg."

So that's what I did until I had neutralized the wound, and all the while I'm doing this, must have been at least three hours, Peters was yelling, "Hurry up, hurry up, I've got to get back to Dog Company!"

Well, you know damn well Peters isn't going anywhere for a long while. But that's the way those Marines felt, most of them anyway. They knew they were fighting for their lives, and the thought of a whole Marine Corps division being annihilated was incomprehensible to them.

Right in the middle of my work on Peters, Colonel Roise came in. I may be wrong, but I think Peters was a particularly good friend of Roise's. He stood there watching me dabbing the wound. I looked up and could see the tears rolling down the colonel's cheeks, no sobs, just tears.

On second thought, maybe it was the cold. I don't know. But all of us were miserably sick of the whole operation at that time. We didn't know if we'd ever get to the coast. All we knew was we had a long way to go.

Whatever, Peters did get to the ocean and eventually was sent home. About four years later I saw in a Marine Corps journal that he had lost his leg. Don't ask me why, but I felt guilty about it. Maybe it was because every Marine I treated made an impression on me. None of them ever became just another face. I can honestly say that.

Another officer came into our tent who was probably a battle fatigue case. His platoon had been particularly harshly handled, really clobbered. He would just sit there, glaring into space. I let him stay in the tent for several hours, even gave him some of our precious brandy.

You see, he was a special case. His dad was an Army general. He definitely did not want to leave his men, yet he knew he was exhausted. Finally he said to me that he was feeling better, and back he went. He stayed in charge of his platoon all the way to Hungnam.

It was like that in our battalion, and I think a good deal of this spirit was due to Lieutenant Colonel Harold Roise; 2/5 was the rearguard of the whole division from Yudam-ni to Hagaru-ri and I'll never forget the job Roise did in taking that responsibility. Magnificent! What an officer!

Here we were, really in the rear ranks, and every day before we'd start our march, he'd come over to me.

"Doc," he'd ask, "are all the wounded taken care of? Have they all been seen? Are they all ready to go?"

Sometimes I'd have to say no. Maybe there'd be two or three men up on a hill, waiting to be picked up.

"Okay," he'd say, "let me know when you get them. We're not leaving any of our Marines for those bastards."

Can you imagine, holding up the movement of a whole battalion like that? There're a lot of former Marines alive today who owe a lot to Roise.

And every time we'd stop, there he'd be, looking for the safest spot for me to set up. No place was really safe, but he'd do the best he could. Hal Roise was sure as hell the epitome of what a Marine officer should be. And the troops knew it.

But there was nothing he could do about the cold. Not only would our blood freeze, but everything else. The corpsmen would stick the morphine bottles in their crotches to keep them from freezing.

In this arctic weather, the chest wound could be very critical. You see, if the wound would allow any of that frozen air into the lungs, well, believe me, that air shouldn't be there. I developed a method of taping a condom over the wound. There were plenty of them available, though God knew what the men were going to do with them where we were.

Then I'd put a small slit in the condom with a bayonet so air could leak out, but as the air tried to get in—remember, that wind was tremendous—the condom would flatten, keeping most of the air out. I don't know if this saved anybody in the long run, but we would try anything.

Another sight I saw that can show you how bad the weather could be was this tall Marine who'd been hit in the face. It was a worse-looking wound than it actually was, but he'd bled a lot. As you know, when blood comes out, it's red. But with this frozen weather, it was pink.

Now, do you remember that cotton candy we used to get at the circus? This kid looked just like he had a huge piece of that cotton candy on the side of his face. At first I didn't know what to make of it. When I realized what had happened, I gently cut the ice off and slapped a dressing on the wound. I wonder, did Hawkeye on "M*A*S*H" ever see a sight like that?

Anyway, we did make it to Hungnam, and the happiest guy in our battalion had to be Sam Jaskilka, CO of Easy Company, who would eventually retire as a four-star general. Sam had actually received his orders to go home just before we were trapped by the Chinese. To make things even more interesting, his wife was pregnant. I never found out if Sam got home in time for the delivery or not, but he did get home in one piece.

Well, after we arrived at the coast, we quickly went aboard ships. I'd walked the entire seventy or so miles from Yudam-ni in subzero weather and didn't even have a sniffle. Twenty-four hours after boarding that tub, I caught one hell of a cold, didn't shake it for weeks.

I stayed with the 5th Marines until April. Then I came home, along with a friend whom I'd gone over with, Stan Wolfe, a surgeon in the 2nd Battalion of the 7th Marines. Stan had also gone through hell with the 7th.

However, there is one more thing I'd like to tell you. When I was growing up, my family was very strict on language. Profanity was definitely taboo. I also developed a very bad stammer. It stayed with me until I got with the 5th Marines. Then all my inhibitions about profanities went out the window, and so did my stammer.

AUTHOR'S QUESTION: Do you stammer now?

ANSWER: Fuck, no!

Maggie Higgins

The Korean War had its share of outstanding war correspondents, but no one in the class of World War I's Floyd Gibbons* or World War II's Ernie Pyle.†

There is one name, however, that has stood the test of time rather well: Maggie Higgins. Her fame derives partially from the fact that as one of the very first women to serve as a front-line reporter, Maggie stood out at all times. In the early 1950s the tremendous change that World War II had brought to women in American society was just beginning to be felt. A war correspondent known as Maggie was indeed a rarity.

Under the auspices of the now-defunct *New York Herald-Tribune,* Maggie arrived in Seoul before the first evacuation from the South Korean capital. From then on she covered the Korean War until she returned to the States in 1952.

As an outstanding journalist, Maggie seemed to possess the essential qualities that are needed to endear oneself to the people at the top. Her first conquest was General MacArthur. It was to Maggie that this great commander made one of his immortal statements. It was on June 29, 1950, less than a week after the war started, when he said to Maggie, "Give me two divisions and I'll hold Korea." Mac must have been dazzled by Maggie's smile when he uttered that sage remark.

---

*An outstanding personality, Floyd lost an eye at Belleau Wood with the Marines.

†The most famous of World War II correspondents, Ernie was killed while covering the Marines during the Okinawa campaign.

One of Maggie's great admirers among the Marines is Ray Murray, former CO of the 5th Marines. He greatly laments the fact that Maggie was not allowed to stay with the Marines during the eventual long retreat from Yudam-ni to Hungnam.

"I was really sorry O. P. Smith felt that Maggie had to be flown out at Koto-ri," Murray told me. "It would have been great PR to have her march down with us. Maggie may have been a woman, but she was as good a journalist as any of the other ones we had with us. She called them the way she saw them."

Murray certainly should have known Maggie by the time the Marines had reached Yudam-ni. She had been with his regiment at Inchon, had gone in with the early assault group at Red Beach. She had stayed with the 5th through the retaking of Seoul. But when she was with them at the Chosin, it was a different story. General Shepherd tells us why.

"I had flown into Koto-ri to get an on-the-spot appraisal of the situation. I told General O. P. Smith that I would be marching down to Hungnam with the troops. Hell, I'd known O. P. since the end of World War I. I thought he'd welcome me, maybe figure I'd be able to take some of the responsibility off his shoulders. I was wrong. O. P. didn't like my idea at all."

"'General,' he said, 'please don't march down with us. We have no idea how many Chinese there are out there. We have a long way to go. We could still be overrun; no one wants a lieutenant general of Marines killed or captured. I'll probably be flying out tomorrow myself. We've got to have a perimeter set up when these men get to Hungnam. I'll give you an accurate report on how things are, then you can get on a C-47 and take off.'

"Smith may have been junior to me, but he was right. You should never interfere with the commander in the field. I'd only be in the way. I spent a good deal of time talking to various Marines, trying to get a picture of the situation, then headed for the plane.

"Just as I was about to get on board, my old friend Lewie Puller showed up. He had a very irate Maggie Higgins in tow. It was easy to see he was quite interested in getting rid of her.

"'General,' he said, 'please take this woman down to Hungnam with you. General Smith doesn't want her with us.'

"Poor Maggie, she'd already been chased out of Hagaru-ri. Now she was to go all the way down to the sea with me. I knew her quite well. She wanted me to tell General Smith to let her stay with the troops.

"'Oh, General,' she pleaded, 'this is the biggest story of the war. I don't want to miss it.'

"I looked over at Lewie. He had this beaten look on his face and he's shaking his head. He took one of Maggie's arms and gently interlocked it with mine.

"'Please, Maggie,' he said, 'go with General Shepherd.'

"Now it was time for me to be fatherly.

"'Oh, come on, Marguerite, I flew up here so I could go down to Hungnam with the troops. But General Smith has shown me that I'll only be in the way. You know everyone loves you, but General Smith has enough to worry about. He's got the lives of all these men on his mind.'"

Lem finally convinced Maggie that the two of them had better get on board, and they did. They just sat there for several minutes. Then they started to hear mortar fire.

"What's going on?" Lem asked the pilot.

"'We've got to wait until they rid the area of Chinese machine gunners, sir. They are on both sides of the runway.'"

Shepherd then turned to his companion. He put one of his arms on her shoulder.

"'Maggie, if we're going to die, let's die in each other's arms.' She laughed. You must remember that Maggie was fearlessly crazy."

The plane did take off and it was fired upon, but not hit. It made it to Hungnam. A year or so later, Shepherd was made Marine Commandant. He continued to make his periodic trips to the Marines in Korea until the war ended. Maggie eventually returned to the United States, wrote a great book on her days in Korea, married an Air Force general, and settled down on a farm in Virginia.

But when the Vietnam War came along, she became restless. She had become quite well known by this time, and had no trouble getting back into harness. While in Vietnam, she contracted a rare Oriental disease and died.

But when you talk about her today with the venerable General Shepherd, he just smiles and shakes his head.

"O. P. should have let her stay with the troops. She would have been a Joan of Arc to those Marines on the way down."

John Babyak and Emil Dlwgash: The Steel Town Marines

The Marine Corps has always had a plentiful supply of recruits from the steel towns of western Pennsylvania and eastern Ohio. Many of these Marines trace their ancestry to central Europe. While at a reunion of the Chosin Few, I ran into two of these gentlemen from the Youngstown, Ohio, area. They were Emil Dlwgash and John Babyak.

Emil served in the 3rd Division of the Corps in World War II. He was wounded on Iwo Jima. When he was discharged after World War II, he joined the Marine Corps Reserves. He was, of course, recalled to active duty after the Korean War broke out. He was once again wounded and sent home for good. He is now retired from the General Fireproofing Company.

John, the younger of the two, joined the Marine Corps after high school in 1948. He ended up in the 1st Marines from Inchon to Operation Killer in 1950. He received a Letter of Commendation at the Reservoir and a Bronze Star at Operation Killer.

He injured his spine very seriously in an automobile accident two years ago while working for Hydro Security. He is not paralyzed, but another jolt to his spine could be extremely dangerous.

The economics of the area where these two men grew up have

changed drastically since their youth. The Youngstown Steel and
Tube Company is no longer the giant of the area. However, it is still
a very fruitful place for Marine Corps recruiting. When I asked the
Youngstown telephone information for John Babyak's phone number,
they told me there were four John Babyaks listed.

SERGEANT EMIL DLWGASH
F Company, 2nd Battalion, 7th Marines
CORPORAL JOHN BABYAK
D Company, 2nd Battalion, 1st Marines

JOHN: You know, it's a funny thing, but in 1950 if there was
anyone disliked by the Marines any more than Harry Truman, I
don't know who it could have been.

EMIL: How about Douglas MacArthur? Do you know that in
1944 he wanted to move the whole 3rd Marine Division to Leyte and
use us as policemen? That's right, he wanted to use it as MPs.
Halsey and Nimitz quickly put a stop to that.

JOHN: Well, just after we went into Inchon, Truman said that all
we were was the Navy's police force. And he also said we had a
better PR department than Joe Stalin.

EMIL: Oh, that caused a big stink. But nevertheless, we went
and fought his war for him. I guess that's what *Semper Fidelis* really
means.

JOHN: Yeah. Well, in 1948 I thought I was going to parade for
that same Harry Truman, but I ended up getting shafted.

I was at Camp Lejeune at the time. The word came down that
we're to start practicing for a big review by the President. No one
is excited about that until we hear it's going to be in Miami,
Florida.

Wow! This means some beach time and all those beautiful
girls down there. We started drilling in earnest, and I mean dress-
blues drilling and all the nitpicking that goes with it. Our captain
is riding us pretty hard, but who cares, we'll soon be on our way
to Florida.

Then came the bombshell. The captain called a group of us together.

"I'm sorry, men," he said, "but we're not taking as many men to
Florida as we thought. You men are not going."

Okay. I'm only five feet five and a half inches, but I don't think I look like a Munchkin out of *The Wizard of Oz*. But as I look around, it becomes obvious that they have picked all the tall guys to go and are going to leave the rest of us at Lejeune.

This really pissed me off, so I got permission to see the captain. His name was Doty. After I stated my case about the short guys not going to Florida, I could see he was embarrassed.

"Look, John," he said, "the colonel wants to make a good impression on the President, and he thinks the taller Marines can do it. I know it isn't fair, but that's the way it is. I'll make it up to you men when we get back."

Well, Doty was a very fine officer, the kind of guy who really practices that leadership stuff the way they tell you Marine officers are supposed to. When he came back from Florida, he gave all those who didn't go five days extra leave.

Then, about six months later, he called me into his office. There was another officer there. His name was J. J. Thomas. He was an Annapolis man. Both of us loved sports and we used to gab about it a great deal.

Well, when I walked in they told me to sit down. Then the captain started in.

"Babyak, we have been checking your record. We think you should go to OCS."

Jeez, they could have knocked me over with a feather. All I had been trying to do was be a good fire team leader. I didn't feel I was qualified to be an officer, but, above all, I *didn't want* to be an officer. I had to think fast.

"Sir," I said, "about six months ago I was told I didn't have the military bearing to parade in front of the President. Now you're talking about something that is really important. You're talking about me being an officer, someone who would have the responsibility of a platoon under fire—the lives of all those men."

Oh, I'm talking a mile a minute, my hands in the air like a little ole Eye-talian. They kept trying to sell me the idea, but I'm just not buying. They finally gave up on me, read my ass off a little, and sent me out.

By this time it was the spring of '50 and I had less than a year left on my cruise. I liked the Corps, but it never was my intention to be a career man. If I'd gone to OCS, I would have had to ship over.

Now for the funny part. Did you ever hear of "convenience of the government"? Well, that's what I was by the end of my enlistment. Couldn't go home anyway. I was in the middle of Korea. All discharges were frozen.

Anyway, when we first heard about the trouble in Korea, several of us had to go to a map to find that damn place. We had to learn a great deal about Korea and in a hurry.

EMIL: Well, it seemed to me that a good deal of your outfit was a finished product when war broke out. I was in the reserves when the thing started, as were a lot of others in the "Glorious 7th." I was with the 3rd Division during World War II, so I was no stranger to the Corps, but we had men in the 7th who had never gone through boot camp, I mean had never been to either Parris Island or San Diego, never been on real active duty. They'd done nothing but attend meetings in the reserves.

JOHN: No question about that. Many of us had never seen combat, but we had served together for quite some time. We had been together on the Med cruises. We were the ones who had enlisted between the wars.

EMIL: But there weren't enough of you. The Corps had gone from half a million when the Japs quit in '45 to around 74,000 when the Korean War broke out. I don't think the government ever let it get that low again.

JOHN: I guess not. But what I got a big kick out of in Korea was my reason for joining the Corps. I had graduated from high school in Youngstown, Ohio. This is very much a blue-collar town. It's the kind of place that is dominated by the steel industry. Well, things were not good in '48. There were just no jobs available. So, rather than just hang around, I decided to join the Corps. It had the big reputation.

So what happens? I am up to my rear end in snow, with God knows how many Chinamen trying to kill me, when I got this letter from home. It says there are plenty of jobs available back in Youngstown. I wasn't a likely candidate for any of them. That's the way it goes, I guess.

EMIL: As we used to say, "Was this trip really necessary?" Well, of the three infantry regiments of the 1st Division, the 7th might have been the last to land in Korea, but we were the first to meet the Chinamen, in any size anyway.

JOHN: That's right, it was near Sudong, on your way to the Chosin. You had a firefight with them. I remember that.

EMIL: It was a lot more than that. We had a first-class shootout for a couple of days. We took a lot of casualties, but we really shot the hell out of them. Then, I think it was the third of November, our airplane pilots really racked them up like bowling pins. After that, the Chinese seemed to disappear. But we should have realized those chinks weren't playing games, not throwing as many men at us as they did.

JOHN: We heard they were testing us with the lives of their men. That was the only thing they had a surplus of—men.

EMIL: Oh, when they hit us late in November, they surely had men, thousands of them. We were up near Yudam-ni at the time, and if the 5th Marines hadn't got there when they did, we'd still be there.

I was a sergeant at the time, in charge of four mortars. We called them "four-deuces [4.2]." You could tell when one of them was fired by its burst and its sharp crack. It was a damn good weapon. The last thing we wanted was to have the Chinese grab one, which was always possible because those gooks were all around us just about every night. We squared things away as best we could when dawn would come, but night was hell. Anyone who averaged more than two or three hours' sleep was lucky.

By this time we were being supplied strictly by air drops. I remember once getting all this barbed wire. What the hell could we do with barbed wire? This wasn't France in 1918. And the ground was frozen solid. John's regiment was coming up to meet us on the MSR, trying to keep the route open, but our first job was to get Hagaru-ri. It was one tough trip, I'll tell you that.

JOHN: We didn't link up with the 5th and 7th until up around Koto-ri. That's where our engineers had to put up that Treadwell bridge. That was one hell of a job, but the gooks had blown the one that had been there. There was no way you could have gotten through without a new bridge. They sure put it up in a hurry.

Right after the bridge went up, a Marine in our platoon went bananas. This guy's uncle had been a Marine in World War II. The whole family must have been batty, because the uncle had brought back a Japanese skull from the Pacific to use as an ashtray. Naturally, this guy figures he's got to get a Chinese skull. Keep everything in the family.

It wasn't going to be too hard to do, because you could always find a dead Chinaman. The guy goes to one of our trucks and gets an ax. Then he lops off the poor chink's head.

Next he takes a ten-gallon can of water and starts to heat it to burn all the flesh off.

Fortunately, we weren't all screwy. One of the Company D guys told the captain what this nut was doing.

Jeez, did the captain hit the roof! He made the kid throw the skull away, then he really lit into him. Oh, he was calling him everything under the sun. He had that kid scared shitless. And that was the end of the skull-hunting. These were the kind of officers we had. They weren't about to put up with any of that crap.

Another good one was our platoon leader, Second Lieutenant Howard Foor. We called him Bugs. He had great leadership qualifications, but the poor guy never got a chance to really develop them.

When we were around Koto-ri, we ran into this roadblock. We couldn't see any chinks, though. I turned to talk to this big red-headed kid who had just joined up with D Company, when, wham, he takes one in the head. It seemed to lift him right off the ground and his body rolled over into a ditch. Poor kid, I never knew his name. Then the Chinese fire got real heavy.

"Look," says Foor, "we've got to take that hill where the fire is coming from. We'll have to flank it."

Jeez, I can't see how the hell we can flank it, but we start to try. As I said earlier, I'm only five feet five and a half inches. Well, I got this big parka on that reaches down to my ankles and I'm slipping on the ice all over the place. I'm having more trouble with the parka than with the gooks. It's hell.

Anyway, as we're trying to maneuver into a flanking position, Foor is doing his best to lead us. All of a sudden this gook jumps up out of nowhere and riddles the lieutenant with one of those damn burp guns. The G-D things look like they cost $9.95, but they sure can shoot.

Just behind the lieutenant there was a BAR man named Jannti. He was a good friend of Foor's.

Hell, when he sees what happened, he takes that BAR and

puts a whole clip in the Chinaman's gut. He liked to cut the gook in half.

In the meantime we're still trying to concentrate on the hill, but as far as I can see, there ain't no way we can take it.

Then George Company comes along and joins us, but it's still no soap. It's obviously a tough nut to crack.

The next thing we know, a company of Royal Marines [British] shows up. If you ask me, these Brits are salty as hell. They give us this "cheerio" business and tell us not to worry, they'll take the bloody hill. They had a lot of guts, I'll say that for 'em, but they can't take it either. I don't remember if we eventually used the 11th Artillery or our planes on the Chinese, but there was no way we were going to get that place without more men and a great many more casualties.

One more thing about leadership. I honestly think the 1st Marines had one of the greatest combat leaders who ever lived as our colonel—Lewis "Chesty" Puller. I mean, he was the Man.

After the Chosin I got a letter of commendation that was personally presented to me by Colonel Puller. He looked me right in the eye, gave me the letter, and shook my hand.

"Thank you, son," he said, "our Corps needs more men like you."

Well, I was on cloud nine. Can you believe that? I mean, being thanked by the one and only Chesty Puller!

Then, shortly before I left Korea, I received a Bronze Star when my fire team wiped out a gook machine-gun nest that was holding us up. This happened in South Korea after we'd left Hungnam. And who do you think pinned the medal on me? That's right, the same Colonel Puller. His face lit up when he got to me.

"Well, son," he says with a big grin, "I see you're up here again. You must be quite a Marine!"

Wow! He *remembered* me. Can you beat that? All the decorations he gave out in Korea, and he remembered me.

EMIL: All the enlisted guys loved Chesty, but not all the officers. He'd been in the 7th Marines, you know, on the Canal, in World War II. That's where he was so badly wounded.

One thing we all got a bang out of was when he heard we were going down the MSR, he disagreed. He thought the 1st should join up with the 5th and the 7th and we could flank the Chinese. How the hell are 20,000 men going to flank over 100,000? None of us would have gotten out. But that was Chesty.

And speaking of getting out, when we got to Hagaru-ri, they started airlifting the wounded out.

JOHN: That's right, and that guy Almond told Smith not to take the time to build the airstrip when we were going up. But Smith told him baloney, he was going to build it anyway. Thank God he did! Those Army [Air] Transport guys did one hell of a job taxiing our men out.

EMIL: Well, there was one plane that didn't take any Marines out. That's the one that took out the mortar, that's right, just one mortar.

When we got to Hagaru-ri, I was told to take the 4.2 that had fired the most shells over to the airstrip. Christ, we had been firing in constant support of the rifle companies. The one that had fired the most had fired one hell of a lot of shells. You know how it works. You fire so long, then you move your mortars and start firing from another angle. The four-deuce was one hell of a killing machine. You didn't want the chinks knocking them out.

So we showed up at the airstrip with our base piece. It was in awful shape, but that was the one they wanted. Do you know, they wanted to fly this beat-up piece of junk out as quickly as possible? I couldn't believe it. I went up to this Army major to find out the score.

"Sir," I asked, "what is going on? This is a piece of junk. God knows how many rounds it has fired. It's had it!"

Well, these two doggies—one was a major, the other a captain—were nervous as hell. They no sooner had landed than they wanted to get the hell out of there.

"That's why we want it, Sergeant. Back in Aberdeen they want to know how much punishment one of these can take in combat. Please hurry and get it aboard, and good luck."

Well, I think their plane was on the ground between ten and fifteen minutes. They got out of there so fast I figured they must have a couple of sweet things waiting for them back where they were going. They left on a C-46. Its cargo was two Army officers and one beat-up 4.2 mortar.

JOHN: You can't blame those doggies, though. I'd have gotten out of there if I could.

EMIL: Well, I was taking my men, there were twelve of us, back to our unit when a captain grabbed me.

"Don't bother to settle down," he says. "You and your men are replacements for Fox Company."

Oh, that's a jolt. We'd been in constant combat for what seemed like several days. We sure didn't want to go into a rifle company, particularly Fox. The word going around was it was jinxed. They'd lost a lot of men at Fox Hill up near Yudam-ni, and had continued to take casualties on the way down the MSR. However, when you're told to do something in the Corps, you do it.

As it turned out, Fox *was* jinxed—for me, anyway. I was no sooner there when I got hit. We had just come down a hill when this Chinaman jumped out of nowhere with a BAR. Don't know where he got it, but he had it. He didn't really know how to use the thing. He was firing it in every direction, and wham, the sonofabitch hits me. He wasn't even looking at me when I was hit.

JOHN: Well, I marched all the way down in one piece, but, my God, it was cold. It was so bad it could stun your memory. Above all, you'd try to stay awake. With that weather you could go to sleep and not wake up. You'd just plain freeze to death.

There was a time, near Koto-ri, when we were moving south, when this Marine yells, "Hey, there's a gook!"

Sure enough, sitting on a hill, about 300 yards away, there's a chink. He's got a rifle in his hands, but he's not making any motions toward using it. We approached him very carefully, ready to fire at his slightest move.

When we got real close, it was obvious what had happened. The poor bastard had frozen to death. He was stiff as a board. I think it was then that I realized those Chinese were just as cold as we were.

EMIL: Yeah, I heard that when you started to get close to the sea, you could see groups of Chinamen wandering around in a daze. They'd had enough.

JOHN: I'll tell you one thing, by the time we got down there, I'd had enough, too! Nobody had to tell me to get on that ship twice. The next time we met the chinks was in South Korea, and it was a different story.

But, you know, as I look back on the whole thing, I have mixed feelings. Take that old expression, "My country, right or wrong."

Okay, I'll go along with that. But why do they have to keep the troops in the dark? We're not idiots. Remember that crack Mac-Arthur said about being home for Christmas? When we were going north, we're all saying to ourselves, "What Christmas does that joker mean, certainly not 1950."

And what really pissed me off was when I found out that the Chinese had specifically told us to stay away from the Reservoir. Sometimes I feel the guys in the ranks are smarter than the big wheels. At least we were a lot closer to the action. I sure as hell wouldn't have sent troops to the Chosin.

EMIL: You're probably right. Anyway, I'm just glad I didn't get called up for Vietnam. I was hit on Iwo Jima, then at the Reservoir. Three strikes and you're out, you know.

Who's Sleeping
in My Rack?

A small minority of the Marines in each platoon at boot camp are picked for sea school; here they are trained to be seagoing Marines. This duty, a bit of an anachronism, is a throwback to the days when Marines aboard ship were sent up in the rigging so they could pick off the enemy gunners during sea battles.

Today, these Marines man the 20 mm guns on the capital ships and perform in such capacities as brig guards and captain's orderlies. This is where the term "seagoing bellhops" came from. It is also considered good duty by Marines, especially when compared to the foxholes.

I had both sea duty and the infantry in World War II. Believe me, sea duty is better, unless you want to earn the Medal of Honor. Very few seagoing Marines are awarded the CMH these days.

A Korean War Marine who also served both aboard ship and as a rifleman is Bud Cain. I met Bud at a gathering of Marines in Woodbridge, New Jersey. He told me of an ironic sighting of his former ship while he was in Korea.

"It was near Wonsan in North Korea," Bud remembered. "We'd been sitting off the coast in our transports for what seemed like forever. Now we were in our landing crafts, headed for the shore. I could look over on my left and there she was, the USS *Missouri*, the Mighty Mo, my former ship. I'd been a member of the Marine detachment on her for almost two years when I got the brilliant idea to transfer off her. I must have been nuts.

"Well, as we were going in, I could clearly see two Marines on the *Missouri*, waving at us. I turned to my fire team leader.

"'Lookit, see those two gyrenes on the Missouri. I'll bet one of 'em is going to sleep in my old rack tonight. I'll be digging a hole in the ground somewhere, maybe have some gooks shooting at me. Not that guy on the Mighty Mo. He'll have clean white sheets, a soft pillow, and he'll wake up to a good hot breakfast.'"

At this point in Bud's narrative, a Marine named Bob Hill joined us. An old shipmate of Cain's, Hill had stayed on the *Missouri* after Bud had left, and was still on her when she was off Wonsan.

"Oh, for Christ's sake, Bud," he said, "I remember watching you guys go in at Wonsan, and I did take over your rack after you left us. But, Bud, you are wrong about the breakfast. You know damn well that our toast would frequently be cold."

Bud looked at his old pal.

"Is that so?" he said. "What the hell do you think we were having for breakfast up at the Reservoir? Caviar?"

Barber of

Fox Hill

The British have a way of honoring their heroes. They have such figures as Kitchener of Khartoum and Montgomery of El Alamein. In Bill Barber we have an authentic American hero. Hence the title "Barber of Fox Hill."

Born in eastern Kentucky, Barber had already served a decade in the United States Marine Corps when his command, F/2/7, was assigned the task of defending what was to become known as Fox Hill against an overwhelming number of Chinese troops.

Rising high above the surrounding area, the hill was located in such a way as to dominate the MSR between Yudam-ni and Hagaru-ri. In case the Marines were to retreat, it was essential that this area be under their control.

Starting early in the morning of November 28, the hill came under attack and was to remain so over the next four to five days. Although Barber does not go into detail about the ferocity of the fight, it was extremely bloody.

It was a struggle dominated by rifle, machine-gun, and mortar fire. In some cases it turned into a very primitive struggle with pistols, entrenching tools, bayonets, and even fists.

Above all, there was Barber. It seems that every command decision he made was the right one. Though he attributes this to luck, he was still the one who ordered these correct moves.

Seriously wounded during the second night of the siege, he nevertheless stayed in command, and he always seemed to be in the right place at the right time.

I asked him how it was possible for his one reinforced company to hold out against such incredible odds.

"Well," he answered, "it was certainly due, in part anyway, to our superior firepower, plus the lack of any artillery or air power on the part of the enemy. But," he added, "the main reason was the military stupidity of the Chinese. Their tactics were extremely bad."

In any case, the hill was held. When his reinforcements arrived, Barber was even able to send out a patrol in their support.

When it was all over, eighty-six of Barber's original 237 men were on their feet. According to what Barber considers a conservative estimate, they had killed or wounded more than 2,000 Chinese troops.

Captain Barber was evacuated to Japan by air from Hagaru-ri, and from there to the United States. He'd been in Korea about thirty days, long enough to be awarded the Congressional Medal of Honor.

Colonel Barber retired from the Corps in 1970.

CAPTAIN WILLIAM BARBER
F Company, 2nd Battalion, 7th Marines

You want a comparison between the Japanese on Iwo and the Chinese at the Reservoir? What makes this difficult is the roles they were playing. On Iwo we were the attacking force and we greatly outnumbered the defenders. At the Chosin it was the Chinese who were the attackers.

The Japanese on Iwo were typical throughout the Pacific. They were tenacious. They held on and made us pay the price for every inch. All they had to do was look at the armada we had surrounding the island to know they didn't have a chance. But if we wanted to take the island, we'd have to come to them and take it.

On the other hand, the Chinese were in a different position. And they were fundamentally stupid in their tactics.

For example, we were attacked in the same position and almost at the same time every night. They made plenty of noise before they would charge, yelling, blowing bugles, and so on. They made no attempt at surprise whatsoever.

There was only one time that they made an effort to flank us, and that was pretty weak. All I had was a Marine rifle company. If they'd tried to flank us with strength, I don't know if we could have stopped them. Mass attacks with no artillery or air support can be extremely bloody to the attackers. Fox Hill was no exception.

Besides, the company I was in command of was in top shape. We were not looking to die a glorious death for an emperor, like the Japanese. We wanted to hold that hill. It was a good company, full of guts and hope.

And I should have known Marines by then. I'd enlisted in the Corps in 1940 and had risen from the ranks. I was what is called a mustang.

I was living in eastern Kentucky when I went into the Corps. Then, like now, this wasn't a part of the country with a booming economy. I'd managed to get through two years of college, but couldn't see how I could scrape up the money for the next two.

Hitler had gone into Poland by then, and Japan was kicking the daylights out of the Chinese. The Marines looked like a good outfit. I decided to go into the Corps so I'd be ready when the United States got involved.

When the Japanese attacked Pearl Harbor, I was a corporal at Marine Parachute School at Lakehurst, New Jersey. I stayed there until 1943, when I was chosen for Marine OCS at Quantico, Virginia. After earning my commission, I was sent to the 1st Parachute Regiment at Camp Elliot, near San Diego.

Then the Marine Corps disbanded its parachute regiments. I was sent overseas to help form the newly created 26th Marines of the 5th Marine Division. The only campaign of the 5th was to be Iwo Jima. I went ashore a second lieutenant. When the island was secured, I'd been wounded twice and was a company commander.

When the Korean War broke out, I was a captain in charge of the marine barracks at the Philadelphia Navy Yard. The Marine Corps was just about as combat-ready as anything the country had. It was inevitable that we would be involved as quickly as possible. That brigade we sent over in a hurry did a tremendous job at Pusan. They were the cream of the Corps.

I went over a little later, joining F/2/7 as CO on November 6, 1950. The 7th was at Sudong, about halfway between Hungnam and Haguru-ri.

My job was to make my presence known. The first thing I had to know was which of my officers and noncoms had the moxie and the knowledge to lead. It meant a lot of practice. Some of my noncoms were World War II veterans. They were excellent. As we moved up, I always had a lot of patrols out, was constantly practicing the coordination between the company and the supporting artillery and, in

general, trying to improve the efficiency of the company. By the time
we were needed, we were in pretty good shape.

The attack came on November 28. I was told by Colonel Lockwood [CO of the 2nd Battalion] that my company was to guard positions over Toktong Pass, between Yudam-ni and Hagaru-ri. A lot was
going on up around Yudam-ni, but I didn't know this. Lockwood
drove me in his jeep to the place where F Company was to set up.

This was the first piece of good luck we had. If someone hadn't
spotted this area as a very important position, the Chinese would
really have been able to shoot the hell out of the 5th and 7th Marines
when they came down the MSR a few days later.

Then came another break. My company was able to borrow some
trucks from the 11th Marines so they could arrive in place before the
darkness set in.

There was still another piece of good fortune. I knew the men
were tired. I almost said the hell with it. The ground was frozen; why
not leave them alone? Nothing was going to happen that night. But
no, at the last minute I changed my mind. Just to be on the safe
side, I gave the order to dig in.

Oh, did the men bitch! I couldn't have been elected dogcatcher.
But dig in they did. When the Chinese came, we were ready for
them.

We ended up with an oval-shaped perimeter that was as strong
as you could have with one company.

Actually, it was a reinforced company. We had machine guns
and mortars from Battalion. All in all, at least 240 Marines.

There was still another incredible piece of good luck. I didn't
think we were going to be attacked, and if we were, I didn't have the
foggiest notion which direction the attack would come from. Yet,
purely by chance, I put my strength in the line facing Yudam-ni. I
had just one platoon facing Hagaru-ri. Hell, our supply trucks were
coming from Yudam-ni with their lights on till after midnight.

Well, at 0120 I got word from my strong point that they were
hearing noises. Of course, it could be Marines coming down from
Yudam-ni. But my 3rd Platoon commander [Bob McCarthy] said
they were the enemy.

"Are you sure?" I asked.

"I am now," he answered. "I'm going to open fire."

Well, once we started firing, so did the enemy. Petersen's platoon, next to McCarthy's, became involved. It was a real old-fashioned shooting match. It seemed every one of the enemy had a burp gun. McCarthy's group was badly shot up, but the enemy losses were astronomical. We had to give up some high ground but, on the whole, held the line. The next morning one of my platoon leaders, John Dunn, organized a counterattack and retook what we had lost that first night.

By now we knew we weren't facing North Koreans. The attacking force was definitely Chinese. There was no way of knowing how many were out there. All we knew was there had to be a tremendous amount of them.

Now for another piece of good luck. The radio we usually had, the SCR300, would not reach either Hagaru-ri or Yudam-ni. Both towns were about seven miles away.

So, when I found out where my company was to be posted, I put in a strong request for an Angry 9, the radio we used for our naval gunfire coordination. I had to persist, but I finally got one.

This allowed me to get through to both Yudam-ni and Hagaru-ri. At least I was able to get the word to Regiment that we were under heavy attack.

When daylight did come, we could clearly see the Chinese pulling out to the northwest, the area they had come from. We could see them moving back, but they were out of our firing range.

It was now time for me to take stock of our situation. I had suffered many casualties, most of them wounded. As we were trying to defend this area with one company—we needed a battalion—the loss of those men hurt us.

But what a job they did! One of them, Hector Cafferatta, was awesome. God knows how many Chinese he'd hit. He also did a tremendous job in throwing back at the Chinese their own hand grenades. The last one exploded too soon, taking one of Cafferatta's fingers with it. Cafferatta was a big guy, nicknamed Moose by the troops. He ended up with the Medal of Honor.

I kept calling for air support, but didn't get any till the afternoon. When it did come, it was the Australians who came. They did a great job.

That same afternoon I got a message from Colonel Litzenberg, giving me the option to move down to Hagaru-ri.

While this certainly was an attractive suggestion, I knew by now the extent of the Chinese attack at Yudam-ni. Fox Company was holding a very key piece of terrain. We were set up in a pretty good position. If we pulled out and left this position to the Chinese, God knows what would have happened.

While there was no way for reinforcements to get to us, we could be supplied by air drops. While the men were all bitching about not getting enough materiel, in reality we certainly got our share.

Besides, I couldn't very easily get my wounded out, even though the rest of us could have made it.

Our artillery was really superb. I think it was How Battery of the 11th Marines. They were down near Hagaru-ri, but they were able to zero in on the Chinese whenever I asked them to.

Well, the second night it started all over again. This time part of the Chinese did hit our flanks, but not with as much strength as they hit our center.

They seemed to be coming at us in battalion strength. We'd done a good job in neutralizing their battalion that hit us the first night, but on the second night they charged with what was left from the night before, plus a fresh battalion. This was when I was hit.

It was an unusual shot. First it went through the arm and rifle stock of Bob McCarthy. It was rather well spent, but it had enough drive left in it to lodge deeply in my hip. I later learned that it just missed important nerves and blood vessels, but I was too involved in the battle to pay much attention to it. I had to keep moving.

After the battle, our people made a lot of the fact that I stayed in the fight. My citation even has me being carried to the various positions in a stretcher, which is a part of the fight that I don't remember at all.

Besides, a lot of my people were getting hit. I know Elmo Petersen was hit twice, once in the shoulder. He didn't quit.

And Joe Brady. He'd been hit in the hand. Yet, when we had some much-needed mortar shells air-dropped 500 or so yards from our perimeter, Brady was one of our men who went out after them. He cradled two of the shells under his good arm and started zigzagging back to our lines.

Joe had been a halfback at Dartmouth College. When he was inside our perimeter, I pulled him aside.

"Joe," I said, "I bet you never made a run like that at Dartmouth!" He laughed.

Wounded or not, staying in the fight was the norm. We had picked up a lot of weapons, mainly '03 rifles and Thompson machine guns, from the dead Chinese near our lines. I guess the Reds had captured them from the Nationalists. Many of our seriously wounded Marines asked for them, saying that if things got real rough, I could count on them.

Well, the morning after the second night, we were still in position, but we'd suffered more casualties. However, so had the Chinese. As I looked out at them, they seemed to be confused. Then one of my men pointed to this mass of dead Chinese.

"Captain," he said, "look at that dead Chinaman." He was trying to point out the man he was talking about.

It was rather hard to see who he meant—there were so many dead ones out there—but I finally located the right one.

Well, it seemed that one of our men had shot their bugler. The dead guy was still clutching that damn bugle. Many of the Marines made fun of the Chinese bugles, but each bugle call meant something. If you wanted to confuse them, just shoot all their buglers; they'd be lost.

Anyway, I now started to pay some attention to my hip. The pain could get so bad I'd have to take morphine. I could still get around, but I'd had to keep going to keep my circulation moving. I knew it wasn't fatal, but the bullet was still there and I knew I was going to be in for a rough time. I had a great first sergeant, Charlie Dance, and a top-notch executive officer named Charlie Wright. I know Wright was also hit, but it was a day or two later. These two helped a great deal.

Anyway, I kept my command, but I told my officers to watch me. If I said something that didn't seem like me, they were to call me on it. If I really went off the deep end, someone was to take over.

In the meantime, it was getting colder than I'd ever seen it. We were getting ammunition by air drops, but it would mean nothing if our weapons didn't work.

Luckily, I had a couple of gunnery sergeants who really knew weapons. I had them keep circulating, showing the men how to keep their weapons serviceable. This was particularly true of the BARs. We'd be in real trouble if we lost our BARs.

Our machine guns were also important. They were from the battalion's weapons company, heavy water-cooled guns. In gaining them, I also got a very good sergeant. He was a reservist from Tennessee. His name was John Henry, a good name for a Tennessean. His guns were very effective.

In addition, I had some eighty-one mortars, also from the battalion. Once again I got a good man, a PFC O'Leary. He'd been a mortarman in World War II. What he didn't know about mortars hadn't been invented yet. He had a knack for range estimation for mortars and everything else.

In addition, we had Fox Company's own machine guns and mortars. We were a formidable force, all right, but to hold out, when you consider what we were facing, took all we had.

In the meantime, I realized we were isolated. The Marines at Yudam-ni had started their march down the MSR. I know people like General Smith and Colonel Bowser were concerned about us, but they didn't have a good picture of our situation. The one who did was our colonel, a man named Litzenberg.

Now, as far as I'm concerned, I never knew a better man than Homer Litzenberg. He was tough, fearless, a marvelous tactician—in short, a real tower of strength in every way. I can't imagine a commanding officer being any more effective. I was sure Litz would not leave us at the top of that hill.

By the third day we had more or less developed a routine. I was trying to make sure the men changed their socks every day, things like that. We didn't want anyone getting frozen feet.

The care of our ever-increasing wounded was a real problem. The blood plasma was all frozen. It was tough to see a young Marine bleed to death, but it happened. The corpsmen would keep the morphine in their mouths to stop it from freezing, but there was nothing they could do about the plasma.

Our corpsmen did a great job, though. One of them was a man named Ed Jones. He was always working on someone. He was killed trying to get a wounded Marine under cover.

As expected, the third night found the Chinese coming at us again. This time we had plenty of ammunition and had grenades. As I remember, we let them come into a can't-miss range, then opened up.

My God, it was slaughter! I believe they were coming from the south this time. We had fired illuminating shells that lit up the whole area. John Henry had his machine guns in an ideal position. The Chinese didn't have a chance. I guess the enemy found this out in a hurry, because the assault ended up without the intensity of the first two nights. It was just a big turkey shoot for us.

The next morning our morale was surprisingly high. My wound was bothering me a great deal, but the mood of my men cheered me up. It was even better when I saw a great deal of air activity. Our planes dropped a large supply of material and ammunition, and our Corsairs hit the Chinese with everything but the kitchen sink— napalm, bombs, and bullets.

The exit from Yudam-ni had started in force. We later found out that General Smith called it an advance to the rear. Whatever, it brought up a serious question for me. I sent the word out to the troops.

"Listen, men," I told them, "I know damn well we're going to be relieved, and soon. We've got to be very careful *not* to fire on our own troops. No one wants any dead Marines on their conscience. Now let's try and clean up this mess!"

Well, you never saw Marines turn to on a police detail so cheerfully. Even some of the wounded helped.

That night we were waiting for the attack. But outside of sniper fire, nothing really materialized. I actually think the troops were disappointed.

On December 2, I received radio contact from Ray Davis, CO of the 1st Battalion, 7th Marines. He told me that we were to be relieved shortly.

"Colonel," I said, "watch out for that rocky ridge to our left. It's still loaded with Chinese."

Then I sent out a patrol to keep the Chinese busy while the 1st Battalion came from the right and drove them out.

A day or two later we joined the column going to Hagaru-ri. My wound was bothering me greatly, but I insisted on walking those seven or so miles with my men. I later received the Congressional Medal of Honor for our stand at Fox Hill. But my real honor was commanding F Company, 2nd Battalion, 7th Marines in that fight. Those men were magnificent.

Due to my wound, I'd turned over my command to First Lieutenant Jack Dunn, the only one of my platoon commanders who hadn't been hit on the hill.*

---

*Ironically, Dunn, who hadn't received a wound at Fox Hill, was killed between Hagaru-ri and Koto-ri on December 6. The Chosin campaign was like that.

I was evacuated by air from Hagaru-ri to Hungnam. From there, I was flown to Japan. I'd been in Korea about a month.

There is one thing that happened just before I left my company that I won't forget. A young PFC came over to me.

"Captain," he said, "I guess those chinks had a bellyful of Fox Company."

Amen to that.

The Helicopters

When Sal Cavallaro (C/1/5) took a hand grenade in the face on the outskirts of Seoul, it was a Sikorsky helicopter that evacuated him back to a base hospital in Inchon.

"It probably saved my life," says Sal.

This same experience was shared by hundreds of other Marines during the Korean War. Once again I turn to Lieutenant General Victor "Brute" Krulak (USMC Ret.) and Brigadier General Gordon Gayle (USMC Ret.) for the story of the Marine helicopters. First, Gordon Gayle:

"We had helicopters in Korea before the Army did; used them to carry supplies, evacuate wounded, and reconnoiter areas, especially out-of-the-way places.

"One time, when I was the exec of the 7th Marines, we had to get a battalion across this river, can't remember which one. So we called in the helicopters and got the job done in four or five hours.

"Another time we moved a whole battalion from reserve to the front lines and took the other battalion back to reserve.

"We called it Operation Bumblebee. You see, a bumblebee can't fly, according to aerodynamics anyway. We felt the same about our helicopters. But both seem to do pretty well.

"Back in the late 1940s, Bill Twinning, one of the smarter Marines, looked into the future.

"'In this new age we live in,' he said, 'we've got to deploy troops with the greatest possible rapidity. The answer is the helicopter.'

"Brute Krulak was another early believer in the chopper. When they had a demonstration in front of Breckenridge Hall in Quantico to show how a helicopter could pick up a man, it was Krulak they picked up."

And indeed Krulak was a believer, probably the first American military officer to see how important the helicopter was to become to the United States.

"The other services laughed at us," Krulak told me, "when we sent the first helicopters to Pusan. At first we used them for reconnaissance and evacuating our wounded. Then in the summer of '51 we brought the first helicopter squadron in the world to Korea and put them into combat in an attack by a company in a mountain area. This was followed by using them in support of a company in a night attack on the Chinese. We called the first assault Summit, and the night attack was Black Bird.

"Well, as soon as the Army saw what our helicopters could do, they wanted a piece of the action and said, 'Resources such as the helicopters should not be committed to a single unit. They should be under the auspices of the whole 8th Army.'

"We raised such a fuss that they left us alone. They started to buy their own, but I don't think theirs were as good as ours. Of course, none of them in the early '50s were anywhere near as good as what we have now, but they did a great job for us."

At any rate, the Marine Corps was the first branch of the services to utilize the helicopter in combat.

Joe DeMarco:
The Toktong Ridge
Runner

"Both my parents came from Italy," Joe told me, "around the turn of the century. Hard-working immigrants, they raised seven sons and four daughters, a very hard thing to do during the Depression. Five of my brothers served in the U.S. Army during World War II. One of them was shot up pretty badly in the Philippines."

All of Joe's brothers had been drafted. Joe's father could understand this. But, in 1948, when Joe enlisted in the Marines, he was baffled. He said to Joe, "In the old country they say you gotta go in the army, you go. But here no one says you gotta go in these Marines. Why you go? You don't like your home, your family, whatsamatter?"

Joe had a hard time convincing his dad—mainly because he didn't know himself—but he succeeded.

Signing up for a three-year cruise, he spent most of his early Marine Corps days honing his electronics skills. Then came Korea, an experience that he had not counted on.

"Of course, I didn't want to go to Korea. But I knew when I left for Parris Island that if there was a war, Marines would be involved."

Joe spent a year in Korea, came home, finished out his enlistment, which he had extended an extra year, and was discharged as a staff sergeant.

He has managed to return to the San Diego area on several occasions, usually alone. When he visited the West Coast in 1985, where he now has a daughter living, his wife agreed to accompany him.

"Thank God for that. She had a great time. She died a few months after we returned. I still miss her."

SERGEANT JOSEPH DEMARCO
B Company, 1st Battalion, 7th Marines

Three or four years ago I was talking to this young fellow who works with me at Wang Laboratories in Lawrence, Massachusetts. He's a member of the Marine Corps Reserves. What does he have on his desk but a copy of *Leatherneck* magazine. I hadn't seen it since I left the Corps back in '52. Jeez, it's great! The Corps never changes, just the names. I asked the wife to renew my subscription. Renew? That's a hot one, I hadn't subscribed for thirty years. Anyway, I now read it from cover to cover.

Well, December 1948, I was working for one of my brothers in industrial catering. I got a phone call from Gus, a very close friend of mine. We'd grown up together in the large Italian area of Lawrence. He was working in his father's grocery store.

"Joe," he said, "when you quit work, come on down to the store. I've got a big surprise for you." Big surprise, I couldn't wait! I jumped into my Chevy and drove to the store, even sideswiped a snowbank on the way.

"So, Gus, what's this earthshaking surprise?" I asked.

"I joined the Marine Corps."

"You did what?"

"Yeah, ain't you coming?"

"Hell, no, what do you think you asked me to do, go out and have a couple of beers?"

"Look, Joe, why don't you see if you can pass the physical?"

"Listen, if you can pass it, so can I."

At any rate, he got me to go to the recruiting station in Boston, and much to my amazement I failed the damn thing. I was underweight and my blood pressure was high.

"Go on home," said the doc, "eat a lot of bananas, drink lots of milk, and take some tranquilizers. Then come see me."

Now it was a challenge. I did what he told me to do and returned a week later.

Things had improved, but I still was a little off in both the weight and the blood pressure. This didn't bother the doctor.

"It's good enough for me. Let 'em worry about you at Parris Island."

So that's how I got to boot camp along with my buddy Gus. The second day there I looked at Gus and just shook my head.

"We're a couple of stupid assholes."

"You can say that in spades!"

Well, we got through that place, but Platoon 28, 1948, was no picnic, I'll tell you that.

We were given our ten-day furloughs and ordered to report back to PI. We had enlisted for three years, and as far as we knew, we'd been slated to spend all those years at Parris Island. Hell, we even thought of going AWOL permanently, but decided that was a sucker's play.

When I got home, there was my father and mother to greet me. I had on my dress blues. My father had never seen dress blues before.

"Hey, Joey, you an officer?"

"No, Pop. This is the Marines' dress uniform."

I don't think my father really believed me. He had to take a picture of me in my dress blues.

"I want my relatives in the old country to see my Joey in his officer's suit," he said.

From then on, whenever I'd come home, I had to wear my "officer's suit" for Pop.

When I got back to Parris Island, I was told to report to radio school at Camp del Mar in Oceanside, California. They had told us that Gus and I would stay together, but he was sent to clerk-typist school at Camp Lejeune. So much for what you're told when you enlist.

From then on, I went the regular Marine routine until February of '50. Then I was offered a shot at high-speed radio operators' school at San Diego. The only catch was I'd have to sign on for an extra year on my enlistment. I told them thanks but no thanks. Then they went to work on me.

"Think what it'll mean to have these skills when you're discharged. Besides, your buddy, Ski, has already signed on." So I figured what the hell, why not, and I went along with them.

Now for the ironic part. Normally I would have put my three years in by February of '51. By that time my outfit had just left Hungnam for Pusan in Korea. All discharges had been frozen. What are you going to do?

Well, I finished the operators' school first in my class. The fact that the chief instructor was from Sommerville, Massachusetts, didn't hurt, but, frankly, I was a crackerjack radioman. I seem to have a natural penchant for it.

As the top man, I more or less had my choice of billets. They kept offering choices such as Camp Lejeune, but I kept refusing them. I was a corporal in a casual company, which meant I could go to Hollywood almost anytime I wanted. I always was a stargazer. Things were going great until the first sergeant called me in.

"We're got something for you, Joe. How would you like to go to the 1st Division?"

"Hey, wait a minute. Everyone knows where they're going."

It was now the middle of July, and the scuttlebutt had the 1st going to Korea as soon as possible.

"Joe, now we're not asking you, we're telling you!"

So the next day I went the forty or fifty miles up the coast to Camp Pendleton. I was assigned to Communications, 1st Battalion of the 7th Marines. The regiment was under the command of an old-time Marine, Homer Litzenberg, while the 1st Battalion Commander was Ray Davis. Colonel Davis was a great leader, but he certainly was no recruiting-poster Marine. He was not very tall, and he used to wear his piss cutter [overseas cap] at a crooked angle. I was not impressed when I first saw him, which just goes to show you how wrong you can be. By the time I left the 7th, I was convinced that Ray Davis just might be the greatest Marine who ever lived.

In July of '51, the 7th was a paper regiment that the Corps was trying to fill up in a hurry. Colonel Davis had been a regular officer in charge of the reserves in the Chicago area. Of the three infantry outfits in the 1st Division, I think the 7th probably had a higher percentage of these reserves than the other two. It was quite an experience to watch these men operate.

I was lying in my fart sack one morning when this buck sergeant came over to me. He had never spent any time on active duty, but he'd also never missed a reserve meeting. Regular attendance at those meetings usually meant promotion.

"Would you mind sweeping the floor, Corporal?" he very politely asked me.

I was stunned.

"Corporals don't usually do that, Sergeant. But I'll very quickly have it done for you. And by the way, we call it a deck, not a floor."

"Of course, thank you, Corporal."

Jeez, our communications chief was a postal inspector from San Diego. We had reserves up the ass. It would come out in the wash during our hikes. We had one just about every day. A twelve-mile job is not considered a long one for regular Marines, but it knocked the hell out of these reserves.

I was due to be assigned to a company. Abel had this real rugged guy as its captain. He carried a K-Bar in his boot. Charlie Company [had] another rough guy, but Baker, jeez, its company commander looked like he'd come out of a bandbox.

His name was Myron Wilcox. His last post had been embassy duty in Paris. He looked pudgy and he wore glasses. Naturally, I was assigned to Baker Company and once again I was wrong. Anyone who says that first impressions are usually right is full of baloney. Wilcox was a good man.

Well, we headed for Japan as soon as possible, but we spent only a few days there. By the time we got to Inchon, the 1st and 5th Marines had already landed and were well on the way to Seoul.

At this time a good buddy of mine, another communications Marine named Ronald Strohman, had become ill. He couldn't seem to hold anything down. The doctors said he was just seasick. I could see it was a lot more than that. I managed to get some fruit juice from the Army—it wasn't easy—which he did seem to digest, but he was still in a bad way. I decided I better keep my eye on him. He was made a message center runner, which is just about as easy a job as you can have. Then this lieutenant stepped in.

"Listen, this guy Strohman is faking. He's all right. Send him to Charlie Company. They need radiomen."

So away went Ron. We all knew that Charlie Company was a jinx for radiomen. Hell, they lost more of them than Carter had pills.

Anyway, a week or so later Charlie went up a hill and came down again. When they came back, Ron wasn't with them. He was never seen again.

Well, most of our officers were good guys, and the relations between them and the enlisted men were excellent. We did have one guy who was a real wiseass, a first-class loser. I think he was the same guy who sent Ron to Charlie Company.

This guy was something else. He always looked spick and span.

When someone asked him how he kept so neat, he just smiled. "My men do all my laundry," he said.

Every day, even if we were short on water, this idiot would take five gallons for a shower. Once again, his men would be forced to get it for him. Some of them weren't getting enough drinking water.

He really got it one time, though, when Colonel Davis went on a patrol with us. Major Tom Tighe, one of God's noblemen, was also going. Tighe appreciated our lack of water and hadn't been bathing, just like the rest of us.

At any rate, he spots this lieutenant. You couldn't miss him, not with his immaculate clothing and those flying boots he used to wear. The rest of us were still wearing our leggings.

"Hey," said Tom, "you come with us. I never see you doing any work. Come and earn your pay."

Before we left, we were told to take our blankets, we were going to be gone overnight. The colonel, however, was scheduled to go back to our headquarters.

Well, we went quite a distance. Then Colonel Davis changed his mind. He decided to send his runner back for his bedding. The wiseass heard Davis tell his runner to go back.

"You there, get mine also. It's in my tent."

Jeez, you could see Davis fuming.

"Lieutenant, you were told to bring your bedding. If you want it, go back and get it."

Oh, the men loved the colonel, you can bet on that.

Later that night the wiseass came over to me.

"Joe, do you have an extra blanket?"

"Sorry, Lieutenant, I can't help you."

That was it for the Lieutenant. He was sent back to the States. I hope they put that guy in charge of a mess kit repair unit.

Well, we joined the fighting around Seoul. It wasn't fun anymore. That's where we lost Ron.

After Seoul, we started to move out. Then the word came through to return to Inchon. We were moved by boat over to Wonsan, on the east coast in North Korea. Then we marched up the coast to Hungnam. From there we started out in a northwesterly manner toward Yudam-ni, a town on the northwestern side of the Chosin.

We met our first real resistance about thirty miles up the MSR. We weren't sure who the enemy was. I wasn't, anyway. All I knew was there were a lot of them. We later found out they were Chinese, probably testing us.

I spent more of the time with Captain Wilcox. I had surely changed my mind about the captain. He was a real professional. We'd go out on night patrols. You could easily see he knew his business. Sometimes we'd get back to our lines quite late. I'd be bone-weary. That radio could get heavy. Wilcox's hole had already been dug for him. I guess he got sick and tired, seeing me spend half the night digging mine. He put out the word.

"Tonight I want you guys to dig a hole for Joe also. The poor bastard is just as tired as I am when we get back."

Now, normally a radioman would spend a couple of weeks with a company, then go back to Battalion for a while. Another radioman would take over. We were rotated that way. When my time was up, Baker's executive officer, Joe Kurcaba, made a request.

"Look, Joe, you fit right in with us. Everybody thinks you do a great job. Why not stay with us?"

Well, I liked Joe, liked everybody, so, what the hell, I stayed. Then came the night of November 27. The hell had begun.

I was bedded down, had even taken off my Mickey Mouse boots. Then I heard those damn bugles blowing and all the small-arms fire and mortars. I got on the radio trying to find out what in hell was going on. I could hear Lieutenant Chou Ein Lee trying to get his platoon up. None of this legendary, "Come on, you guys, do you want to live forever?" crap. Lee was more to the point. He was less colorful.

"What the hell do you think we're here for? Turn to."

I stayed on the radio while Wilcox had the phone part, also trying to get information. I can't remember how long this went on, but it ended with a mortar shell. Those damn chinks could put them in your pocket.

It scared the shit out of me, stunned me completely. I hadn't been hit. Then I looked over at the captain. I could see that the phone had been broken, the receiver was dangling in air. Wilcox was a mess. His jaw was shattered. The poor guy was in awful shape. He was eventually evacuated. Thank God he lived, but he must have had a lot of painful time in the hospital.

The next day or two were brutal and confusing. I'd had enough. I figured it was time to go back to Battalion. Jeez, when I got there, it was no better. We were soon told that orders had come from X Corps to get our asses back down to Hungnam. Well, how the hell are we going to do this? The Chinese seem to be on all sides. We're up near Yudam-ni. Hungnam is maybe seventy miles away. Plus we've got all these fuckin' Chinamen to deal with.

There's another problem. Our battalion has really drawn the short straw. Two companies of the 7th, Charlie and Fox, are out on a limb. Our battalion is ordered to pick them up on the way down.

First came Charlie. We literally had to fight our way to them, but we got through. They'd had a real rough time but were still intact. They'd done a great job. They were very low on ammunition when we got there. Another heavy Chinese attack might have finished them. We got there in the nick of time, just like in the movies. Now it was time for Fox, over near a place called Toktong Pass.

We had to be mountain goats to get to them. Those damn slopes were covered with snow and ice. You had to hold on to the guy ahead of you or you'd fall on your ass.

I'm now lugging the TVXA [radio] for the colonel. Every now and then he'd stop and get under a poncho with a map. He had this little light and was trying to figure out where the hell we were. It was pitch dark and just about as cold as it could get. How he could orient himself I don't know, but he did.

About two in the morning we got into a real firefight. We're cranking up that TVX as fast as we can, but Davis had a habit of depressing the microphone, which makes it tough to turn the transmitter. I kept telling him to release the microphone. Finally I yelled:

"Goddammit, Skipper, release the button!"

The colonel looked a little sheepish.

"Oh, I'm sorry, I'm sorry."

Finally we got through to Litzenberg. We could hear Homer talking.

"You know, Ray, you're getting close to Barber [the besieged captain of Fox Company]. Why not go right in?"

"I know, Homer, but I got to let my men rest for a couple of hours. We've just had a firefight with the Chinese. The men are exhausted and frozen."

Litzenberg always listened to Davis.

"All right, Ray, you know best."

So we rested for a few hours, then we took off again. By now it's daylight. We kept going until we came to this huge field of snow. In the distance we can see a wooded area.

"Okay," says the colonel, "Fox Company is over there. Let's go."

As we're moving through the field we start to receive some fire from the Chinese. But, you know, I was so tired and cold, just plain miserable, I didn't care. You can get that way.

At any rate, we got to Fox Company, and the place looks like a Hollywood battle set. Those guys had been fighting from an oval perimeter. They're standing up and cheering us. There are dead and wounded Marines all over the place. One I'll never forget was this corpsman, or doctor, lying there with his scissors in one hand and a roll of bandages in the other. He was dead. He must have been hit in the head just as he was going to bandage some wounded Marine.

I spotted Captain Barber. He was hobbling around, using a stick for a cane. He'd obviously been hit in the leg or the thigh. He's talking to Davis, trying to figure out how we're going to get his wounded out. And there were a lot of them. There was only one officer not hit.

Then some planes came in, dropping supplies and ammo. Hell, they even dropped some 105 mm shells. Why, I don't know. This was a rifle company. Someone yelled, "Watch out!" Jeez, this crate hit a Korean lieutenant and killed him. Then a helicopter tried to come in, but it crashed. It was quite a sight.

Many of these guys are still cheering us. I thought to myself, What the hell are they cheering for? Don't they realize we've got another seven miles or so to Hagaru-ri? And then where are we? It's a long way to the sea.

I spotted this wounded guy I'd served with earlier.

"Hey, Joe," he says, "got any water?"

Well, of course, I didn't. It's all frozen. So I took off my helmet, filled it with snow, and put it over a fire. Christ, do you know how much snow you have to melt to get a glass of water? Plenty! So I spent the next few hours melting snow for these poor guys.

I don't know if it was the next day or the day after, but Davis finally said, "Let's get the show on the road." We took all our wounded from our battalion and those of F/2, but not all the dead. Contrary to what you may have heard, we left many bodies there.

At any rate, the long road down to Hungnam somewhat rolls

together. I can remember one point when we had to leave the road and take a hill. Among the things we found was a German machine gun. I was working the radio with Major Tom Tighe, the guy I'd mentioned earlier. We all called him Tom Thumb. What a winner, a guy you really loved.

So Tom pulled out his .45.

"I think I'll blow the water jacket to pieces. Then you guys can dismantle it and throw the pieces away. We don't want it, but we sure as hell don't want to leave it for the Chinese."

He squeezed the trigger, but there's nothing but a click. He does it a few more times, but there's still nothing.

"Major," I said, "are you sure there's a clip in it?"

"Of course, what do you think I am, an idiot?"

Sure enough, it was loaded. We examined it. Can't remember what was wrong, but it was probably fouled up when it was issued.

"Can you beat that?" he said. "I've been carrying that goddamn thing since Inchon and it doesn't work. Thank God I didn't need it in a tight spot."

Then we came across this big bunker that had some Chinese in it. The chinks weren't like the Japs; they would surrender.

"We'll have to corral these guys and take them with us," said Tighe. "What a pain in the ass!"

As he said this, he leaned on the piling they had to hold the structure up. Wham, the whole thing caved in. Those poor bastards, there was no way we could dig them out.

"Too bad," said Tighe, "I guess we don't have to worry about them after all."

Okay. I mentioned Ron Strohman earlier. There was another communications man I used to pal around with. His name was Don Short. The three of us used to hit the slop chutes in San Diego before we went over.

Don was from the Hollywood area. He'd been one of the Marine extras in that film *The Sands of Iwo Jima*. He had pictures of himself with John Wayne and with Forrest Tucker. He had them stashed in a jeep.

One night, coming down from the Chosin, the chinks blew up the jeep. Oh, was Short pissed off!

"Those bastards blew up my pictures of me and the Duke. Those crummy sonsofbitches."

Can you beat that? We still don't know if we're going to end up dead or in a prison camp, and this guy is worrying about his pictures.

The food supply was brutal. We had a lot of those Charms candies. I ate them till they were coming out of my ears. Haven't had one since. If you were lucky, you had a can of beans. You'd keep this under your armpits all day, then warm it up over a fire at night.

When we got to Koto-ri, they had mess tents set up for us. It was luxurious as hell. Then this officer came by.

"Enjoy," he said, "but remember, we still have a hell of a long way to go." This brought us back to reality.

Shortly after that, I was told that one of our company's radios had gone on the fritz. I was ordered to volunteer to bring them a new one. It was quiet, no big deal. I started off with one of our chaplains. His name was Father Van Antrep. I think his father had been mayor of Detroit at one time.

Anyway, a Chinese mortar shell landed near us. This was bad news. I've already told you how good those chinks were with mortars.

"Father," I said, "you are not supposed to be under fire."

"I don't think the Chinese know this, Joe. Let's get the hell out of here."

So we took off. Wham, one of those shells landed very close. If it had been any closer, we would have been goners. As it was, we both got shrapnel up the ass. It seems to me that the father was hit worse than I was, but neither wound was very serious.

I got a corpsman to fix me up. It was just a couple of deep cuts. The shrapnel was easy for the guy to pick out. I could have gone to sick bay, but the Chinese loved to throw their mortars at those places. It would have meant a Purple Heart, but hell, we had guys get those for cutting their hands on ration cans.

And how Homer loved to give out those Purple Hearts! We'd usually have a ceremony where he'd pass them out. He'd get all choked up, real crocodile tears. I guess he figured the more Purple Hearts, the more we were fighting. Just look at the casualty figures of the 7th Marines' officers alone. That will show you what we were doing.

Well, we did get to Hungnam. Then we were evacuated to Pusan in South Korea. In the meantime we'd been switched from the command of General Almond to that of Matt Ridgway. He had taken over the 8th Army when General Walker was killed in an automobile wreck.

The 8th Army was to stabilize the front against the Chinese who were moving into South Korea. This is where I got my court-martial. What a joke! I was waiting for my third stripe at the time. I was also pretty salty.

It was in central Korea. Colonel Davis had taken a patrol out, with me as the radioman. We were slated to be gone for three days, but it ended up eight days. We got back after midnight on a Sunday morning. I figured I'd sack in the whole day.

Jeez, at 6:00 A.M. this staff sergeant comes into the tent.

"All right," he yells, "drop your cocks and grab your socks, all outside for muster."

What the hell is this, Parris Island? Besides, in three years I'd never heard of a muster on Sunday.

"Forget it," I answered. Then went back to sleep.

Well, that really cut it. Now it's the first sergeant who comes in.

"What the hell is this? You have willfully disobeyed an order from your superior. You are on report."

I said something like "Bullshit," but I knew I was in trouble. I was too tired to care.

A few days later I saw Tighe.

"Sorry, Joe. It looks like you're going back to private instead of up to sergeant."

A couple of weeks later I was up in front of a very stern Major Thomas Tighe. A captain is acting as my counsel. I didn't know what to say; all I could do was stammer.

"Captain, for Christ's sake," says Tighe, "take the prisoner outside and tell him how to act during a court-martial." Out we go.

"Look, Joe," the captain says, "go back in there, tell the major exactly what happened, and throw yourself on the mercy of the court."

Back in we go, and I'm still tongue-tied.

"What Corporal DeMarco means to say," said the captain, "is blah, blah, blah." He told Tighe what had happened.

Tighe said, "All right, dismissed."

I saluted and walked out. I thought I saw Tighe covering his mouth to stop from laughing.

A week later I received my third stripe. I was amazed.

Going in at Inchon: the perfect amphibious landing. *(United States Marine Corps)*

7th Marines at Hagaru-ri. "It wasn't much of a town." *(United States Marine Corps)*

The 1st Marine Air Wing protecting the Marines at the Reservoir. Without them, the 1st Division would never have gotten out. *(United States Marine Corps)*

The Reservoir, 1950. Going up wasn't bad. *(John Gaddit)*

Coming down was. *(John Gaddit)*

A welcome cup of hot coffee, 1950.
(John Gaddit)

The 5th and 7th
Marines have just been
told they are to
backtrack to Hungnam
from Yudaru-ri.
*(United States Marine
Corps)*

Hungnam, 1950. What to
do with all these Chinese
prisoners?
(Robert Mosher)

Mick O'Brien a month after the Reservoir. *(Mick O'Brien)*

The Fire Brigade arrives at Pusan, August 2, 1950. *(United States Marine Corps)*

Jim Brady (right) and the eastern front, 1951. It was like Vermont. *(James Brady)*

The celebrities were there: Jack Benny, right. *(Robert Mosher)*

A bogus wound, 1951: this Marine was trying to win his girl's sympathy. *(Peter Santella)*

Left to right: Lt. Col. Raymond G. Davis, Lt. Col. Webb D. Sawyer, and Col. H. L. Litzenberg Jr., shortly after Sawyer received his promotion, 1951. Ray Davis got the Congressional Medal of Honor for the Chosin.
(United States Marine Corps)

Ray Murray congratulated by Major General Oliver Smith for getting the 5th Marines from Yudam-ni to Hungnam.
(United States Marine Corps)

That old bandit, Syngman Rhee, inspiring the Marines. *(Jack Orth)*

Three happy interpreters. "One was a double agent." *(Peter Santella)*

A Seoul Honeywagon. "One of our guys threw a hand grenade in it."
(Peter Santella)

Have a Blatz. It was green beer. *(Peter Santella)*

The once beautiful city of Seoul. *(Peter Santella)*

Hospital Ship U.S.S. *Repose*, a haven for many Marines. *(Jack Orth)*

The big move, 1952. *(Peter Santella)*

The big move, 1952. 1st Marine Division moves from the eastern front to the western front. *(Jack Orth)*

General Lemuel C. Shepherd Jr., Commandant of the Marines, is followed down sandbag steps by Major General Edwin A. Pollock, Commanding General of the 1st Marine Division, 1952. *(United States Marine Corps)*

Liberty. "The youngest pimp I saw in Korea." *(Jack Orth)*

A captured Chinese peace poster, 1953. *(Jack Orth)*

Spring '53. The western front. Note armored vest. *(Jack Orth)*

Left to right: Naval Corpsman Burt McDowall, Cpl. Jack Orth, and Don Comton. A night on the town. Comton was killed at Vegas, spring of '53. *(Jack Orth)*

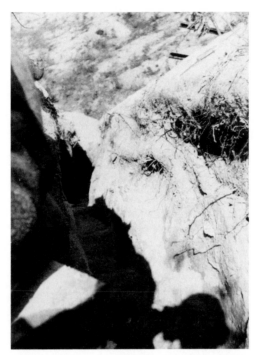

The Trench Line at Boulder City, spring '53.
(Jack Orth)

"We called it Dagmar." You can see why, 1953.
(United States Marine Corps)

France, 1918? No, Korea, 7th Marines, 1953. *(United States Marine Corps)*

Cleaning up after the Armistice—risky business. 1953. *(Jack Orth)*

Remembering a hero, 1953. "Lieutenant Valentine was the bravest man I knew." *(George Broadhurst)*

George Broadhurst. He was hit on the last day of the war. *(George Broadhurst)*

What had happened was the case went up to Colonel Litzenberg. It had to. But Davis had called Litzenberg and pointed out what had happened. He asked Litzenberg to tear the thing up. As I said earlier, Homer always went along with Ray's suggestions. Tighe knew this all the time. From then on, every time I saw Tom Thumb, he'd smile.

"Good morning, Private, how are you today?" He had to have his little joke.

Well, in September of '51 I was rotated home. A year or so later I saw a picture of Ray Davis being presented the Medal of Honor by Harry Truman. All I could think was if Davis didn't deserve it, nobody did.

By 1972 he was Assistant Commandant of the Marine Corps. Then he retired. I wrote him a letter telling him who I was and congratulating him on such a great career. I didn't think he'd remember me, but he did. He sent me an autographed copy of *The History of the United States Marine Corps,* and told me if I was ever in Atlanta to stop by. We could have a couple of mint juleps.

There is another guy I'll never forget, and that's Joe Kurcaba. He was a mustang. Joe took over Baker Company when Wilcox was badly wounded. Joe was killed on December 8, 1950. Peace to his ashes.

Integration

There were no Negroes living in my hometown when I grew up. Therefore, the absence of black faces in my platoon at boot camp did not affect me one way or another. It was not until I left Parris Island, in November of 1943, that I really discovered segregation.

This happened at a lowlife honky-tonk dive in Port Royal, South Carolina. As I went into the men's room, I noticed a sign that said Whites Only. I thought this was really overdoing things, since it was obvious that only whites were served at the bar as it was. Besides, the way this rest room smelled, I could hardly imagine blacks clamoring to use it.

Anyway, I figured it was time to find out how the Corps felt about blacks. The sergeant I asked was from southern Georgia.

"Sergeant," I said, "I don't remember seeing any colored [a 1943 term] at Parris Island. Do we have any in the Corps?"

"Yeah, goddammit, we started taking them in last year. But don't worry, you'll never serve with any of them."

I figured it would do no good to tell this fellow that it would not bother me if I did serve with blacks. The point is, he was right. During my tour of duty, I never did serve with a black Marine.

Move ahead to the fall of 1948. I was a student at Kenyon College in Gambier, Ohio. The civil rights movement was in its infancy, but it was there. The black students on campus were no longer an oddity.

Ninety or so miles north of Kenyon, the Cleveland Indians were enjoying a magnificent season. Sparked by their outstanding center fielder, Larry Doby, they were making a very serious run at the American League Pennant.

The Indians' owner, Bill Veeck, a former Marine, had brought the hard-hitting Doby to the Indians that year. Doby was the first black star to play in the American League.

In mid-season Veeck pulled another coup. He signed Satchel Paige, the wonder pitcher of the Negro League, to a Cleveland contract. Veeck did not know for sure how old Satch actually was, but he knew that Paige could still pitch. Before the season was over, the Indians had won both the American League pennant and the World Series. Baseball had become one way for blacks to climb out of their isolation. The same could not be said of the Naval Services. However, the next year was to change that drastically. General Krulack recalls the incident well:

"It was a general order from the Secretary of the Navy. It went like this: 'Henceforward, no member of the Navy Services shall be promoted, reduced, billeted, messed, disciplined or otherwise administered in regard to race, color or creed.' That was it. Segregation was over and done with.

"At the time I received that order [September 1949], I was the CO of the 1st Command Service Group, some 2,600 men. This was a logistical outfit stationed at Camp Pendleton. In my command I had one black unit. It was named the Depot Company. I knew that had to change at once. I sent for my chief of staff.

"'Have you read this order?' I asked him.

"'No, sir.'

"'Then read it. I want you to immediately reduce the Depot Company to one Marine. Check the spec numbers of each man and transfer them to the units where they are best suited. And report back to me when it is done.

"Next I went to see my boss, General Graves Erskine. The general was from Alabama. He had the well-earned reputation of being very explosive. At any rate, I presented myself to him.

"'Sir,' I said, 'in compliance with the Navy Department's order number such-and-such (whatever the hell the number was, I can't remember it), I have reduced my Depot Company to one man and transferred the others to various units throughout my command.

"Erskine got red in the face.

"'On whose authority?' he bellowed.

"'The Secretary of the Navy.'

"'Is that so? Well, you don't know what's in that safe over there.'

"'No sir, I don't. But I do have this order from the Secretary of the Navy.'

"'Get out of here!'

"'Yes sir.'"

At this point General Krulak chuckled.

"You know," he said, "he never did tell me what was in the safe. Well, next I went to Dave Shoup,* Erskine's chief of staff. I told him about the order. I got the feeling that Shoup thought it was a hot potato, didn't want to touch it. Then I went back to my office.

"At about four o'clock, Erskine's G-1, a friend of mine named Murray Hayes, came to see me. He was all smiles.

"'Brute, I can't talk now, but I want to tell you the old man [Erskine] has called the Commandant [Gates] to tell him he has complied with the order. It's a done thing. You want to leave Erskine alone for a while, though.'

"That was it. Throughout the Corps it was the same. We were integrated and that's all there was to it. I don't remember it being a problem in Korea. It wasn't until Vietnam when we had such a row over civil rights in the States; part of that turmoil was bound to get to southeast Asia, and it did.

"I was a lieutenant general by then, and my orders concerning any race trouble were explicit. I wasn't going to get involved with any rednecks or Black Power advocates; I was simply going to fire the commander of the unit where the unrest occurred. A position like that got results. As I recall, we had fairness at every level."

Thus, the Korean War was the first time that black and white Marines served together in combat units. By the time of the Armistice, the black presence was very much a part of every battalion. Today, some 20 percent of the Corps is black.

---

*A World War II hero, Shoup was later Marine Commandant.

Bob Smith:
The Black Pioneer

The Marine Corps was lily white until 1942. Then came President Roosevelt's order to take in blacks; they could segregate them, but they had to take them in. It was not the most popular order in Marine Corps history; there were too many Southerners in the Corps. But like it or not, there it was, a direct order, and it had to be obeyed.

During the next three years, some 20,000 black Marines served in the Corps, all in labor battalions. They suffered 87 casualties during World War II.

This, then, was the structure of the Marine Corps when Bob Smith enlisted in 1949. It was soon to change. An order came from Washington, desegregating all units. It was earthshaking, all right, but there were problems.

"You can't change men's minds with an order," Bob told me, "it takes time and lots of it."

Over the next twenty-three years, Smith saw not only his Corps but also his country change. He served in the 7th Marines in Korea, not as a laborer but as a squad leader in a rifle company. When Vietnam came around, he was a sergeant, and when he'd had enough soldiering, it was First Sergeant Robert Smith who retired in 1972.

He now lives in northern New Jersey with his wife and their two children. He is employed by the U.S. Postal Service.

PFC ROBERT SMITH
C Company, 1st Battalion, 7th Marines

I was in the Naval Reserves, serving aboard the USS *Missouri*. We had a detachment of U.S. Marines aboard, and they impressed me greatly. It seemed more of a man's life to me than the Navy. The services were not as yet integrated, but you could see it coming. I had decided to make a career out of the military, and the Corps looked like the best place. So in 1949 I enlisted in the Marines. I spent the next twenty-three years in the Corps and never regretted my decision.

I was first sent to Montford Point at Camp Lejeune, North Carolina. They had the black boot camp there. The only whites I saw at Montford were the officers. All the noncoms were black, and they could be tough as the devil on a young boot.

There was one sergeant in particular who was mean—I mean just plain mean. The first or second day I was there, I was walking when I was supposed to be running. He came over to me with this "I am God" look on his face.

"Boy, I better motivate you."

So he gave me a big kick in my rear end, and believe me, he had big feet.

"Now *run!*"

Oh, he was all "yessuh, yessuh" to the white officers, a real Uncle Tom, but he could sure take out his hostilities on the black boots.

"As you were, colored boot." That's what we were called in those days.

This guy was also a career Marine. I ran into him several times throughout the years. I don't think he ever changed. He'd been brought up a certain way and had no education. I don't think he realized he was living in the past.

There were, and still are, several whites in the Corps who feel the same way. I can remember drinking with a couple of 'em in a noncommissioned officers' club after I'd made sergeant. One of them brought up this man's name.

"Oh, he's a real Marine," he said. "He can sure keep those blacks in line."

"Do you mean he can't handle the whites?"

"Well, uh, I didn't say that."

"But you sure implied it."

That was the end of the conversation.

You see, I think it's all a matter of education. You have prejudice today and always will have. Look at Ireland. They're all white Irishmen. Nevertheless, they're killing each other. All over religion. That's some kind of religion.

But if you look at it from an educated standpoint, it's all foolishness. I've served with plenty of Marines, white and black, who I've thought were idiots. I've tried to stay away from these people.

Once the order came down to integrate, though—which was also in 1949—more and more Marines started to accept it, but not all, not by a long shot.

Well, after I left boot camp, I was sent to Camp Lejeune as an MP. There was one other black guy in the MP Company. It was tokenism, all right, just the two of us in the whole company. Many of the whites were ready for the change, some were not. As I said before, I'd just stay away from the idiots who were upset over the change.

The big test came when the North Koreans crossed over into South Korea. There were somewhere around 70,000 Marines on active duty then. When I'd enlisted a year before, I'd gone in on one of those one-year deals. I'd liked what I'd seen of the Corps and had signed over for a full enlistment just as the war started. The Corps changed overnight. It needed more Marines and plenty of 'em.

Confusion was the order of the day. I was sent out to Camp Pendleton and placed in a tank battalion. It wasn't until my records caught up with me that they realized I didn't know a damn thing about armor. So I was transferred to Charlie Company, 1st Battalion of the 7th Marines. The 7th was basically starting from scratch. Charlie Company probably had as high a percentage of called-up reserves as any company in the 1st Division.

Our colonel was a man named Homer Litzenberg. We called him Weeping Willie because he'd get very emotional when he'd make a speech. Our battalion commander was a light colonel named Ray Davis. He wasn't a big man, not as far as Marine colonels go, but he was one hell of a big Marine. He ran a good show. He got the Medal of Honor. He earned it.

My platoon was made up mainly of reserves from Missouri. Several of them had never been on active duty. Because I was a regular, I was made a fire team leader, even though one of the men in my fire team was a corporal. The team didn't cotton to me being a black man, but that didn't bother me at all. I had the strong-mindedness to assert myself. Once they realized I was the boss, I didn't have any trouble to speak of.

The officers were another story. I had some disagreements with them that I couldn't win unless I made a big issue out of it. There were a couple of times when I could have gotten one officer in plenty of trouble, but I couldn't see any sense in it. We all knew we were going to Korea in a short time, and harmony was a lot more important than a few small incidents.

As the days went by, it became more and more obvious there was another division in our company, perhaps more evident than the black and white one. This was the difference between the regulars and the reserves. Regardless of color, the regulars were naturally apt to stick together, as were the reserves. I had three liberties before we shipped out, one to Tijuana, another to San Diego, and on the third we just drank beer at Oceanside. I went on all three with a black and a white regular.

Well, San Diego wasn't much, but Tijuana was what today you'd call X-rated. I don't want to talk about it, let's just say that place made Sodom and Gomorrah seem like Sunday school.

Oceanside was the place where we had fun. The three of us walked into a bar and ordered drinks. When we finished, the bartender, he must have been a real redneck, deliberately broke our glasses.

So what do we do but order another round. We drank up and started to leave. The asshole did the same thing. Consequently we ended up drinking there for the rest of the evening. We broke them on the glasses.

There were six blacks in our company. A couple of them just didn't know what was happening. I stayed away from them, just as I did from several of the white guys who wouldn't accept what was going on. Anyway, on the twenty-ninth of August we left the States for Korea. It was there that we found out we were going to have a lot more trouble with the North Koreans and the Chinese than we'd had with each other. And when we got to the Chosin, we were to have more trouble with the weather than with anything else.

Well, first we went to Inchon. We landed six days after the 1st and 5th Marines. Our job was to head east until we linked up with them around Seoul.

On our way up to join them, I saw a frightening sight. It was the tank I had been assigned to when I first arrived at Camp Pendleton. The damn thing had been destroyed, and it was obvious there were no survivors.

As for Seoul, we never did get into the city itself. We went north of Seoul to a town called Uijongbu, chasing the NKPA. We took some casualties, but not many. That NKPA seemed pretty shot up to me.

After that place was secure, we went back to Inchon, went aboard LSTs, and headed for Wonsan in North Korea. It was bad enough to sit off Wonsan for about two weeks while the harbor was being cleared of mines, but we ended up missing the Bob Hope show. The great entertainer had left by the time we got ashore. Missing his show really pissed me off, but not as much as something that happened later on.

Anyway, around the first of November we started north on what came to be known as the MSR. We went through some valleys and reached a point somewhere near Sudong. Then we got the jolt of our lives. We ended up facing an intact enemy force.

You see, we were convinced the NKPA was a shattered force. So what in the hell are these guys we're facing? We soon found out. It was either a regiment or a division of Chinese troops. They were called volunteers, which was a joke. We later found out that we had shot them up so badly they had to be taken out of the fight. But we didn't know this at the time. All we knew was we had won a victory and that the Chinese seemed to have disappeared. Next we started up this huge plateau.

On the tenth of November, several helicopters appeared on the scene. We'd been on C-rations for many days and sure as hell didn't expect what we got. Those helicopters were loaded with hot meals. Whoever thought headquarters would be celebrating the birthday of the Corps where we were? It was beautiful!

The next day we started up that damn plateau again. When we got to the top at Koto-ri, the weather turned overnight. It must have dropped sixty degrees and it was going to get worse. We had a lot of

Southern boys in the 7th who had never conceived of weather like this.

We continued to move north until we reached what my company called Turkey Valley, right outside of Yudam-ni. We were now leapfrogging with the 5th Marines.

The night before Thanksgiving we were told to expect turkey the next day. The thought of a cooked meal for a change was mighty appealing.

We went out on patrol the next morning. It was a long, cold day. As we headed back to our area, there was just one thought on everybody's mind, our turkey. Then came the letdown—no hot turkey. We were ready to start another war. Our lieutenant was as mad as anyone.

"Where the hell is our turkey?" he yelled.

"Sorry, sir, I guess they forgot about you guys. They gave yours to a unit of the 5th Marines that had just come through."

Well, if I was pissed off at missing the Bob Hope show, this was the most riled up I think I was in my twenty-three years in the Corps. So were the other guys in our platoon. I ended up eating frozen shrimp, peas, and carrots. I didn't eat shrimp again for about twenty years. A few days later we were in deep trouble, but I was still upset about the turkey.

We were down around Turkey Valley—some people call it Turkey Hill, but it was really a valley—when we started to move up to join the unit of the 5th that had gone through us. We hadn't gone very far when the Chinese hit us.

My God, it was unbelievable! Every which way you looked, all you could see were Chinamen. I had an M-1. I fired it so much that the barrel was almost burned out. It seemed that every shot hit someone. If you fired low, you'd get someone in their front ranks, if you fired high, you'd hit someone in the rear. They'd stopped our advance, but we'd stopped them cold in their tracks.

The next morning, just about everywhere you looked, you could see dead Chinese. It seemed obvious we were surrounded.

To make things worse, the thermometer kept dropping. Each Marine is doing his best to keep warm. I know I have a real problem with my feet, and I'm trying to keep them from freezing.

The problem was the damn shoepacs. Where the leather and the rubber met in the pacs was the spot that hurt my Achilles tendon. This made me put too much pressure on my toes. The sweat would pour down on my toes and freeze.

All right, do you know the difference between frostbite and frozen? Frostbite means the destruction of the tissue. This means amputation. Frozen, if it is caught in time, can be thawed out. A lot of people don't know that. What I was trying to do was keep my feet from getting frostbite. And while I'm doing this, the damn weather is getting worse and worse.

In the meantime we got all these Chinese all around us. And we've taken a lot of casualties. I later heard the rest of the 7th is calling us "Suicide Charlie." We had to clear the hills of all these Chinese who were on all sides of us. Things get a little hazy from here on. All I can remember is constantly fighting and being worried about my feet.

I finally ended up in a jeep we were using as an ambulance. My feet are definitely frozen, but when we got to a tent near Hagaru-ri, a corpsman had thawed them out.

I'd been made a squad leader before we started up the MSR, so they now gave me another squad. As you know, they say every Marine is a rifleman, and we proved it at the Reservoir. My new squad had cooks, bakers, truckdrivers, everything you can think of, but they all had M-1s. There was no rear echelon.

We made it down to Koto-ri and I rejoined what was left of Charlie Company. I don't recall much action the rest of the way down the MSR, but the Chinese were always there.

Eventually we got to Hungnam and were evacuated to Pusan, in South Korea. By the middle of January we started to move north again. We were making a river crossing and the ice gave way. It didn't take long until my feet were frozen again.

So, back I go to sick bay, where they once again thawed out my feet. I returned to Charlie Company, but there was good news awaiting me.

"Smith," I was told, "your number has come up. You're going to be sent back to the States." I let go with a beautiful scream, "Up yours, Korea!" I roared.

[At this point, Smith made the appropriate sign with his left hand in the crook of his right elbow and his right hand pointed upward.]

Now, do you remember when I told you about that bartender

back in Oceanside who'd break the glasses after serving us? Well, the other black guy who was drinking with us that night was killed in Korea. When I was next in Oceanside, I tried to find that bar so I could tell that asshole what had happened. I couldn't locate it, but what the hell, that bartender probably couldn't have cared less.

One more thing. Years later—I think it was after I'd come back from Vietnam—I ran into that sergeant who'd motivated me with his foot. I had my wife with me.

"Well, Smith," he said, "aren't you going to introduce me to your better half?"

"No, Sergeant," I answered, "I don't think I will."

Mick O'Brien
and Task Force
Drysdale

Many of the United Nations countries furnished troops for the
Korean War. Most of these soldiers fought extremely well. The stand
of the British at a place called Gloucester Hill—named after the
Gloucestershire Regiment—during the April 1951 Chinese offensive
is legendary.

The Turks, mentioned several times by the Marines, were simply called "wild men."

To Jack Jefferson, an American soldier in the 2nd Division, they
were great fighters, but, as Jack says, "My God, they were filthy! I
remember that when one of our regiments replaced them on the
lines, we had to do one hell of a cleaning-up job. But when it came to
close-up fighting with the gooks, they showed no mercy."

The Princess Pats from Canada were also outstanding, as was
the French Battalion. France had her hands full in Indochina at the
time, but they firmly supported the Korean War.

The one non-U.S. unit that will always be closely associated
with the United States Marines is Task Force Drysdale, some 235
men of the Independent Commandos of the British Royal Marines.
They were under the command of Lieutenant Colonel Douglas B.
Drysdale, and were very prominent in the fighting between Koto-ri
and Hagaru-ri during the Chosin campaign.

I received a letter from one of these Royal Marines while I was
putting together this book. His name is Michael (Mick) O'Brien and,

as a retired Colour Sergeant, he now lives in Cornwall, England. In this letter he writes of his days in Korea.

"We were under U.S. Navy operational command. We operated from U.S. ships, carrying out raids on the east coast of North Korea, blowing up railroad bridges, tunnels, and [performing] other tasks."

When the Chosin emergency arose, O'Brien was one of the Royal Marines in Task Force Drysdale.

"This was a piece of history in itself," writes O'Brien, "as the last time the British Royal Marines fought alongside the U.S. Marines was in the Boxer Rebellion. We were also fighting the Chinese in that debacle back at the turn of the century.

"Well, as for the Chosin, I remember it well," O'Brien continues. "We were fighting side by side with the U.S. Marines as we tried to get from Koto-ri to Hagaru-ri. There were the long, cold, dark nights that became like daylight as the Chinese attacked, blowing bugles and whistles. The bright lights from their flashing gunfire lit up the sky. The next day we could see dead Chinese everywhere and plenty of our own fallen."

What O'Brien is writing about is the attempt of Drysdale to get through to the 5th and 7th Marines at Hagaru-ri.

Chesty Puller had put together a group made up of the British Marines, George Company of Puller's 1st Marines, Baker Company, thirty-one U.S. Army infantrymen, and seventy men of the U.S. Marines 1st Division headquarters. Drysdale was given the command.

They moved about four miles north before running into an extensive Chinese force. The Communists cut the task force in two. Drysdale was seriously wounded, but he did get the bulk of his command through to Hagaru-ri. The cut-off group, which included Lieutenant Colonel John McLaughlin, USMC, became separated from Drysdale and was captured. McLaughlin's conduct in captivity was exemplary. After the war ended, he was awarded the Legion of Merit.

Above all, O'Brien tells of how proud he is that when the 1st Marine Division received a Presidential Unit Citation, the forty-one Independent Commandos of the Royal Marines were included in the citation.

"When I was at the Chosin," says O'Brien, "a young American sergeant gave me a Marine emblem. I wore it in my green beret for the rest of my service and now proudly wear it in my jacket lapel. I wouldn't take $1,000 for it."

That sounds rather good, coming from a member of a Marine Corps that was founded before there was a United States.

John Saddic: The Lebanese Marine

Both of John's parents were born in Lebanon. They settled in Philadelphia, where John was born. When World War II broke out, he joined the Marine Corps and ended up as a machine gunner in the 22nd Marines of the 6th Division. He was seriously wounded near Naha on Okinawa.

After being discharged, he joined the Marine Corps Reserves so he could go down to the Philadelphia Navy Yard every now and again and drink some beer with his buddies. He was married when the Korean War started. His wife had just presented him with a son. He never thought he would go to Korea, but as he says, "What are you going to do?"

His feet were injured severely at the Chosin by the subzero temperatures. After a long stretch in a naval hospital, he was once again discharged from active duty. He did not rejoin the Marine Corps Reserves.

Today he runs a very successful mill supply stocking distributing firm outside of Philadelphia. Still happily married, he has been a grandfather for many years.

I asked John whether, if he could do it all over again, he would still join the reserves after World War II. He looked at me as if I were crazy, and smiled.

"Of course," he said.

SERGEANT JOHN SADDIC
11th Marines

When I went down to Parris Island in '42, I was only seventeen years old. Some of the men in my platoon were twenty-five, twenty-six years of age, with a couple of them even older. I looked at these guys as old men, everyone my age did. We even called a couple of them Pop. I'd look at them and say to myself, Okay, you guys have had your shot. Most of you are fathers; you've already produced someone to carry on your name. But what about me? I've had nothing!

Oh, I'd bumped up against a few girls, but as far as having a lasting relationship, zero. I felt that if I'd gotten killed then, I would have been cheated. Let those old guys get killed, not me.

Then, after I was called back for Korea, *I* was the twenty-five, twenty-six-year-old guy. I had a wife—still have her—and a baby boy. The shoe was on the other foot, Right?

Now, the seventeen-year-old kid, he has no responsibilities. Right? If I get killed, who will take care of my wife and kid? Let those seventeen-year-old kids get killed, not me.

You figure that out.

Okay. New Year's Eve, 1949. I had gone to a party with my wife and my oldest boyhood friend and his wife. We had knocked down several drinks when the conversation turned toward the Corps. My friend had a brainstorm.

"John," he said, "you know I'm in the Marine Corps Reserves. We meet down at the Philadelphia Navy Yard. There are several of your buddies from the 6th Marine Division down there, and they're always asking for you. Why don't you join up? We have one hell of a time. We get paid thirty dollars a month for doing almost nothing. It'll be a snap for you."

"Jeez," I said, "that sounds great! It'll give me a night out with the boys."

So that's how I got back in the Corps. Everybody thought it was great, except my wife. She always was smart as a whip.

"Are you off your rocker? Haven't you had enough of all that killing? There's bound to be another war, and you'll be the first one called up."

"Oh no, not with all my experience," I told her, "me, a Purple Heart machine gunner. I'll spend the war training kids."

Well, I trained kids, all right. On the ship going to Korea we had some machine gunners who had never fired a machine gun. We tied a wooden duck to a line we had hanging off the fantail. I showed these kids the score off the ass end of our ship. And it was the same with the mortar men. We must have scared the hell out of the fish.

Well, June 21, 1950, was the happiest day of my life. My wife presented me with a son. I was still on cloud nine when those bastards crossed over into South Korea. I didn't think much about it, but my wife did. She was still in the hospital, but she gave me the word.

"John, you better get ready because you're going to go. I just know you are going to go."

Well, just like that, our unit is called up. My wife was right; so what else is new?

Now I'm beginning to panic. Hell, I had no dough then. I was going to Villanova on the GI Bill. Who was going to support my wife and son? She couldn't very well work, with the baby and all.

You see, at this time you had to be a sergeant or above to get a family allowance. I was just a corporal. So I went over to welfare to state my case.

"Do you own a car?" they asked me.

"No."

"How about furniture?"

"Yes."

"Sell it."

Sell it? I thought they'd gone bananas. Here I am with a brand-new baby and they want me to sell my furniture. What the hell's going on?

My next step was to go to the Red Cross. And you know what they told me? "Go to welfare; we can't help you."

Oh, for Christ's sake, talk about the runaround, I was getting it in spades.

Then I got a brainstorm. I decided to call the *Philadelphia Inquirer* and ask for the editorial department. They'd usually eat up a human-interest story like this.

"Look," I said to this editor, "I'm a World War II Purple Heart veteran of the Pacific. My unit has been called up over this police action in Korea. I'll go, all right, but I'll be a sonofabitch if I'm going while my wife and child are begging on the street. I've called both welfare and the Red Cross and they gave me the brush-off."

Oh, did this guy get excited!

"What's the matter with those idiots?" he said. "I'll call you back within the hour." He did.

"Call the Red Cross; I think you'll get a better reception now. Ask for Mrs. What's-her-face."

So I called the Red Cross and it turns out Mrs. What's-her-face is the same broad I talked to earlier. Now she's singing a different tune.

"Oh, Mr. Saddic, of course we'll help you out. We didn't realize the full story, blah, blah, blah . . ." She's falling all over me.

About three months later, Congress got into the act. Now you didn't have to be a sergeant or above to get a family allowance. So the Corps took over from the Red Cross.

But a year or so later I've been to Korea and have been sent home with frozen feet, I got a call from the Red Cross. They want to know when I'm going to pay back the loan they had given my family a year before. I think it was fifteen dollars a week for three months. Now they've really got me pissed off, but I kept my cool.

"Gee," I said, in my altar-boy voice, "the man at the *Inquirer* didn't say anything to me about a loan. I'll have to call him and check this out." *Inquirer*—I'd said the magic word. You know, like Groucho Marx used to say on his television show, the magic word.

"Oh," this guy said, "if you didn't know it was a loan, forget it. Glad to have you back in Philadelphia."

Ah, the power of the press.

Back to June of 1950. And, by the way, if you remember 1950, here's something else for you to think about. For years they had been kicking our Philadelphia Phillies around. But by 1950 they'd come up with a team they called the Whiz Kids. Our group didn't want to go to war. We wanted to go to Shibe Park.

Anyway, we went down to Camp Lejeune in Jacksonville, North Carolina. Here they told us we would have extensive training before leaving for the West Coast. But it soon became very apparent this was bad dope. The scuttlebutt had us going to Camp Pendleton out in Oceanside, California, as soon as possible. I called my wife, Linda, and told her she better get down to Lejeune in a hurry if she wanted to see me. So she got ahold of a mutual friend and down they came. It was a pretty crummy drive from Philly, but they arrived on a Friday. We later figured out that she arrived at the camp gate at about the same time our troop train was leaving for the West Coast. That's how fast they were moving us. I didn't see Linda again until I got back from Korea.

After we got to Oceanside, we were told once again that we would have a lot of time to train and organize our outfit. All I knew was, I was a machine gunner in the 11th Marines, the artillery regiment of the 1st Division. I was a squad leader in a group that was set up to guard the guns from a charging enemy.

Well, once again we'd be given a lot of bullshit. Now they've changed our plans again. We were to leave for Japan as soon as possible. They'd set up a camp over there with the terrain quite similar to Korea. It was in Japan we were to become a real fighting division.

Now, can you believe this? Japan ended up being more of the same. I should have known this when we were still at sea. If we were really slated for a long stay in Japan, why not wait for our machine-gun practice there?

Okay. We land in Japan. The first thing they do is give out port and starboard liberty. I was starboard. As we were going down the gangplank, this gyrene taps me on the shoulder.

"If we're going to train a lot in Japan, why the hell are they loading all those ships?"

Christ, he was right! We no sooner got back on board than we headed for the assault on Inchon. Many of those who made that landing may have still have had hangovers. The short time we were ashore, a lot of the guys tried to drink Japan dry.

After all, it was only ten weeks earlier that a good many of the Marines who went into Inchon were civilians, serving in reserve units not only in Philadelphia but throughout the country. During those ten weeks they'd been hustled all over the lot. There was no real camaraderie like we had in World War II. I guess the main reason they did so well was their pride in the Corps.

But bitch, my God, did we bitch! Many of the men in my unit had learned to gripe in World War II, and I mean they already had degrees in bitching before Korea. It got so bad our captain figured he'd better call a meeting. His talk to us was a classic.

"Look, you guys," he said, "I know you're pissed off about being here. So am I." (He was also a World War II vet, a tall, lanky guy from Texas.) "But we're here and that's it.

"Now," he continued, "let me tell you something. Let's say you're back in the States and you want to get laid." (As you can imagine, this broke the guys up.) "You go to a cathouse and you pick out some broad. You give her the three or five dollars, whatever the going rate calls for, and go upstairs.

"Okay. Did you ever think that maybe the whore doesn't want to get laid at that point? Maybe she's tired or sore, something like that. But she's taken your money, so she spreads her legs and makes believe she loves it. She makes you think you're the greatest lover since Errol Flynn.

"So that's exactly the position we're in. We're getting fucked, just like the hooker in the cathouse. And, like her, we can't do anything about it. So, relax, do the best job you can, and, for Christ's sake, remember you're Marines!"

Jeez, you should have heard the laughter and the cheering. The men loved the way he put things. From then on, especially up in the Chosin, when we were freezing our nuts off, every time we'd see the captain, we'd push our heads back, put both hands behind our heads, and moan, "Oh, Captain, oh, oh, I love it, I love it!" He'd just smile and utter some brilliant remark like "Attaboy."

So, after Inchon and all that vicious fighting around Seoul, they stuck us aboard LSTs. The scuttlebutt is really flying. The rumor we all loved was that the war was almost over and we were headed home, which brings me around to one of my favorite bitches about Korea.

In World War II we normally had a pretty good idea about what was going on. The company commander, the platoon leaders, even the sergeants, someone would keep the troops apprised of what the score was. Not in Korea. Here's what I mean.

When we were up in the Reservoir in late November, we'd been seeing Chinese for several days, but I had no idea of their involvement in the war. It wasn't until I saw all these planes dropping supplies to us that I knew something was screwed up. Why had gear stopped coming to us via the road from the south? I asked one of our sergeants what was going on.

"Hell," he said, "don't you know? The road's cut off. We've got these fuckin' chinks on all sides, thousands of them."

That's the way it was in Korea. You didn't know what was going on until it happened.

Well, we left Inchon sometime in October. Much to our surprise, the LSTs we were on were crewed by Japanese, that's right, the guys who were shooting at us just five or six years before. Remember, the original Marines in Korea had a tremendous amount of World War II men in their ranks. One of these vets, he must have been about six foot three, goes over to one of these Japs.

"Look, you little sonofabitch," he roars at the little Nip, "a few years ago you were probably shooting at me. I'm about to toss your ass overboard. Let the sharks have their dinner."

Of course, the Jap doesn't speak English. All he knows is that the rest of us are laughing our heads off. So he starts laughing too, and bobbing his head up and down. To top it off, the little guy has thick glasses and buck teeth. He looks just like the Japs we used to see in the cartoons during World War II. Then he starts saying something like, "Ah so, ah so."

All this was too much for the big Marine. He also burst out laughing. We never did find out if he was going to throw the Jap over the side or not, but it's a good thing he didn't. After all, the Japanese were our host.

Well, we headed out from Inchon not really knowing where we were going. No more rumors about going home. We knew we were heading for another combat landing.

Then we got a pleasant surprise. The landing was a lark. Hell, we just walked in. It was at a place called Wonsan, over on the east coast of North Korea—no combat whatsoever. But when we started out for the Chosin, things were going to change—my God, how they changed!

Can you imagine a situation like this? The thermometer is beginning to drop, yet we continue to go north. By the time the Chinese hit us, it was below zero. I've been told that before we got back to Hungnam, it was thirty below zero. All I know is, it was colder than a witch's heart.

When we'd march, our body fluids would be working and our feet would be sweating. We couldn't change our socks—we'd be wearing two or three pairs, and they'd freeze to our feet. The chinks would be wearing rubber sneakers. They're better in the cold.

And, by the way, the worst thing was trying to take a leak.

You're trying to find your pecker through six inches of clothing. You know what happens to it in frigid weather? It shrinks so it feels like it's gone into your belly. That's tough. And when you take a crap—well, you don't read any newspapers. Boom, boom, it's over. You try to clean yourself off and get your pants back on. I can't remember much diarrhea. Maybe it's because we were strictly on rations. But, I'll tell you, those bodily functions were murder as it was.

Okay, let's go back to Philadelphia. A month or two before we were called up, my wife and I went to a fortune-teller, one of those gypsy women you had a lot of in those days. She told me that my lucky day was going to be November 29. We both laughed. I told my wife maybe I'd make a big killing at the track that day.

Back to Korea. It's November 29, my lucky day. The Chinese start to zero in on us with mortars. Everyone was trying to find a hole to dive in. I spotted this cart, so I jumped under it. This guy in our outfit, can't remember his name, but he was from Texas, sees me and yells over, "Hey, asshole, don't you know you're under a cart full of land mines?"

Oh, for Christ's sake, *this* is my lucky day? I hightailed it out of there and jumped into the first hole I could find.

And, you know, as I was looking for a good hole to jump into, I quickly decided to do something I'd been thinking of for the last day or so. I'd stick my hand under my body in such a way that when I jumped, I'd be sure to break it. We'd heard they were evacuating our wounded by air. If I did this, I might even get home and see my wife and new son.

Ya know, at the last second I couldn't do it. Don't ask me why. One shell that had wounded me in World War II had killed five of my buddies. I'd done my share. There were millions of guys back in the States who hadn't done a fuckin' thing. Let them come to Korea! And I'll tell you something else. I'm not the slightest bit ashamed of thinking about it. Ask any guy who's been in combat. You're bound to think that way at one time or another. But in the long run, most guys don't do it. After all, you have to live with yourself.

Well, speaking of those planes that were coming in to get our wounded out, they were one of the reasons we were able to fight our way down to Hungnam. All day long we'd have complete control of the air. Our Marine Corsairs were kicking the hell out of those Chinese. We loved watching it.

You see, in a situation like we were in, with the miserable weather and all those gooks, we were always looking for anything that would take our minds off our problems. Give me a pencil and I'll show you what we did.

If a Corsair would come in like this and get rid of its bombs, napalm, or start strafing,

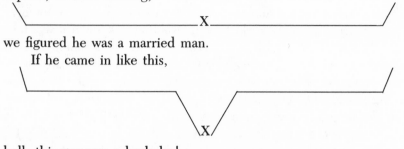

we figured he was a married man.

If he came in like this,

hell, this guy was a bachelor!

Anyway, we'd cheer like hell every time they came over. These guys were keeping the gooks off our ass. We were all for them.

But the cheers were few and far between. That Chosin campaign was one mess after another. There was one I'll never forget. It was horrible.

It happened one morning when we'd been trying to keep the gooks off our back. We started following this trail of blood. You could see where the blood increased, and you could tell by the footprints that the guy was staggering and that he was a Marine. We were afraid of what we'd find, and we found it. There was this young Marine propped up against a tree. You know how guys will push back their helmets, like the guys in the cigarette ads? That's what this kid looked like, just like he was resting, only of course he was dead. I thought of myself in World War II. This kid had just begun to live. I thought of the telegram that would go out to his parents. What a waste!

There was one bright spot on the road down that did give me a tremendous ego trip. We ran into some British Marines who were brewing some coffee. Jeez, did it smell good! One of the Brits called us over.

"Hey, Yanks," he said, "want some good coffee?"

We jumped at the chance. That joe wasn't going to stay hot long, but while it did, it was great. Well, there I was, sitting on the tripod of a 105, when I heard this whirring noise. There's a guy with a camera and he's centered right in on me. There I am, with a canteen filled with coffee, and this guy has shown up out of nowhere and he's taking a motion picture of me. The only thing I could do was give him a big shit-eating grin.

Now get this, that picture was shown in the news all over the country. My wife later told me she got several phone calls from guys who had known me in World War II, wanting to know if it was me.

Then, in 1967, a firm called Wolpert made a documentary film on the Korean War. The narrator was a man named Richard Basehart, you know, the guy who played a submarine captain. Well, I'm sitting there, watching this Korean War film, half asleep, when my wife yells, "John, there you are, drinking your coffee!"

Jeez, this gives me a jolt. She's right; there am I on the TV screen with that shit-eating grin. Hell, you'd think I was on a movie lot.

Then, to top it off, when they list all the people at the end of the show, the producer and all that crap, they have a still shot of me drinking that coffee. You'd think I was John Wayne or someone like that. It was great!

Of course, this all happened years *after* the Chosin. I wasn't thinking about anything but that coffee—as a matter of fact, the Brits did give me a refill—and how good it was, when the picture was taken.

Okay, we did finally get to Hungnam and the sea, but we were beat down to our socks. My dogs were killing me. I was scared to death that I'd develope grangrene and they'd have to chop them off. The whole outfit was like that.

Of course, they tried to tell us what a glorious thing we'd done, advancing to the rear through all those Chinese and all that baloney. Bullshit! We knew we'd had the hell kicked out of us, no matter how many chinks we'd killed and no matter how badly we'd been outnumbered.

By now it's sometime around the middle of December. Our morale is pretty low. This chaplain comes over to us and starts to tell us that the Chinese are evil and that we are the best fighting men in the world, that we are fighting for the good, blah, blah, blah.

Oh, he gets no answer from any of us. I mean, I'm worrying about losing my feet and this guy is giving us a pep talk like a high school coach gives between halves. The next thing we expected was to be told to go out and win one for the Gipper.

So, what does this clown do next but say something about it getting close to Christmas and we should all start singing Christmas carols.

Can you believe this? The guy is certifiable. He thinks it's a Hollywood war. We'd just gone through all this crap and he wants us to sing Christmas carols. He starts off with "Oh, Come All Ye Faithful," but he's the only one singing. Christ, is he frustrated!

Then he starts to chew our asses out, but we just stare at him. Finally he looks disgusted and leaves. So much for that rah-rah crap.

Shortly after that, a doctor comes over and looks at my feet. One look, that's all, and he orders me aboard a hospital ship out in the harbor. I'm hobbling aboard when I spot this guy I knew during World War II. We exchange glances. We called each other the same thing, no "hello" or "how are you," just "dumb sonofabitch." Then we smiled.

John Yancey and Hill 1282

Hills, they called 'em hills.
Well, I'm from Rhode Island.
They were fuckin' mountains to me.

                              —Dick Burke, E/2/7

The Korean War was, from beginning to end, a war of hills. Some areas were more hilly than others, but the hills were always there, and controlling the high ground was the main job of the rifle companies.

One of these hills was numbered 1282. It was near the town of Yudam-ni. Easy Company set up its position here on November 26, 1950.

"The ground was frozen," says Dick Burke, "and the digging was very hard. But our platoon leader was one tough Marine. His name was John Yancey and he knew what he was talking about. If he told you to dig in, you dug in.

"Now let me tell you something about Yancey. I'd first seen him back at Pendleton. The Corps was putting together the 7th Marines for service in Korea. They had to do this in a hurry, which meant the 7th was taking in a lot of reserves.

"I had been in the Corps as a regular for a couple of years by then, and naturally I was salty as hell. We'd been hearing some horror stories about these new reserves coming in. You know what I mean, how some of them had never even been to boot camp, things like that. I was doing guard duty at the time. Ironically, what I was guarding were these rations, some of which I'd end up trying to eat later on in that frozen dungheap called the Reservoir.

170

"At any rate, I ended up in E/2/7. We were all waiting to meet our platoon leader. We knew his name was John Yancey and he was a reserve officer. Those of us who were regulars were really pissed off, but what could we do about it? The first thing he did was call us all together.

"'All right,' he said, 'to those of you who are regulars, I know what's on your mind. You're saying to yourselves, "Why the hell do we end up with a fuckin' reserve officer?" Well, you're right, I am a reserve officer, a "weekend warrior," as we're called. But I got this commission the hard way, in the South Pacific in World War II. And I'm not going to have any bullshit in this platoon about regulars versus reserves. We're all Marines and that's it!'"

What Yancey had told his platoon was correct. He had been running a liquor store back in Little Rock, Arkansas, and had left a pregnant wife when he was recalled to active duty. He had received a Purple Heart, serving as a corporal with Carlson's Raiders, and a battlefield commission.

"It wasn't very long," Burke remembers, "before we realized we had one hell of a Marine as our platoon leader, and also a damn decent man.

"We left for Korea on an APA the *Barnfield*. We'd almost reached Inchon when Yancey found out that his baby had been born back in Little Rock. He gave everyone in our platoon a cigar. I stuck mine in my seabag. When my seabag finally caught up with me after I returned home from Korea, the cigar was still there."

In Korea, at Hill 1282, Easy Company's task was simple. If the Chinese attacked, Easy was to hold. And by all reports, everyone there seemed to know the Chinese would attack.

The company was lined up with Yancey's platoon in the center of the hill, Bob Bey's platoon on Yancey's left, and Len Clements's on his right. The company commander, Walter Phillips, and his exec, Ray Ball, were positioned behind Yancey, a position that Phillips felt would give him the best possible vantage point for directing the coming battle.

The Chinese opened up either late on November 27 or early on November 28; it depends which book you are reading. Dick Burke doesn't know for sure, and he doesn't care.

"I do recall seeing Yancey," he says. "The acne on his face, or whatever it was, stood out. He was wearing a shoulder holster for his

.45. He was telling us not to return the small-arms fire that was coming from the Chinese.

"'They just want to know your position,' he's yelling.

"Then the Chinese came at us in force and I was too busy trying to stay alive to notice anyone else."

Again and again the Chinese charged, not a mass charge, but in squads. Mortar fire, grenades, and small-arms fire were everywhere. The Chinese were cut down in droves, but their fire was taking a steady toll on the Marines.

A hand grenade landed near Yancey and part of it hit him in the face, piercing his nose. It was extremely painful and it disrupted his breathing.

It was a long night. When it ended, Yancey felt the Chinese would wait until darkness came before they'd come at Easy again. That was the way they usually did things. This time it was different. Daylight or no daylight, a new bunch of Chinese charged over their dead comrades at Easy.

Once again the Chinese were slaughtered, but the Marines continued to drop. Len Clements (a good friend of Yancey's) was hit in the helmet. Yancey was sure Clements was dead, but the bullet had hit his helmet on the side and had only stunned him. He was knocked out, but eventually came around.

Ray Ball, Easy's executive officer, was not so lucky. Badly wounded, he continued to fire his carbine until he bled to death.

Then came an act that many would call pure bravado. Captain Phillips stuck a bayoneted rifle into the ground, and shouted, "This is Easy Company! And it stands here!"

In one of his books about the Civil War, Bruce Catton tells of a mortally wounded Union Army officer asking his men to give him a Springfield and to brace him against a tree so he could die facing the enemy.

"Perhaps this was bravado," Catton wrote, "but, after all, he was the one doing the dying."

And so it was with Phillips. Moments after he made his statement, he was cut in two by Chinese fire.*

Yancey was trying to form a counterattack when a slug tore into

---

* Phillips's statement and his death are matters of record. He received the Navy Cross posthumously.

his mouth and pieces of a hand grenade sliced his cheek. To his horror, he found that he had lost his sight. He was crawling around when a Marine (Yancey never found out his name) helped him away from the deadly fire. Then he blacked out. He regained consciousness in the sick bay that had been set up at Yudam-ni. Fortunately, whatever had caused his blindness was only temporary.

He was evacuated by air and started the slow process that was to return him to Little Rock. He was awarded his second Navy Cross for his actions on Hill 1282. I had hoped to interview Yancey for this book, but he died in 1986 of natural causes.

But what of Richard Burke, whom I did interview? Burke was badly wounded. In addition, his feet were frozen. He was also flown out, he thinks by helicopter, from Yudam-ni, but it might have been from Hagaru-ri.

"I was pretty much out of it," he told me. "I know I was helped by a sergeant named Dan Murphy. I'm pretty sure he was also wounded. It was difficult not to be wounded with all the lead that was flying around.

"Well, I was a regular, so I ended up getting retired with a disability. I've been working for the Post Office for years. Still, when I look back over the years, I have to chuckle about Yancey. At first we thought he'd be a lemon because he was a reserve. Hell, he just might have been the best platoon leader in the Corps."

Paul Ilyinsky
and John Burns:
The Palm Beach
Connection

When I was in the Palm Beach area, I ran into two Korean War Marines. Although they live almost directly across from each other on the waterway that separates Palm Beach from West Palm Beach, they have completely different backgrounds.

Ilyinsky is the son of the late Grand Duke Dmitri of Russia. It is said that he may be the closest living relative of the last czar. His father, the grand duke, an officer in the Russian army, escaped to England after Lenin came to power in Russia in 1917. There he continued to fight the Germans and was badly wounded while serving with the British Army. Paul was born in England and came to America with his family in the 1930s.

John Burns was born in pre–Disney World Orlando. This was long before central Florida had felt much influence from the North. It was populated by real Southerners. After serving in the Marines during both World War II and Korea, Burns came to West Palm Beach, where he became a very successful attorney.

The two towns where they now live, Palm Beach and West Palm Beach, are as different as night and day. Palm Beach is a town with an uncommonly large amount of wealth but little industry—a friend once told me that Palm Beach's biggest industry is gold—while West

Palm Beach is a city bursting with commerce. Palm Beach is loaded with very rich people, most of whom did not gain their wealth from Florida enterprises, while West Palm Beach symbolizes the new industrial South.

On Sunday night in Palm Beach, one goes to the Colony Hotel to enjoy the jet-set rhythm of the very popular Marshall Grant and his orchestra. On Sunday night in West Palm Beach, you go to bed early to get ready for a very busy Monday.

An interesting sidelight is the fact that in February 1986, Paul, a six-year member of the Palm Beach town council, decided to run for the first councilman's job. This is similar to the office of mayor. His opponent, the incumbent, a woman and a direct descendant of the Emperor Charlemagne, seemed to want to keep things as they were, while Paul wanted to bring Palm Beach into the twentieth century. He was beaten.

John Burns, on the other hand, whose offices are right next to the West Palm Beach City Hall, is greatly amused by the politics across the waterway.

"It's not exactly Tammany Hall they have over there, you know," he said. "I don't think they have any smoke-filled rooms. Ski is on the right track, but I doubt if Palm Beach will change in my lifetime."

John's use of the appellative "Ski" is quite interesting. Paul Romanov Ilyinsky spent almost seven years on active duty as an enlisted Marine. Like many of his fellow Marines, he was known simply as "Ski," or, as he advanced in rank, "Sergeant Ski." It is highly doubtful that any of his buddies in the Corps realized they were addressing a Marine who could possibly lay rightful claim to the title of Czar of all the Russias.

.

GUNNERY SERGEANT PAUL ILYINSKY
1st Marine Division

Like a lot of the other reserve units called up in July of '50 for the Korean War, ours was in an utter state of chaos. We were supposed to be a rifle company, but we were completely understaffed. We were the Charlottesville, Virginia, unit. I was attending college there at the University of Virginia. One of our platoons was being commanded by a Marine pilot. He was a great guy, but he knew nothing about a rifle company. That's the way things were.

Shortly after we were mobilized, the word went out that I had actually been to South Korea. Well, you know how scuttlebutt like that can fly around. Pretty soon I was supposed to be an expert on all phases of the place. I had become a celebrity, all because I had spent two weeks in Korea during my first cruise in the Corps.

Now let's go back to August of '45. I was a seventeen-year-old boot, having just arrived at Parris Island for my recruit training. We all figured we'd be involved in the upcoming invasion of Japan, when Truman decided to try to end the war with our brand-new atomic bombs. Thank God he succeeded! Many of the Marines wanted to go home right then and there. But not me. I was a regular, if you please. I wasn't going anywhere but where the Corps told me to go until my enlistment was up.

I ended up at Link Training School, where I learned to fly and also became an armorer. When the chance came to go to the Pacific, I jumped at it. When I got to Hawaii, I was put in charge of the Marine pilots' rifles and pistols. It was good duty, all right. I was a buck sergeant by then.

So one day a guy called Jim Bullock, the squadron commander of the transport outfit I was assigned to, came over to me.

"Sergeant Ski, how would you like to go to China?"

Oh, this sounded great. Naturally I agreed. I would still be the armorer, but I'd also be a jack of all trades, if you know what I mean.

Well, as it turned out, I spent the better part of the next year flying all over the Pacific area. Not only did I get to Seoul, but to Saigon, Tientsin, Thailand, Midway Island, everywhere you can imagine. I'd find out where one of the planes was going and I'd bum a ride.

One of these jaunts that I can clearly remember was our trip to Tsingtao. The 6th Marine Division was getting ready to pull out, and the situation was all fouled up. There were rows of John Deere tractors just sitting there. None of the Chinese knew how to service them, and they had no fuel anyway.

And the cartons of Lucky Strike cigarettes, there were thousands of them. They were probably headed for the black market. It was a hell of a mess.

Now for Korea. I was told that our squadron was going to carry a large supply of penicillin to Seoul. I had never been there, so I went along. Our pilot had never been there either, so naturally we developed engine trouble. It always seemed to me that at the good liberty towns, or ones that no one knew anything about, our pilots were always doing that.

We ended up spending about two weeks there. I had a chance to talk to several Korean people. God, how they hated the Japanese! They'd tell me how oppressive the Japs had been to them during the occupation. They seemed to like us very much. As far as they were concerned, we were the ones who'd thrown the Japs out of Korea.

There was one thing they were apprehensive about, and that was the division of their country. I can't remember any of them predicting a major war like the one that developed, but they seemed to know something was brewing.

"We're one people," a police captain told me. "To make two countries out of Korea is asking for trouble." How right he was.

All right, back to July of 1950. I was a gunnery sergeant in the reserves by then. Our skipper, a Marine by the name of Bill Miller, and myself and a lieutenant went down to Montford Point at Camp Lejeune as an advance party for the Charlottesville unit. When we got there, the gate was locked. We showed the sentry our orders. He was baffled.

"Beats the shit out of me," he said. "All I know is this place has been locked up ever since I've been at Lejeune. My orders are not to let anyone in. You better check with the colonel."

So, we went to see the colonel. His name was Masowlski and he was a hell of a guy. We walked into his office and presented ourselves.

"Jesus Christ, Captain," he said to Miller. "A goddamn war has started!"

"That's right, Colonel. And I have my company coming down by train tomorrow."

"Where are you going to put them?"

"My orders say Montford Point."

"Oh, for Christ's sakes, we haven't used that place for almost a year. We better get over there and open it up."

We got into his jeep and went back to the Point. He told the sentry to open the gate. Then we got a shock. There were no mattresses. The racks were loaded with rust, the springs hanging through the bottom. The place was in shambles.

We decided we'd go to the mess hall for a cup of coffee. We must have been dreaming, the place had been closed for months. Keep in mind that many of our men coming down the next day had never even been to boot camp. I don't think they expected what they found.

Anyway, you know what the Corps says, "You do with what you have." When the men got there, they were put to work. For food we had them bring in sandwich wagons, you know, the ones you see at factories at lunchtime. It all was a hell of a way to introduce some of these lads to the Corps.

We were like that for a week or two, then the men started to go to other outfits. I believe several of them ended up in the 7th Marines out at Camp Pendleton. Then came my turn. I was sent to something called AES-46, right near Lejeune, at a place called Cherry Point.

What had happened was some guy had looked at my spec number. This told him that I knew everything about Link trainers, so I was back to what I'd been doing in '45. I didn't like it at all. Fortunately for me, there was a captain there named Bill Rupp, whom I had served with in the Pacific. I pleaded my case.

"Captain," I said, "you've got to get my ass out of here. I am a gunnery sergeant and all I'm doing is swabbing the decks around here."

"Okay, Ski, how would you like to go to Korea?"

"Sure, why not?"

So, if you please, that's how I got to Korea.

MacArthur had made his left end run at Inchon by then, and the 1st Marine Division had secured Seoul. I was back to being an armorer, which was another MOS of mine.

I was sent to an airfield a little south of Seoul, where I ended up doing a little bit of everything. These F4U's were coming from the carriers we had off Korea. They'd do their job in support of the Marine ground-pounders, then land at our field for refueling. Some of them would be shot full of holes, which we'd patch up. We soon became experts at getting those Corsairs ready for combat again. When they were fit, off they'd go on another bombing run. It was actually a triangle they'd be flying between the carriers, the target, and our field. Our job wasn't a dangerous one, but it was an absolute necessity.

We also had some transport planes there. When the Chinese came into the war in force, these transports went up to that airstrip the Marines had built at the Chosin to get some of our wounded out. They came back to our field near Seoul with a full load.

Now, what happened then shows you what the Marine Corps is all about. After the planes had landed, they'd start to unload the wounded and they did it by the seriousness of each case. There was no bullshit about it. The first Marines off would frequently be PFCs. There was none of that "officers first" business, not in the Marine Corps anyway.

Well, I guess I'd spent six months or so there working my butt off when the colonel sent for me.

"Ski," he said, "how would you like to have a commission?"

"Oh, I'd like that very much, sir."

"That's fine, you should be an officer. I'm going to recommend you and I'll have three other senior officers write letters in your behalf. You're going to be leaving here shortly, but these letters will eventually catch up with you."

The colonel was right. A few days later I received my orders for Tokyo. When I reached Japan, I was told that I was now a member of the Marine MPs. It dawned on me that I had done a stint as an MP at Camp Lejeune several years before. I guess someone had spotted this fact in my record book. I must have had one hell of a lot of MOS's in that jacket of mine.

And, incidentally, I had recently made master gunnery sergeant. If you want to talk about good duty, you can start with having three up and three down and being an MP in Tokyo in 1951. For Christ's sake, you were a king! The Japanese were going all out for the American dollar, and that city was really hopping.

There had been one big change. The U.S. and Japan had agreed that Japan would take over the prosecution of all civil crimes committed by the American military personnel. No more slapping of the wrist for breaking up a Japanese nightclub. The Japs weren't severe, but you did have a lot of Americans spending a week or two in a Japanese jail. This was something that had not happened before.

The Japanese had a system that was different than the American one. Instead of a jury they had three judges. The defendant had a lawyer, as, of course, did the prosecution. First one lawyer, then the other, would present his case. The three judges would then make their decision. I'll say one thing, though, I always found those judges to be damn fair.

At the end of '51 I came back to the States. I reported in at

Treasure Island and was immediately called in to see the commanding officer.

"I've got some letters here about your becoming a commis-
sioned officer," he said. "We should have this straightened out by
the time you get home."

I'd forgotten all about what the colonel had said to me in Korea,
but the Marine Corps had not. My mother was living in Palm Beach,
so I helped start a Marine Reserve unit in West Palm Beach. It had
taken so long for them to get me my commission, they skipped second lieutenant and made me a first lieutenant in the reserves. By the
time I retired, I was a lieutenant colonel. I'd held just about every
rate and rank in the Marine Corps from private to lieutenant colonel
except second lieutenant.

Now I'm going to do you a favor. There's a great Marine living
right across the inlet from here, in West Palm Beach. His name is
John Burns. He was my colonel in the West Palm Beach reserve unit
after the Korean War. John had a hell of a record in Korea. See
Burns, you won't regret it.

Paul was right.

FIRST LIEUTENANT JOHN BURNS
A Company, 1st Battalion, 7th Marines

So you've talked with Paul Ilyinsky across the water in Palm Beach.
Did he have socks on with his loafers? [I hadn't noticed.] That's how
you tell the difference between Palm Beach and West Palm Beach.
We wear socks with our loafers; they don't. Paul is a good Marine,
though, socks or no socks. He was in my reserve unit after we both
got back from Korea, must have been in it for twenty years. He
retired as a lieutenant colonel. I also had long service in the Corps,
both on active duty and in the reserves, retiring as a colonel.

It had all started in '43 when I went into the Marines as an
eighteen-year-old boot. I was going to win the war. Then came a
major disappointment. I did my best to get overseas while the war
was going on, but was unsuccessful. You don't tell the Marine Corps
what your duty is going to be; they tell you. I made up for all I
missed in World War II during the Korean War, though, so I guess
it evens out.

Shortly after World War II ended, I got a chance to pick up a Marine Corps Reserve commission by taking an eight-month course at Chapel Hill, North Carolina. I passed the course, got my commission, and stayed at Chapel Hill until I graduated.

I had just finished my first year at law school when the North Koreans crossed over into South Korea. I wasn't going to miss out on this one. I had no intention of staying in law school while the Marines fought in Korea. I got back in the Corps as soon as possible, and was immediately sent to Quantico for a refresher course.

In the meantime the war in Korea had gone full tilt. The Commies had pushed the UN forces down to a small area called Pusan, but MacArthur had fooled them with his Inchon landing, and two weeks later the UN recaptured Seoul. Each week brought more good news. When MacArthur announced he hoped to have the troops home by Christmas, I felt I'd once again missed out on combat. Then China came into the war and I knew there'd be plenty of fighting for everyone. Sometime around the first of the year ['51], I received my orders for Korea. I was on my way, but not before one hell of a liberty in San Francisco.

By this time I'd developed two great buddies, Will Curry and Tom Baldwin. Curry had connections with someone whose dad was a big shot at Hertz. When we arrived in Frisco, there she was in a brand-new Cadillac. It was ours until we pulled out.

We immediately took a suite at the St. Francis Hotel, filled the bathtub with beer and ice, and settled in for a great liberty.

Curry knew this Delta stewardess quite well. She got two other Delta stewardesses, and the six of us started to party. We ended up in a nightclub in the Chinese section of town. There was a singer there who can only be described as a knockout. She had on a low-cut dress that left little to the imagination. When they handed out those parts of the female body that men find attractive, she had not been shortchanged. Her dress, definitely of the slinky kind, had a zipper on the back, from top to bottom. On the top it had a rather large tab that seemed to be begging to be pulled.

After one of her singing stints, she came over to our table. Tom Baldwin jumped up and started to dance with her. Wow, was she doing a number on Tom! We used to call it boxing, but I imagine it would be considered tame today. Anyway, Tom loved it.

Next it was Will Curry's turn. Will being a man of no inhibitions whatsoever, I knew there'd be trouble. They were dancing so close together, they looked like one person.

All of a sudden, Will pulled down the tab. The dress fell off and the singer was standing there naked as a jaybird. Christ, everyone is cheering and laughing like hell, except the bandleader. He ran out into the kitchen and returned with a very large butcher knife. It is no longer fun and games.

Oh, this guy took out after Will like a big-ass bird! The naked girl was behind the bandleader, and Tom and I were at the rear of the pack. This guy was yelling how he's going to make a soprano out of Will.

Fortunately, the police showed up in a hurry. They put a blanket over the singer, then arrested her and the bandleader.

"These two," the police officer said, "have pulled this twice before. They want to get you to give them some dough. We suggest you get out of this section of town as quickly as possible." He didn't have to tell us twice.

A couple of days later we left for Korea, but not before we made a pact. We chipped in and came up with about a hundred dollars. We put it in a joint bank account. The last one to return from Korea was to spend it all in one night.

It was March by the time we got to the front. The three of us were assigned to the 7th Marines. It was still commanded by Homer Litzenberg—"Weeping Litz," we called him. He'd had the 7th at the Chosin Reservoir. He went back to the States about a month after we arrived.

Tom Baldwin was an engineer, so he got to the engineering battalion that was supporting the 1st Battalion, 7th Marines. Will Curry and I got Able Company, 7th Marines. They needed a lieutenant for both a rifle platoon and the mortar platoon. We both wanted the rifle platoon, so we decided to flip. I won.

When we joined the 7th, it was in constant combat during Ridgway's counteroffensive to get back to the 38th Parallel. Operation Killer had just been concluded, and we were starting in on what was to be called Operation Ripper. We went through Chunchon and kept moving north, and it was about this time that tragedy struck.

We'd been having problems with the North Koreans, but all of a sudden we ran into some Chinese. They pulverized our mortar platoon, killing my good friend Will Curry.

Later on, my other dear friend, Tom Baldwin, tried to bring me some fresh eggs. We'd had nothing but powdered eggs since we landed. Poor Tom stepped on a land mine and he was gone. I was now the only one left of the three who had made the pact back in San Francisco. War doesn't allow you much time for grieving, but I was utterly crushed.

We had another officer in our battalion named Van D. "Ding Dong" Bell. He is undoubtedly the greatest Marine I've ever known. Lives over in Mississippi now.

Van went into the Marines as a private before World War II. He had sea duty and at one time was the light heavyweight champion of the Pacific Fleet. He'd fought on the islands throughout World War II and had earned his commission by the end of the war. He fought in Korea, and later on had two tours of duty in Vietnam. Van has two Navy Crosses, any number of Silver Stars and Bronze Stars. I'm not sure how many Purple Hearts he has, but it's a lot.

Anyway, Van had Baker Company while I eventually had command of Abel Company. I know we had recently crossed the 38th Parallel, because I believe we were the first battalion to cross it that spring. We had run into a very determined force of Chinese. There was a road going up that separated my company from Bell's Baker Company. There was a hill in front of Baker that Baker wanted. So did the gooks.

It was nighttime, and the only way we could determine who had that damn place was by watching to see which way the tracer bullets were going. I called in for artillery support and was later told my FO team used up a whole trainload of shells that night. With all that fire going out, it lit up the whole area. We could actually see the Chinese marching down the road and not breaking ranks in spite of the pasting they were taking. The next morning you could see rows and rows of Chinese dead.

The ROKs had pulled back on one side of us, as had the U.S. Army on the other. We were sticking out like a sore thumb.

The next day they sent up several tanks to help us get out of there. We were all out of water, so we went over to the tanks to see if we could get a drink. The first guy to step out of the tanks was a fraternity brother of mine from the ATO house at North Carolina. It was like Old Home Week.

There were also some doctors and medical supplies with the

tanks. They checked several Chinese corpses to see what kind of drugs they'd given those troops to get them to walk into certain death like that. They found nothing. Those Chinese were just as disciplined as any troops I'd ever seen.

Bell's Baker Company had also suffered tremendous casualties. When Ding Dong found out that two of his men were unaccounted for, he went back to find them. It turned out they were both shell-shocked, really out of it. He slung one of them over his shoulder and started dragging the other Marine by one of his legs. Miraculously, he got them both back without getting hit. For that and several other things he had done that night, I put him up for the CMH, but it got knocked down to a Silver Star.

Another officer in our outfit was named Eddie LeBaron. Eddie had already played one season with the Washington Redskins. Marine headquarters had wanted to keep him in the States for PR, but he'd have no part of it.

"If they want me to be a Marine officer, I'm going to be a real one. I might as well be playing with the Redskins if I'm going to be in the States," Eddie says. So Eddie ends up on the lines with A/1/7.

After a few months they got on LeBaron again. This time they wanted him to go back to Tokyo and make some film commercials to help sell War Bonds. Eddie agreed only if they'd let him have all the cargo space on the plane coming back.

Eddie returned about a week later. We had just gone into reserve. When we'd done this previously, we'd always be promised a week or so to catch our breath, only to be back at the front a day or so later.

Anyway, Eddie showed up with a big smile on his face.

"Skipper," he said, "I had that plane so loaded with beer and booze, the pilot was reluctant to take off. Break out the troops, we're going to have a ball."

Hell, it was 0100 hours. You can imagine how the men bitched.

"Oh, for Christ's sake," several of them yelled. "We just got here and we're going back up. It's just like the last time." Then I gave 'em the word.

"Gentlemen, thanks to Lieutenant LeBaron, we're going to have a party. Let's break out the refreshments."

The men were stunned for a minute. Then when they saw what we had for them, they let out a big cheer. Eddie was the most popular officer in the U.S. Marine Corps that morning.

There was a lot more to Eddie than just bringing booze to the troops, though. When we went back on the lines, we started sending out patrols again. In one case we got a disturbing call from the patrol's sergeant.

"Skipper," this guy said, "our lieutenant is down. So are two other Marines. I don't know where the hell we are. Can you send us some help?" I had a vague idea where they were, but wasn't sure. Then Eddie spoke up.

"I know exactly where they are. I was out there two nights ago. I'll go."

So Eddie took about six or seven Marines and started out. He got them all back, even the wounded. I can't remember if he was wounded that time or not, but I do know he got hit at least once in Korea, maybe twice.

Nevertheless, when he got back to the States, he resumed his professional football career, played several years as a quarterback for the Redskins.

My point is, LeBaron could have had a cushy job back in the States, but he turned it down. Instead, he chose to be where the action was. Any type of a disabling wound would have ended his football career. He was quite a guy.

Well, as I said, I know LeBaron was hit at least once. As a matter of fact, I can't remember too many Marines who weren't hit, if they stayed there long enough. Of course, I'm talking about the rifle companies.

I caught mine in June. I think it was on Hill 712. The Commies were zeroed in on us with their mortars. We were on the end of a ridge when they opened up.

Once they started in like that, they'd keep them coming for quite some time. A lot of men were getting hit, which caused tremendous confusion. I was trying to get the men the hell out of there when I caught some shrapnel in my face. This took me off the lines for about three weeks. When I got back, they made me company commander. It was mainly artillery and mortars that did the damage, even though we did suffer casualties from small-arms fire.

There was one incident that occurred that summer that I remember quite well, perhaps because it showed how differently people can look at things. We were in a hot spot, hadn't been relieved for quite some time. We knew there was an Army outfit due to take over from us shortly.

So one night I looked behind our lines and saw these lights shining brightly. Someone down there was also making one hell of a lot of noise. The North Koreans also knew something big was going on, and they started in with their artillery and mortars.

Well, hell, I was puzzled. One of my Marines was finally sent down to see what the story was. He came back and reported to me.

"There's a lot of doggies down there, sir. They're putting something up."

I got on my radio and asked to speak with the man in charge. He turned out to be a colonel.

"Sir, this is Lieutenant Burns, A/1/7th Marines. What are you doing?"

"We're putting up our movie screen, Lieutenant."

"You're doing *what*? Do you hear those boom-booms? That's incoming because you've lit up our position. Turn those *goddamn* lights out and stop that racket, *sir*. Tomorrow when you take over, you can do what you want up here, *sir*. But if you don't turn those lights off, I'm going to have my men shoot them out, *sir*."

The lights went out, all right, and I never heard another word about it. But I felt badly for those doggies who were going to have to serve under that nut on the front lines.

You see, that's the type of thing I can remember clearly. Things that are funny now.

Take this young PFC in Able Company. He was a good man, but he was like that guy who was always screwing up in the "Li'l Abner" cartoon strip. He'd do everything right when he was putting together his full marching order pack. Then it would fall apart.

One day, I think it was near the Iron Triangle, we were marching up this road when we started to get some incoming. We all headed for cover. Everything was all right but our friend. He jumped into a slit trench that's loaded with "sweet violets." God, did he stink! He asked me what he should do.

"Take off," I said, "and don't stop until you hit some water. Stay in the damn water for an hour, get some new clothing, and come back."

The lad returned a few hours later, nice and clean, but the men never let him forget it. They'd hold their noses when he'd walk by.

And when I say he was a young PFC, I mean *young*. Hell, I was a company commander at twenty-six! I think the Americans serving in the Korean War, particularly after the early arrivals had gone home, were, on the average, a bit younger than the World War II servicemen.

Another interesting thing about that war was the relationship between the officers and the enlisted men. I think it was a closer thing. I understand it was even more so after the division moved from the east coast of Korea to the west coast in March of '52.

Well, I came back to the States at the end of '51. When I arrived in San Francisco, I went to the bank and drew out the money we'd deposited. I tried to drink it all up, but let me tell you, you can't drink up that much liquor in one night. Besides, my heart wasn't in it. I started thinking of Will and Tom and became very sad.

Hungnam

In mid-December of 1950, the Americans started the evacuation of Hungnam. It was, to say the least, a gigantic undertaking. The 1st Marine Division had been joined by what was left of the U.S. Army 7th Division, the intact Army 3rd Division, and the bulk of the 1st ROK Corps, a total of more than 90,000 troops.

In addition to this host, there were many thousands of North Koreans who did not want to be left to the mercy of the Chinese Army. All told, close to 200,000 human beings were to be shipped down the coast to Pusan in South Korea. It was to be the largest UN evacuation of the Korean War.

Every available ship was pressed into service. What equipment could be loaded was put on board. Over 10,000 tons of equipment left Hungnam. The remaining gear was blown sky-high when the UN pulled out. By December 26 it was all over.

This evacuation has been compared to Dunkirk in World War II. There was a big difference, however. At Dunkirk the Allies escaped a Nazi trap. At Hungnam, the Chinese were delighted to see the UN depart. There was no way the Communists could have forced them out, not in December of 1950, anyway. This factor has always raised a question: Should we have pulled out or should we have stayed?

General Lem Shepherd, who was there, is undecided on this question.

"I was at a little gathering we were having for Ned Almond's fifty-eighth birthday on December 12," Lem related to me. "General [Oliver P.] Smith, the commander of the 1st Marine Division, Carl

Ruffner, X Corps chief of staff, and a couple of other Army generals
were there. I know Ned didn't want to pull out. I can't remember
about the others. But we had our orders and that was it. I do feel we
could have stayed there with no fear of the Chinese overrunning us,
but with China now in the war it was a political football."

John Hitt, a sergeant in the 1st Marines, is more outspoken.
"Gave it back to them, that's what we did. After we'd fought our
asses off over it. Hell, the 3rd Division [U.S. Army] had set up a
perimeter there that was ironclad. The Chinese were finished at this
point. By the time they were reinforced, we would have had a
Gibraltar there the whole Chinese army couldn't have touched."

Lieutenant General Krulak is of like mind.

"The Chinese were finished, near Hungnam anyway," Brute remembers. "We were interrogating this prisoner. The interpreter
asked him if his legs were bothering him.

"'No,' he answered. "A couple of days ago they hurt a lot. But
they no longer hurt at all.'

"Well, the man had gangrene in both legs. They didn't bother
him because they were dead. In a day or two the rest of his body
would also be dead. A great many of his comrades were in the same
shape.

"Granted, the Marines may not have been in great shape, but
there was nothing wrong with most of them that a few days' rest
wouldn't cure.

"The position we had was utterly defensible. We had plenty of
naval gunfire, complete air superiority, plenty of ammunition and
food. Our firepower was greatly superior to that of the Chinese.
Hungnam was easy to supply from the sea. In short, everything was
going for us.

"Why, then, didn't we stay? Well, nothing breeds fear faster
than fear. As far as Washington knew, we were facing hundreds of
thousands of Chinese hordes waiting to pounce on us. They felt we'd
be slaughtered. Nothing was further from the truth.

"In my opinion, we lost an opportunity to change the history of
the war. We were to pay for this blunder with thousands of American
lives over the next two and a half years."

William G. Thrash:

The Guest of Mao

On top of old Smokey
All covered with flak,
I lost my poor wingman,
He never came back.
For flying is pleasure
And dying is grief.
A quick-triggered Commie
Is worse than a thief.

"Do I know Bart DeLashmet? Of course I do. He was a lieutenant in the Army's 25th Division. Bart was from my neck of the woods. He was from Mississippi and I was from Georgia. We were in the same prison camp, up near the Yalu. Ask Bart about those winters. He must have been as cold as I was."

Lieutenant General William Thrash, USMC (ret.), told me this while I was visiting him in Southern California. When I got home I called Bart, who now lives in Darien, Connecticut. I asked him about the winter weather up by the Yalu.

"Cold, my God, it was cold! And Thrash, those Chinese made him stand naked out in that weather. But he never did break for them. Thrash was a real hero."

General Thrash now lives in Corona Del Mar, about halfway between Los Angeles and Oceanside. He runs his own business and is enjoying life to the hilt. Among his golfing buddies are Ray Murray and Ross Dwyer. They can all break ninety, which is quite good golf for men who are well into the back nine of life.

General Thrash saw very active service in the three wars that occurred during his Marine Corps career. Just before I left, I asked him if he could draw any comparisons among the Marine flyers of the three wars.

COLONEL WILLIAM THRASH
U.S. Marine Air Corps

In World War II we sang some of the dirtiest songs I've ever heard in my life, just absolutely filthy songs. In Korea we would sit around all night and sing ballads. Things like "Old Number Nine."

> *Blood on the parachute,*
> *Blood on the ground,*
> *Great big puddles*
> *Of blood all around.*

Not a filthy word in any of them. I guess we were all a little bit older than in World War II, maybe somewhat more sentimental.

But then in Vietnam, they didn't sing at all. I was the wing commander at the time. They'd invite me to the officers' clubs and we'd just sit there and drink.

Of course, they'd eventually get drunk. I had forty-six clubs for the wing throughout Vietnam. I had to raise the price to fifty cents a drink to stop them from pouring the booze over each other's heads. But sing, never!

Well, after graduating from Georgia Tech I decided I wanted to be a Marine flier. They needed aviators, all right, but in '39 they didn't have enough planes to go around. I didn't actually get to Naval Flight Training until the summer of '41. That's where I was when Pearl Harbor came along. I was a second lieutenant at the time.

From then on, things happened fast. By the time I finished my flight training, I was a captain. When I went out to the South Pacific that fall, I was a major. In other words, I had gone from second lieutenant to major in less than a year. Great Scott, at that rate I should have been Marine Commandant by the time the war ended! I wasn't, but I was a lieutenant colonel, which is not bad for a twenty-eight-year-old Marine.

After I returned to the States, I was sent to the Naval War College. Shortly after I got there, I was demoted to major. I may have been the first major to finish the course at the Naval War College in Newport, Rhode Island.

By the time the Korean War started, I was back to lieutenant colonel. I was an instructor in the Aviation Section at Quantico. I wasn't at all surprised when Ray Murray's regiment was quickly sent to Pusan. That's what being a Marine is all about.

I was sent to Korea in the spring of '51. I was the group tactical officer of MAG-12, which meant that I was more or less the flying operations officer. Our problem was, we had only four regular officers in the group. I was one, Lynn Stewart was another. He kept the airplanes going. Jay Hubbard was also one. Can't remember the fourth.

This meant that I was doing a tremendous amount of flying. Two or three of the reserves were World War II types who had kept up their flying between the wars, but many of our men had not.

We were stationed at K-18, way up on the east coast, about ten miles behind the lines. We had about seventy planes there, mostly World War II Corsairs.

It was easy to feel sorry for many of these reserves, though. Most of them had guts, but they didn't belong there. They'd come to me and shake their heads.

"Goddammit, I haven't really flown much in five years. I didn't want to come out here but, dammit, I'm here. Let's go and get it over with." They had guts, all right.

There was one thing that saved our butts. Between the wars, money was real tight. For part of this time I was in aviation planning. We weren't getting many new planes, if any. But they still had money to overhaul what we had.

Well, by God, I went to work on this. We had Corsairs stashed all over the country and we made sure they were in good shape. We had trouble locating some of them. Remember, this was before the age of computers. We didn't really know where they all were. But we found out. Hell, I think we overhauled every plane in the Naval Service before we were through. It was something. By the time I went to Quantico, we had 1,482 aircraft that were immediately ready to operate.

Well, when I got to Korea, I started flying missions at once. Good Lord, I'd frequently fly two of them a day. And I'd work with the reserves. Christ, I'd at least take them up for a few spins around the field before they'd go on a mission.

Then I'd take them on a hop over the lines.

"Listen," I'd say, "stay right on my wing. Don't lose me, *don't lose me*. Everything will be all right."

Some of these guys were impossible. If one of them was a threat to himself, I'd go to my exec.

"Jesus Christ," I'd say, "it isn't a question if this guy is going to kill himself, it's a question of when. Get him out of that airplane."

It was a situation like the film *Dawn Patrol*. Errol Flynn would have to send his new pilots up against the Germans when the kids would have had ten or so hours' flying time.

In our case, that Chinese antiaircraft fire was getting better each day. I didn't want to lose any young fliers if I could help it.

Most of our missions were bombing the Chinese or North Korean supply lines and flying close ground-to-air support for our troops. We'd take 250- or 500-pound bombs, load them, and take off. Our Corsairs were the F4U's. They'd be in trouble if we ran into some Chinese jets, but I don't remember seeing many of them—a few, but not many.

I flew these missions until December. The word had gone back to headquarters that I was trying to win the war singlehanded. It wasn't really true, but I received orders that the time had come for me to come off the lines. I was told to go down to the Wing as the G-3 assistant.

Well, as I told you, the enemy's antiaircraft fire was getting hotter all the time. We were losing a plane or so on each mission. We had an antiaircraft officer of our own who was concerned.

"Colonel," he said, "why don't you take me up with you? If I can see what they're throwing at you, and what their fire pattern is, I might be able to tell you how you can avoid it. Can't hurt."

I figured, "Why not? I'll go on this last mission. Then I'll report to Wing." I loaded the antiaircraft officer on a TBM and we started off.

When we reached the enemy lines, we ran into a buzz saw. The air was full of flak. I guess I zigged when I should have zagged. I think it was a 20 mm shell. But, at any rate, I knew we were in trouble. It took out the fire wall and, worst of all, it knocked out the oil lines.

"Get ready to get out," I said. "I'm going to try and make the ocean, but if we can't, we're through."

Then the prop stopped.

"That's it. Let's go!"

Hell, I landed right in the middle of a Red Chinese reserve division in about three feet of snow. I whipped out my trusty .45. Then I started to look around. There were about twenty Chinamen pointing their weapons at me. Well, people will ask me what I did next. Very simple. I gingerly put my pistol back in my holster and stuck up my hands.

I later found out that Dick Still, another pilot who was stationed at K-18, who had also gone along with us, had landed about half a mile away. He was captured at the same time. Our antiaircraft officer was never heard of again.

Anyway, this group of Chinese just kept staring at me. I expected them to open up at any minute. As far as I was concerned, I had just bought the farm. I think I was more numb than scared. My brain seemed paralyzed. No heroics, just numb.

One of the Chinese then came over and knocked me down. He stuck his burp gun next to my face. My mind was just kind of floating on air.

Then, for Christ's sake, another Chinaman ran out with a camera and took a picture of the scene. It was probably used in Chinese newspapers under the caption, "Yankee Marine Dog Cowers Under Brave Chinese Soldier," or something like that.

Next they took me up to see the general of the division. He couldn't have been more cordial. He spoke good English.

"As long as you're in my command, you will be fed well, no one will touch you. You will not be harmed and you will have a warm place to sleep. Try to escape and you will be shot."

Well, that sounded like a good deal. Besides, I was towering over most of the Chinese. It would have been a snap to spot me if I tried to escape.

I spent close to a month there with the Chinese Army, and let me tell you, I was impressed as hell. These troops were well trained and very disciplined. Dick had joined me by then. Neither one of us was bothered at all while with the army.

Then they started to walk us to a place called Pyongyang. This was well into North Korea. Now we were out of the army's jurisdiction. We were at the Chinese Political Interrogation Headquarters. Things were different. Here they wanted us to dig in the coal mines. They were eight of us. This one young pilot said, "No way!"

"I was brought up in the coal mines in West Virginia," he told us. "They have no shoring in those mines. That sucker is going to cave in."

We knew it meant trouble, but we all refused to go into the mines. What we didn't know was that the grade of coal there was excellent. It was the place where the Japanese had got this silky type of coal that they had used in their ships years before.

Wow, did they ever kick the hell out of us! Fists, boards, everything you can think of. They really worked us over. But the Chinese, in a way, don't really have the stomach for downright torture. Oh, they'd starve you to death. Then they'd just shake their heads.

"Too bad," they'd say, "he just didn't take care of himself. Too bad."

Of course, the food was pretty scarce there. It wasn't that those Chinese were living high on the hog. They weren't. But, my God, we were hungry!

Well, I stayed there about three or four months. We were all pilots and the Chinese were all ardent Communists. They worked on us every day. What they really wanted was for us to come around to their way of thinking. Can't remember that any of us did.

As for the mine, we never did go down in that hole. Two or three days after we'd refused, it caved in. I don't believe they mentioned it again. They lost face on that one.

Now, in case you are wondering why so many of these Chinese spoke English, it was simple. They had been houseboys for the old 4th Marines in Shanghai before the war. They were always asking us if we knew some of the old China Station hands. I felt it would be wrong to tell them yes, even though I knew some of the men they asked about.

We had a regular system set up. They'd ask us how many planes there were at our field. We'd tell them we didn't know, that we'd been shot down on our first mission. We'd try and stonewall them as best we could.

At any rate, everything changed in the spring of '52. I was sent up north, near the Chinese border. Here they had a very large prison camp, officers in one section, noncoms in another, and the ranks in the third section. They had destroyed our rank structure. But as a colonel I was the senior officer, for what it was worth.

Of the three, the PFCs' camp was the worst. Christ, those poor kids were dying like flies! The Chinese would try and play off one guy against another.

Leadership was desperately needed there, but the Chinese would allow none of it. As soon as one man would step forward, the Chinese would knock him down.

For the officers, it was political preaching. God Almighty, did they preach! For months on end they gave us this crap. By now it was getting cold again. The food was horrible. We were living like pigs and we still had to listen to that communistic bullshit.

So I talked to some of the other officers, the Army, Navy, the British Gloucesters, the Australians, one officer from every outfit in our section. This guy would pass it on to the others. That was it. We told the Chinese we were going on strike unless they stopped this communistic claptrap.

That did it. They stopped our food for a while. Then they gave up. They knew we weren't buying that goddamn Communism anyway. But they wanted the ringleader. So they started working on each man and they weren't very nice about it.

Finally, one American broke. He gave the Chinese my name. I ended up spending most of the rest of the war in solitary confinement.

I was completely isolated from the American POWs. Actually, I was in the cellar of a house near the camp. The Chinese would come see me. They were trying to make me confess to dropping germs in North Korea. What a joke! The only germs I'd had contact with were the ones passing around the prison camp.

Every now and then they'd get frustrated as hell at me. They'd strip me balls-ass naked and make me stand out in the snow. They'd watch me shake like hell. When I'd stop shivering, they'd pull me inside. You see, when you stop moving, that means you're beginning to freeze to death. They didn't want that. They'd pour cold water on me, then warm me up. The questioning would start again.

"Did you drop germs on the people of Korea?"

"I don't know what you're talking about."

That was it. Outside I'd go. It was pretty tough on a boy from Georgia, I'll tell you that. But they were clever. They knew just when to bring me back in so I wouldn't freeze to death.

When it first happened, the indignity of it all was mortifying. The thought of standing there with my privates waving in the breeze was embarrassing beyond belief. Then I figured the hell with them. After all, I wasn't at a full-dress ball in Washington, D.C.

By this time my clothing had changed drastically. When we got to the Yalu River, they'd taken away my flight suit and my thermal boots and given me a great big cotton-padded uniform. That was bad enough, but guess what they gave me for my boots? Sneakers, that's what! Back home in Georgia they'd call me a lousy horse-trader for that one. Believe me, though, it wasn't a voluntary swap.

One thing that helped me a lot was something that Dick Heisinger had told me back at Quantico. Old Dick was a prisoner of the Japanese in World War II. I asked him what it was like.

"When you're dealing with the Oriental, don't ever show any emotion," he told me. "If they knock you down, just take your time and get back up. If they hurt you, try not to show it. But don't beg, don't curse them, and don't fight them. Just be a stoic." I tried to follow this advice, but it wasn't always easy.

Take the time they tried to scare the daylights out of me. They'd been bugging the hell out of me again about germ warfare. I'd made up my mind that if it was at all possible, I wasn't going to play ball with these clowns.

Well, they came into my cellar and started calling me some ugly words. I'd say they thought I was against the people of the whole world. They were going to rid this planet of such a vile creature.

So they took me outside, where they had a squad of Chinese soldiers lined up. I didn't see anyone with a camera, like before. This was the end. Of course, I was scared to death. But this time I was composed. "For Christ's sake, Bill," I was saying to myself, "show these SOBs you can die like a man."

"Thrash," one of them said, "one last time. Will you admit that you dropped germs on the Korean people?"

"I did *not!*"

Then the soldiers started going through the "ready, aim" routine. Just as their officer was going to say "Fire," this big Chinaman, he looked like Big Stoop out of "Terry and the Pirates," came over and clouted me on the side of the head. Then they picked me up and took me back to my cellar.

An hour or so later I was alone in my dungeon when it struck me, hell, they weren't going to kill me. I was worth something to them alive, not dead. Everything seemed to explode. I laughed and laughed, couldn't stop. Someday I would be going home.

Physically I was all right. I'd lost about fifty pounds, but outside of constant cases of diarrhea—it went with the territory—I seemed to be reasonably fit. The most amazing thing were my teeth. They were turning black, so I figured they were going to fall out. They didn't. I later found out many of the POWs did lose their teeth. Why not Bill Thrash?

Well, there were two or three Korean kids living in the house above my cellar. They knew things were not very pleasant for me, so they'd punched a hole in the cellar wall and were always shoving garlic in for me.

Of course, garlic also goes through you pretty fast. Sometimes the guard would let me out so I could let go, but a good deal of the time I had to go right there in the cellar. The ground was the floor, so I'd then bury it. Hell, my floor was a regular septic field. But I kept my teeth and I never had worms, either. You just can't fathom the effects of garlic on the human body. I hope those kids have had a good life.

The regular food, when we got it, was cabbage. I can't look at it today without getting sick.

Meat? No, sir. From the day I got to the Yalu there was no meat at all, not till the last month or so. Then they gave us two pigs. One of our Brits said he'd been a butcher. He'd take care of those porkers. Then a doctor in our camp came around.

"No, no," he said. "Trichinosis."

What were we to do? We were hungry as hell. Those pigs made our mouths water.

"Doc," I said, "is there any way we can fix them so they're edible?"

The doctor was as hungry as we were.

"Well, look, take those suckers and boil them for twenty-four hours. I guess you can eat anything if you boil it enough."

So, that's what we did. And the good doctor ate as much as anyone.

We would occasionally, but not very often, get soybeans. This was the real protein food of the Korean people up where we were. The Chinese guards were probably getting a lot of those beans. They also had some corn, but we very rarely received any of it. All in all,

I'd say our food supply was somewhat below that of our guards, and those poor Chinamen were barely on a subsistence diet.

As for escape, I couldn't see how you could do it, not after they had you in one of the camps up near the Yalu, anyway.

In the first place, being a Caucasian, you'd be bound to stand out like a white horse walking down Main Street.

Then they had their search teams, all of the school kids in North Korea. I don't know what those people do for sport, but they must have a lot of sex because, God Almighty, there were kids all over the place.

So, what the authorities would do if a prisoner was missing was close the schools and turn loose the kids. For these youngsters it became a game. These kids would fan out, charging through trees, mountains, fields, everywhere. It became their "kick the can."

Then, when they'd find the prisoner, they'd start cheering. Along would come some Chinese soldiers and haul the guy back to the camp. He'd be thrown in solitary confinement for a month or so, and that would be it.

Another thing that made it impossible to escape were the guards. They'd be stationed every quarter of a mile or so on the roads. If a villager wanted to travel to the next town, he'd have to have a pass. North Korea was a real police state. This meant the prisoners could not use the roads. The North Korean people sure as hell weren't going to feed the guy. All in all, I'd say that escape was an utter impossibility.

Well, it was in April of '53 that they took me out of solitary confinement and stuck me back in the camp and, much to my surprise, as the senior officer, put me in charge. I know damn well that by this time the Chinese were as sick of the war as we were. Their officers in our camp wanted to put their houses in order. We even started to receive regular rations of potatoes. Life was getting better.

Then came a bit of a problem. We later heard that things at Panmunjom had hit a snag when that old bandit, Syngman Rhee, started releasing the prisoners down in South Korea who didn't want to go back to North Korea or China. But eventually things got straightened out. The Chinese then called me in to tell me we were going home.

"But," they said, "you're the senior officer. If there is any trouble, we'll take you off the train and send you back to China."

"Well," I said, "I'll take that responsibility if I can set the rules."

I knew we'd be going back in those little Toonerville Trolley boxcars of theirs. This would be no picnic.

"Those car doors must be left open," I said. "No locking us in. Periodical stopping of the train so the men can go out and relieve themselves. Give us ten minutes to stretch our legs. If you stop in a village, I'll make sure that our men have absolutely no contact with the locals. Believe me, all we want is to get the hell out of here. If you go along with me, there'll be no trouble."

The Chinese went along with my request immediately. I think they were as anxious to get rid of us as we were to leave that dung-heap.

So, that was it. We had no problems whatsoever getting out of North Korea. Just a long, boring train ride, but a trip when our spirits continued to soar with each mile.

As we got closer and closer to freedom, everyone was straining to see one thing, and when we spotted it, well, we had a feeling that is hard to describe. It was the flag of the United States of America. Normally, you don't think much about it, but when you spend a couple of years without seeing it, you surely do miss it.

Who Was at Fault?

Victory has a thousand fathers.
Defeat is an orphan.

—President John F. Kennedy

In 1916, Marshal Joffre had fallen out of favor in France. The original hero of the great victory at the Marne in 1914 was in trouble. Many French leaders were seriously questioning whether indeed it had been *his* victory. When informed of these detractors, Joffre simply shrugged his massive frame.

"Who would be to blame," he said, "if we lost?"

And so it is with MacArthur. Today there seems little doubt: it was MacArthur's orders that sent the UN's forces straight to the Yalu. Not only did he ignore the possibility of a Chinese intervention, but he seemed to have had little concern for the calendar. He surely knew of North Korean winters. The winter of 1950 was not the first time that thirty-degrees-below-zero weather had developed in North Korea.

At any rate, should it have been MacArthur's decision alone to hurl his troops toward the Yalu?

Of course not.

The great general's victories at Inchon and Seoul had sealed the doom of the NKPA. He now stood at the pinnacle of his success. Unique as his position may have been, he was still subordinate to the Joint Chiefs of Staff in Washington. While they stood in awe of the man, what about the newly appointed Secretary of Defense, George Marshall? Here was a man who at least equaled MacArthur in every respect.

Then, of course, there was the President of the United States. If anyone had Truman's ear, it was Marshall. A word from Marshall to Truman could probably have stopped the 8th Army from going any farther into North Korea than Pyongyang on the west coast and Won-san on the east coast.

And the United Nations, particularly the British—why were they silent? Prime Minister Attlee was certainly quick enough to come to Washington *after* China had entered the war with both feet. Britain had the closest ties with India of any major power. She had definitely received knowledge of every word Red China had said to the Indian government; that was the reason the Chinese had told India what to expect if any "round eyes" came close to the Yalu.

The Chinese had been emphatic about this. They seemed to be saying, "Let the Koreans now settle this between themselves. But under no circumstances will we allow a European and American army to come to our doorstep."

Why, then, was MacArthur's Army allowed to go north? Why did Truman not tell MacArthur to stop, and, if he refused (which seems quite doubtful to this author), recall him then and there?

He certainly had a precedent. If Harry Truman knew anything, he knew his American history. He was well aware that Lincoln had fired an immensely popular George McClellan after the Peninsular Campaign during the Civil War, called him back for the Battle of Antietam Creek, then fired him again. McClellan was considerably more popular with his troops than MacArthur was with his 8th Army men. Yet the Army of the Potomac did not dissolve after their "Little Mac" was put on the shelf.

Truman always made a big issue of MacArthur's telling him at their meeting on Wake Island that it was very doubtful Red China would enter the war. But why was MacArthur even asked such a question? Ask him about the North Korean army, yes, but do not ask a general, no matter how high his rank, a political question. Or, at least, if you do ask him, get other opinions; do not hang everything on his answer.

And the other opinions, and there were plenty, weighed very heavily in favor of China entering the war if MacArthur tried to conquer all of North Korea.

Well, all of this is now just a page in history. However, it is easy to wonder what would have happened if any of several people had been bold enough to tell the great general to stop. Perhaps, as General Krulak says, the whole course of history would have been changed.

Or, as Sergeant John Hitt put it, "How the hell didn't headquarters know there were thousands of Chinese all around us when every PFC in our outfit knew it?"

Austin Stack:

The Brewmaster

from Queens

Austin Stack has a job today that would make him the envy of just about every enlisted Marine who ever wore the green skivvies. He is president and owner of a very large beer distributing firm, specializing in imported brew. Its name is Franklin Distributors, and it is located in South Windsor, Connecticut.

Aussy, as he is known, was brought up in Richmond Hills, a part of Queens, one of the five boroughs of New York City. He was born in 1930, four years after his parents had left Ireland. Both his father and uncle had been IRA leaders in Ireland's struggle for independence. Sick at heart over the treaty that had split Ireland in two, they started a new life in America.

When the Japanese bombed Pearl Harbor, one of Austin's older brothers immediately joined the U.S. Navy. He went down with the USS *Quincy* at the Battle of Savo Bay, off Guadalcanal. This loss bothers Aussy to this day.

Stack was badly wounded in Korea, near a place called the Iron Triangle. When he got out of the hospital, he was put on limited duty until his enlistment was up.

"It was a real cushy job," says Stack. "I'd accompany the casket of one of the guys being sent back from Korea to his hometown. I'd stay until the funeral, then come back to New York City.

"While I'd be at the poor guy's hometown, I'd go to the nearest VFW post. Hell, I couldn't pay for a drink.

"My problem was I'd have to fortify myself with booze to face the mother of the deceased. It was like going through the loss of my brother all over again. I finally couldn't take it any longer, so I transferred to a guard company."

CORPORAL AUSTIN STACK
B Company, 1st Battalion, 5th marines

When I was told I was going to Korea, it didn't worry me, but I didn't know how to tell my mother. She had already lost a son in World War II.

Both my parents had come from Ireland. I could visualize Mother getting out the statues of the Blessed Mother and praying and crying all the time. So I told her I was going to Japan to be with the artillery. I just couldn't bear to tell her I was headed for Korea as a machine gunner. I don't know how long she believed me, but I tried to keep her in the dark.

Well, in September of 1948 you could join the Marines for one year, then spend the next six years in the reserves and your military obligation would be over. Nobody thought there'd be another war. It seemed to be a good deal, and I grabbed it. Parris Island, Camp Lejeune, Quantico—the year went fast. No big deal. I got out in September of '49 and started taking classes in business at Delahanty Institute. I had hoped to go to Brooklyn College. I was working at the Rheingold Brewery. You remember the Rheingold Girl elections they used to have every year in New York City, don't you?

And then, of course, in June of '50 the shit hit the fan. In July they called up the Marine Reserves. Along with a lot of other guys I was told to report to the Brooklyn Navy Yard.

We were all standing in line at the Yard when the guy in front of me started to shoot the shit.

"Christ, I wish they'd hurry up and get this over with," he said. "I'm a milkman, I've got to get back to work."

"That's tough," I answered, "but I think they're going to swear us in. You're back in the Corps."

"Oh, they'll never take me. I've already got two kids and another due in November. Besides, I've already spent three years in the Corps during World War II." At this time you had to have four dependents to get out of the Reserves.

About a month later I spotted the milkman down at Lejeune. I asked him what happened.

"Oh, for Christ's sake, they won't count the one in the oven. I'll be going home in November."

Talk about stupidity, but they needed warm bodies.

Another guy had false teeth. He took his teeth out and smiled. "They ain't going to get me." Then he bounced his jaw up and down and laughed. He looked like Walter Brennan, the old movie star.

Get him, you bet they did! Even gave him a new set of teeth. I later heard he got to Korea.

The sad part of it was, many of the reservists had seen heavy duty in the Pacific Islands. Now they were going back for some more. The enemy can only miss for so long. Artillery shells, hand grenades, small-arms fire, eventually they'll get you. I wonder how many Purple Heart veterans from World War II were killed in Korea?

Now let's go ahead to Korea in February of '51. A bunch of us are sitting around a fire. There's a young kid there who had gone into the reserves just before the war broke out. He'd been called up immediately and had gone over with the Brigade to Pusan. He'd been with the 5th at Inchon, Seoul, the Chosin, and was now engaged in the Guerrilla Sweep. He'd just got word he was going back to the States.

"That's right," he said, "and *now* they want me to go to boot camp. How the hell can I take a bunch of shit from some guy who's never been in Korea? Semper Fi, I guess." I never did hear if he went to Parris Island or not.

I ended up missing all that early stuff, don't know why, but they caught up with me in November. I went out to San Francisco in December, and there I had a close call with disaster. It all started when a group of us asked a sergeant at Treasure Island when he thought we'd sail for Korea.

"Ah shit," he said, "you won't be leaving for a week or so."

So, what the hell, five of us decided to see San Francisco. We met some real good-looking girls and had a ball. There was one thing that bothered me, but what the hell. It happened when one bar refused to serve me because I was only twenty years old. I'd had a few by then, and I was outraged. I told the clown I'd buy the joint just so I could fire him. Then we left.

At any rate, we got back to Treasure Island and went to our

quarters. Holy shit, the gear is gone, the sacks are stripped, and the mattresses are folded up. The draft had left the day before.

Now we're in real trouble. We think we're going to end up in Portsmouth Naval Prison. We then went to see the top sergeant.

"You guys are lucky," we were told. "We've had a lot of casualties at a place called the Chosin in Korea. They need replacements. We're got planes going to the Pacific all the time."

So we had stops in Hawaii, Johnston Island, Guam, and finally Japan. When we met up with the draft, nothing much was said except that we were going in as replacements for the 1st Battalion, 5th Marines. They had just moved from Masan up the coast to Pohang. They were about to start the big Guerrilla Sweep.

The first guy to talk to us when we joined Baker Company was a first lieutenant, I think his name was Hancock.

"Are you the guys who missed the boat?"

"Yes sir."

"Well, we haven't got any time out here for chickenshit. Just keep your noses clean and I'll see it doesn't go in your jacket. Good luck!" That was it.

At any rate, the sweep started. When the United Nations forces had moved north after Inchon, they had bypassed thousands of North Koreans. Many of these troops were happy as hell to be out of the North Korean Army. Others had become a pain in the ass.

Our company was split into squads. Each squad was given a certain area to sweep. We were given South Korean money and instructed to pay for everything.

We'd been hunting for guerrillas for about a week. I decided to get up early one morning and go out and scrounge for some eggs. I was carrying a carbine and was wearing a .45 on my belt. I was approaching this farmhouse when all of a sudden three guys appear out of nowhere. They were probably North Koreans.

"Oh, for Christ's sake, go away," I'm saying to myself. "All I want is some eggs for breakfast."

Hell, they took one look at me and took off like a shot. I started to enter the farmhouse when another guy walked out, as did the family that lived there. One of them could speak some English. He soon made it clear that the first man had indeed come south with the NKPA and that he had been living in the house. He was also perfectly willing to surrender to me.

Oh shit, who needed this? I took him back to our squad leader, who checked with our captain. We were instructed to hand him over to the local authorities. I was also congratulated for my successful capture of a devious Commie. I never did get my eggs.

That sweep was no farce, however. There were some very nasty firefights with the guerrillas. I heard that a large group of them had surprised three or four Marines from our battalion and had hanged them in a barn. All in all, though, it was like chasing ghosts. Our non-battle casualties greatly outnumbered those from enemy action.

And what were those non-battle casualties? Frostbite! Remember, only two months earlier the Marines had frozen their asses off at the Chosin. Well, the end of January was just as bad. Look out that window. [It was the end of January, near Hartford, Connecticut. A heavy snowstorm had fallen the night before.] How would you like to bivouac in that ground? That's what it was like in Korea, only worse.

All right, by now I was settled down with the 5th. I was assistant gunner on a .30-caliber air-cooled Browning machine gun. The tough part of the job was lugging the gun. The gunner carried the tripod. Believe me, the gun was a hell of a lot heavier than the tripod.

The 1st Battalion's CO was a light colonel named John Hopkins. The men had nicknamed him Twitchy. As a PFC I didn't have much day-to-day contact with old Twitchy, but what I saw of him I liked. Every time he'd come around, he'd ask our platoon leader the same question.

"Are the men getting enough to eat?" he'd ask.

The answer would be yes, which was usually true. Then Twitchy would nod his head.

"Good, Lieutenant, good. Got to keep the men healthy. Hard duty ahead."

Baker Company had several company commanders the six months I was with them; Jim Cronin had it the longest. He was a good egg. Hell, I can't remember having a lemon.

My favorite was a little guy named Bill Kerrigan. If you looked at him, you'd take him for a bookkeeper, but he was hard as nails. Always carried an M-1. He always wanted to know who was doing his job well, and he'd let you know about it.

One time we caught four or five North Koreans in a house down in a valley. They were maybe four or five hundred yards away. All right. We used to keep our tracer bullets in an ammo can. We didn't want to use them too much because they'd overheat the barrel. Well, we opened up on the thatched roof of the house with these tracers. The tracers would be red-hot. They set the roof on fire, and shortly afterward these gooks came out with their hands in the air. By this time I'd been made gunner. I was feeling pretty good about what I'd done when Kerrigan yells over, "Who was the gunner that set that shack on fire?"

Someone yells back, "Stack!"

"Good job, Stack, how to go!"

Most of the officers wouldn't have cared, but Kerrigan wasn't that way. It seems to me he was always there when something was happening.

Now how had I become a gunner? Well, the gunner had been a guy named Franconey. One day we were in a furious firefight with the Chinese. Stuff was flying everywhere. A bullet went through my pack, ruined my pork and beans. A lot of our company got hit that day. We were firing as fast as we could.

Holy shit! The whole gun blows up. Blows the latch cover assembly off and everything. Christ, it was like someone hit me over the head with a baseball bat. Then I look over at Franconey.

He had taken the full blast in his face. Christ, it hit his eyes and his ears, the whole bit. He really had his bell rung! He seemed to go a little batsy.

They stuck him in a helicopter and evacuated him to a field hospital, I don't know where, but he eventually got to Japan. I was hit a few months later and was sent to Japan. I tried to see him, but they wouldn't let me. I did finally get to see him back at St. Albans on Long Island. He'd improved a great deal but was still shaky. I hope he's all right now.

Here's what had happened. Some rounds were sitting up on a trunnion block and when they sit there, the trunnion block is so hot it blows up the other shells, starting a chain reaction.

At any rate, I was then the gunner and we seemed to be constantly on the go. I remember one hill we took, losing some men as we took it. Then we got the word to go on back to where we came from. I mean, what the fuck is this? We lost some good men going up that damn place. What are we going to do? Give it back to them? Look at a map of Korea. Over four or five months' time we went from

Pohang north and northwest to Chorwon. All these moves had names like Killer, Strangle, things like that. But as far as we were concerned, that was all crap for the media.

I remember one time when a bunch of us were sitting around, shooting the breeze. One guy was reading a newspaper, which he carefully put aside.

"Gentlemen, I know you shitheads will be glad to know we have recently concluded Operation Ripper."

One of our guys was from Bangor, Maine. When he heard the word "Ripper," he blew a huge fart.

"There's a rip-per for you!" he said.

You know how those guys from Maine accent their r's. We all broke up.

The war got real serious, though, when the Chinese made a huge sweep down in April of 1951. We were at Wonju when it happened. We'd hit the sleeping bags when Cronin started to rouse us.

"Get your ass up," he's yelling, "we're bugging out."

No one really knows what's happening, but no one wanted to be left behind.

So we started out. As we looked back, we saw this huge flame leaping to the sky. Wonju is burning. I guess they didn't want to leave anything for the gooks.

Now, if there is anyone in the U.S. who hasn't seen *Gone With the Wind* by now, he must have been living in a bubble. Do you remember that scene when Rhett Butler is taking Scarlett home to Tara in a buggy? In the background you can see Atlanta burning. Well, that's what I was thinking of as we're marching out. I told that to all the guys, and everyone agreed. I don't think anyone's morale was really down. It was just another move. I don't think the Chinese got much further, though. If anything, we were pissed off over the fact that we'd have to push them back again.

As a matter of fact, the only time I can remember the morale being really low was between January and March. That period has stuck in my mind, and it wasn't the enemy, it was the cold that broke your back. When we could get hot chow, we used to stick our mess kit in this GI can of boiling water. Then you'd go through a chow line. By the time you'd sit down, the ice was already forming on the food. Coffee? Drink that in a hurry, mate, or you'd have iced coffee.

You know what sticklers the Corps can be on cleanliness. Forget it! Once a month or so they'd try and get you behind the lines for a shower. Christ, they'd have to cut the clothing off you! Your long-johns, particularly the parts that had been next to your armpits and crotch, were so crummy they could walk by themselves.

You'd get in a shower, three guys to a nozzle. They'd turn it on so you'd get wet. Then you'd have to soap down. While you're doing this, you'd also freeze. Next would come the word that the hot water would be on for three minutes while you tried to rinse off. Now would come the battle for the nozzle. Shit, it was chaos!

Then came the crusher.

"All right, you guys, in thirty seconds the water goes off!"

"You sonofabitch! I'm still covered with soap."

"If you shut it off, I'll blow your fucking head off!"

"Listen, you rear echelon shithead, don't you dare!"

On and on the argument would go. In the long run you'd proba-bly get clean, but what a hassle. Then you'd be issued new clothing, stuck on a truck, and be sent back to the lines.

The next time you see a movie with John Wayne killing the enemy in droves, think of all the little things that make war a real hunk of baloney. Glamorous—bullshit!

And, of course, you had the constant danger of combat. It was always with you. Sometimes you'd have some very close calls, but the longer you were there, the higher your chances of getting hit would be.

Take the time in May when I had to go back to company head-quarters. It was a beautiful day and all I had on was my field jacket. I left my pack with my platoon.

I did what I had to do and headed back for the platoon. I was halfway there when I ran into my guys.

"What's going on?" I asked.

"Simple, Stack, we're pulling back."

"Did anyone bring my pack?"

"I don't think so. Semper Fi!"

I mumbled something about what a bunch of nice guys they were, and headed back to get my pack. I did think to get a carbine from one of the guys.

So I got back to where we'd been and picked up my pack.

Holy Christ, there're Chinese all over the place. My heart is pounding like a sledgehammer. Then I realize the gooks are too busy to pay any attention to me. I had picked up my gear so nonchalantly that I guess they thought I was one of them.

You know how it is if a neighbor's dog comes at you, you just stay cool. That's what I did. Then I walked away like I didn't have a care in the world. But I was scared shitless. The guys thought it was funny as hell, but I didn't.

At any rate, after the Chinese drive was stopped, we started moving back into what I'd call north-central Korea. We took a hill without any opposition, which was a blessing. Cronin told us to dig in because we'd be there for a few days. I first dug a hole where I put the machine gun. Then I started to dig a hooch for myself.

Much to my surprise, there was a little hole right near the gun. I jumped in and conked off. The next day Cronin came by.

"Stack," he said, "you better dig your hole deeper; we might catch some incoming mail tonight."

So I went to work. I hadn't dug very far when I saw what looked like a sweater. I yanked at the cloth and this body broke through. For Christ's sake, I was sleeping on top of a dead chink. This was late April, but it was still cold enough that he hadn't begun to really decompose.

The minute the rest of the squad found out about it, they began to give me the needle.

"Hey, Stack, double rations; you have to feed your pal," or, "Stack's got a friend for tea," things like that.

I dug deeper, put the stiff in as deep as I could, and dug myself another hole.

Well, it seemed to be one hill after another. We used to name them things like Baldy, Old Smokey, Big Tits, names like that. There'd frequently be firefights on them, which brings up an interesting point.

When we had to sit in a hole and be shelled, you could be scared as hell. But when I'd be working that machine gun and the old adrenaline would be pumping away, you didn't have time to be scared. You were in a perpetual state of excitement.

Anyway, June came and the weather was beautiful. We had moved over the Imjin River that day, and my feet were all wet. We went up into the mountains and bivouacked for the night. I dug the hole for the gun, set up my own hooch, took my shoes off, and hit the sack. I was with our squad leader, a Marine named Roy Harris, a beautiful guy from West Virginia.

At about 0200 we started to hear firing. We woke up fast. Roy ran down to the hole where the gun was, while I'm trying to get my shoes on. I go running over to the hole as Roy is yelling, "Come on, one of our guys has been hit." There's a tree right next to the gun. I'm at the tree when this gook throws a hand grenade that hits Roy in the face and chest. I get it also, in the arm and the rim of my nose. I go down, but much to my surprise I'm still alive. Just an inch or so higher and it would have got me right between the horns.

I stagger up, but as I do, another grenade comes over and gets me in the ass, so I go down again. I can plainly hear Roy in the hole, moaning. I get up for the second time, but just as I get to the hole, grenade number three comes in. This one really clobbers both my legs, and I fall right on top of Roy. He isn't moaning anymore. There's another guy in the hole and I'm bleeding all over him.

"Throw some grenades over there," I yell to him. "Clean out the area where their grenades are coming from." I manage to throw a couple of them myself, even though I can't really stand.

There's a guy named Hotchkiss over on my left. He's a BAR man who's supposed to be covering our flank.

"Hotch," I yelled, "give 'em a burst, give 'em a burst," and he did.

Then this new kid—he'd only been with us a few days—opens up with the Browning. The only problem is, the gun lights up the whole area. It's like a shooting gallery, particularly with the hand grenades also going off. We're throwing 'em and so are the North Koreans—I think they were North Koreans, not Chinese.

It quiets down some. Then I realize I have to take a tremendous shit.

"You guys are going to have to help me over to that tree or I'll shit my pants."

Once more, John Wayne, where's the glamour? Did John Wayne ever shit his pants?

At any rate, my buddies think it's funny. "Holy Christ," someone said, "the grenades are falling and Aussy is taking a dump."

Well, the guys help me down to the hole. The kid who'd fired the machine gun is dead and so is Roy. But, wounded or not, Harris had done a hell of a good job before he died. He got the Navy Cross posthumously.

As for me, I feel awful. Along with my obvious wounds, I'm getting a tremendous stomachache. A helicopter shows up and takes me to the battalion aid station. From there they whisk me to the hospital ship *Haven*. By this time I'm delirious. All I know is they'd set my broken legs and pulled the shrapnel out of my body. But I still have this tremendous pain in my gut. I give the doctor the word.

"It's my gut, I'm telling you, there's something wrong with my stomach!"

"Now, now, we know what we're doing."

Christ, this went on for a couple of days and I'm really losing my cool, don't know what I'm saying. I got into quite a row with one of the doctors. We're going at it hammer and tongs. I'd had enough of him.

"It's in the stomach!" I yelled, then I puked all over him.

"Stack, I'll have you court-martialed for that."

"Yeah, maybe you'll have me shot, you asshole, but it's still my stomach that hurts."

Court-martial? Can you believe that? What makes this sawbones think I give a shit if they court-martial me? I've been hit by three hand grenades and my stomach's on fire. I think I'm dying. And what's going to happen? I'm going to be fined fifty dollars and restricted to base for thirty days. Bullshit!

Okay. I'm yelling so much they finally decide to X-ray my gut and crotch. It turns out they had missed three small pieces of shrapnel that had punched holes in my colon. Two or three more days and I would have been a goner.

The court-martial? After they had fixed me up with a colostomy, the doctor came to see me. I think he was a lieutenant commander.

"Stack, I owe you an apology. If you hadn't kept bugging us, you would have died. Thank God you did what you did!"

It wasn't easy for this guy to do this. When was the last time a doctor apologized to you?

All right. This was in June. Let me go back to May. We were up on top of this hill. Item Company had been there before us and had a real rough time. They're taking their wounded off the hill. I started to talk to this wounded guy lying on a stretcher.

"Where'd you get hit?"

"In the ass."

"Boy, that's embarrassing. What are you going to tell people back home when they ask to see your wound?"

"Who cares? I just hope I get home alive."

The guy's name was Paine—Painless Paine, they called him. Okay. Now I'm on the *Haven*, and who's in the sack next to me but Paine? He's also got a colostomy. I asked him if he remembers me. Hell, the poor guy's delirious. A day or so later he died. In come two corpsmen and they take away his sheet.

My God, his backside was literally blown off. It was sickening to see. One more for John Wayne. Guys in his movies never get killed by getting their ass shot off.

So these corpsmen start putting cotton in his ears, nose, ass, everywhere he had an opening.

"What the hell are you doing?" I asked.

"Well, once you die, stuff that's in you starts pouring out."

"For Christ's sake, can't you do that somewhere else? That might be me tomorrow. It's not a pleasant thought."

So they took Paine away, but it scared the shit out of me.

To make matters worse, that afternoon a priest came in to give me the last rites. You know, a nice Irish Catholic boy has to have the last rites.

Now I'm really scared. All I can think of is getting that cotton shoved up my ass. Wow! At any rate, next I'm shipped over to Japan and I'm starting to recuperate.

In the meantime, this guy Philip Lieberman, the head of Rheingold Brewery, found out that I had been hit. He calls up his friend, Senator Herbert Lehman, to get the whole story. Lehman pulls some strings and I'm flown back to St. Albans Naval Hospital out on Long Island.

Several months later, two of my buddies from Baker Company are also home and come to see me. It was November, just before I got rid of the colostomy. When I told them how the colostomy worked, they were puzzled.

"But, jeez, Aussy, how about the shit you took *after* you were hit? The one when I held you up next to the tree."

"That was getting rid of stuff already there. And it was a life-saver. If I hadn't gotten rid of that poison, it could have killed me."

Well, from then on, I've always made sure to go as quickly as possible. That's a very bad part of your body to fool around with.

Horseshoe Ridge

Strange things happen when you travel around the country interviewing Marines, all of whom fought in the same war. One of the
most amazing of these occurrences concerned C/1/1 and a little-re-
membered place called Horseshoe Ridge, a few miles across the 38th
Parallel, in North Korea. It was here in April of 1951 that Charlie
Company played its part in hindering what the Chinese had hoped
would be a major spring offensive. I ended up talking with four men
who were connected in one way or another with Charlie Company at
this time. None of these interviews was planned, nor did I know
ahead of time that these men had been in Charlie Company. It was
pure luck. From California, New York, Louisiana, and Maine, they
pretty well bracketed the country.

The Chinese assault itself did not come as a surprise to the Marines, according to Chuck Woodson from Riverside, California:

"We'd been hearing about the coming Chinese attack for days. I
was on an FO team in support of Charlie. Captain Wray, one of the
great company commanders in the Corps, had been getting reports
about it from headquarters. Then, a few days before it began, I was
shifted over to the South Korean Marine regiment on the left flank of
Charlie. I think we were replaced by an Army FO team. I don't
know what happened to them."

Bob Mosler was a career naval corpsman with the 2nd Platoon,
C/1/1 on April 23, the night the attack started. He now lives in a
beautiful wooded area in central Maine. He remembers Horseshoe
Ridge quite well.

"We'd been told to expect a massive Chinese assault aimed at driving the UN forces out of Korea. So we expected it when we were rushed up this ridge to replace an ROK division that had been pulverized by the Chinese. There was an Army artillery unit right behind us. I remember one Marine, you know how Marines are, telling these Army guys to relax now that the Marines had arrived. That was all right, but that evening the Chinese hit us. They gave us quite a mauling.

"I can't tell you how many Chinese were there, but there must have been at least a division. I'd been with Charlie since Inchon, and I can't remember any combat quite as fierce as that night. Our men were dropping right and left, but the damage we were doing to the Chinese was tremendous.

"I remember a platoon leader named Hicks. He was banging on the top of a tank, trying to tell the guys in the tank where to fire.

"Our platoon seemed to be the one that had been hurt the least, so, when we did get the word to fall back, we were the ones told to cover the retreat. My job was to minister to the wounded. I remember going to two wounded Marines as we were trying to make sure we didn't leave any casualties behind. They both had head wounds. One glance told me the first one was dead, while the other was dying.

"There was another platoon in C Company, can't remember which one, where two corpsmen were hit.

"As a matter of fact, by the time I left Charlie, I think I was the only original corpsman left in the battalion."

Floyd Baker, from Louisiana, was with the Weapons Company, 1st Battalion of the 1st Marines, an ammo carrier with the 81 mm mortars. Early on the morning of April 23, his unit was rushed up to support Charlie Company.

"I was amazed," he told me, "to see the South Korean soldiers bugging out. Here we were, in their country, fighting for their freedom, and they're hightailing it like scared rabbits. We knew some of us were going to get killed, and for what? These clowns?

"Well," he continued, "we got into position to be ready for the Chinese attack. Around 2000 hours it came. They're blowing bugles, whistles, and beating drums. Trying to make light of the situation, I turned to the other Marine in my foxhole.

"'They sure could use some music lessons,' I said.

"By now they had us surrounded. We had a security platoon trying to keep these crazy Chinamen away from our mortars. We're keeping those 81's firing like mad. Twice we ran low on shells, so some of us had to go over to the ammo truck and get more shells, crawling part of the way on our bellies.

"Around dawn the Chinese fire slacked off. Then we got word that we'd have to fight our way out. It was as if the Chinese were waiting for us to move. There was an open field we had to cross, one at a time. Some made it, others weren't so lucky. Johnny Savoca was shot through a kidney. As J. J. Baresh was trying to get him on a stretcher, J. J. was hit in an arm and his chest for his troubles.

"A Marine named Bagley from Boston was right behind me. I heard him yell that he was hit, but he wasn't. A bullet had knocked his sleeping bag off his pack.

"There was a guy name of Crow. He was wounded and put on a truck. Then a Chinese sniper put one in his heart. We lost several of our wounded from the snipers.

"We finally fought our way out and got back to our original perimeter. A lot of people were amazed to see us. They thought we'd all been captured or killed.

"I'll tell you one thing, though, it's a good thing you move mechanically when your buddies are getting hit. You just don't have time to realize how scared you really are."

Joe Reisler was a platoon leader in Charlie Company at Horseshoe Ridge. Like the rest of his company, he had no idea what they were getting into.

"They put us in trucks and we drove all night. Everywhere we looked, we could see the ROKs retreating. It reminded me of what I'd read about Belleau Wood, where the Marines would see the retreating French, only I can't remember any legendary remark like "Retreat, hell, we just got here!"* But we knew we were going toward the Chinese.

"They dropped us off at the bottom of our objective. Some of the intelligence people were there, and they had a big map with pins stuck in it. They showed us what to expect from the various Chinese field armies. Then we climbed up a hill to set up our defense on what was to be called Horseshoe Ridge.

"Well, my platoon was on the point of the ridge. I think it was 500 to 800 meters high. We could look down and see the Chinese

---

*Said by a Marine officer at Belleau Wood in World War I.

scurrying around. We called in artillery fire. Our guns opened up and killed plenty of Chinese, but it didn't seem to stop them.

"That night Bob Wray, Charlie's CO, called me up on the portable phones we had. Poor Wray. He'd been at the Chosin Reservoir and had been slated to go home the day before, but with the Chinese about to attack, this was impossible.

"Wray told me what to expect that night, and to try and get some sleep until it started. He was an excellent officer.

"That night it started. It was absolute bedlam. I'm getting reports about one of our machine guns being out, then another. Our walking wounded were beginning to show up everywhere.

"I got another call from Wray, telling me he's sending up a squad from another company. But I knew we couldn't hold. So I said, 'Let's pull back about a hundred yards and regroup.'

"Then my sergeant came up to me.

"'Lieutenant Joe, have you told our flanks that we're pulling back?'

"'No, in all the confusion I forgot about it.'

"He took care of it. Thank God for good sergeants. We dug in, lying on our bellies and firing. An FO told me he was going to call in artillery on the top of the hill we'd just left.

"What a job they did! We could see the dirt flying as they hit our former position.

"We hung on by our fingertips all night. There was so much lead flying around, you couldn't stand up. There was a corpsman lying near me. He looked at me and smiled.

"'Lieutenant, I'd better go to work.' He took off. I never saw him again. The bravery of those corpsmen can never be overstated.

"When daylight came, so did our airplanes. I can't recall how many casualties our platoon had, but it must have been a lot. I know when I got the orders to pull out, no one was unhappy."

As a final note on Charlie Company at Horseshoe Ridge, I received a phone call from Chuck Woodson. He'd recently been at a reunion of C/1/1. It seems that a corpsman, Joe "Doc" Churchill, had been put up for the Navy Cross by Captain Wray. He ended up getting the Bronze Star. Many years later, when Wray, a retired Marine colonel, found out about this, he went to work on what he felt was an injustice.

In August of 1986, the onetime captain of Charlie Company stood in front of what was left of his old command.

"Attention to orders!"

Then he read the following:

"The President of the United States takes pleasure in presenting the Navy Cross to Senior Chief Hospital Corpsman Joe V. Churchill, United States Navy."

Churchill, now a Washington State district judge, could not believe it, but there it was in black and white. The men of Charlie Company all say that Wray was one hell of a great captain. I guess they are right.

C/1/1 did not win the battle of Horseshoe Ridge. The 5th and 7th Marines on either side of them were also hit by mass Chinese attacks. The utter confusion of battle occurred up and down the line. But they certainly took part of the sting out of a Chinese assault that was to peter out not long afterward.

Peter Santella

.

"I'm the police commissioner of New Canaan, Connecticut, and strangely enough we have former Marines throughout the force. They all make good police officers."

The police commissioner's job is only a small part of Peter's life. Having started as a small electrical contractor, he is now the owner and president of a firm that employs eighty people. Partially aided by the twenty-year boom in Fairfield County and greatly helped by a strong desire on Peter's part to give it all he has, Pete has been eminently successful in business.

"One thing I learned in the Corps," says Pete, "is that nothing is impossible if you really want it."

On going to Korea, he can be quite philosophical.

"Many times you'd say to yourself, 'What the hell am I doing here? Why should I be fighting for this stinkin' rice paddy? I don't owe these people anything.'

"But you must remember, World War II hadn't been over very long. The Communists seemed just as bad as the Nazis to us. I think my age group had been bred on the patriotic fervor of World War II. You either went in the service or you were a bad guy. I don't remember anyone going to Sweden to stay out of the service."

These pretty much seem to be the feelings of everyone I interviewed.

PFC PETER SANTELLA
Mike Battery, 11th Marines

The recruiting sergeant at South Norwalk was a big guy, loaded with campaign ribbons. I'll never forget one thing he said to me, as he pointed his finger in my face.

"Listen, son, we're a real close organization. We'll bring you back dead or alive. We never leave our dead behind."

"Jeez," I said, "that's pretty darn nice of you."

What I was really thinking was this guy is some kind of a nut. I really didn't care what happens to me after I'm dead. Besides, no matter what this guy said, I was going to be a Marine.

Well, I was raised in southern Fairfield County [Connecticut]. Many of the people who lived there commute to New York City, but most of the second- and third-generation Italian-Americans don't. We're not New Yorkers. By now we're Connecticut Yankees.

I have a lot of older cousins who live in this area. Most of them served in the Army in World War II, saw a lot of combat. I was jealous of them, felt I didn't do my share. So when Korea came along, I went into the Corps as soon as possible. I was one pretty wiseass kid at the time. This was to change at Parris Island.

A group of us got on the train in New York City. When we reached Washington we had a layover. That's where we picked up the booze. We were still cockeyed when we got to Parris Island, something that did not amuse the noncom who greeted us.

"Well, well," he said, "what do we have here, a bunch of asshole party boys? You're going to really enjoy your stay at boot camp."

Enjoy? That sonofabitch made my life miserable! I hated that bastard. But shortly before we were to leave, I thought he was a pretty good egg. And it was then I had my disaster.

It was around five o'clock in the morning. This other boot started giving me a needle over something. Can't remember where he was from, but we'd not gotten along at all. Maybe he'd gone to military school or something. You might say he was the perfect boot. Finally I'd had enough of his shit.

"Look," I said, "why don't you mind your own business and I'll mind mine?"

Jesus, he hung a sucker shot right on my jaw. I got up in a hurry, almost from instinct. My jaw hurt like hell. I grabbed my rifle and swung it at him. He moved back, so, instead of his head, I hit his kneecap, breaking it. My jaw was broken also, so I guess we both regretted the incident. I know I did. I ended up with six weeks in the hospital. I can't even remember what the argument was all about.

When I got out of sick bay, I was sent to Camp Pendleton for advance infantry training. No chickenshit like PI, but twice as rugged. Next came Forward Observer School at Camp del Mar. Jeez, this was just the opposite.

We were located right next to Highway 101, not out in the boondocks like we'd been at Pendleton. And we had liberty every night. Christ, we had guys at the school who had broads picking them up in convertibles.

I had a great buddy there, a real wild man named Sal Salitino. We'd usually make liberty call together. Our greatest was a weekend on Catalina Island, off Long Beach.

We had only sixteen bucks between us, so we bummed a ride on a Navy launch to get there. We were having a drink at this bar when in walks Robert Mitchum. He was getting a divorce at the time and had these two good-looking dolls with him.

He greets us with, "Hello, jarheads." That did it! We had a great time with him for the weekend. What a guy! When we got back to base, we still had the sixteen dollars.

Now let's go forward twenty-five or so years. A friend of mine, Freddie Steinberger, is opening a restaurant called Fat Tuesdays, here in New Canaan. One of his investors is Robert Mitchum. Freddie invites me to the opening. Mitchum is there also, and I went over to him.

"Do you remember me?"

Mitchum seems confused.

"Let me refresh your memory. Catalina Island, 1951."

"Were you a Marine?"

"That's right."

Mitchum smiled.

"That was one hell of a weekend!"

I agreed.

Well, soon after that blowout at Catalina, Sal and I ended up in the 14th Replacement Draft, headed for Korea. I went into Mike Battery of the 11th Marines. Mike had the 155 mm guns. I can't remember what battery Gus went to, but I know they had the 105s.

We landed at Inchon on November 10, 1951. As this was the Marine Corps's birthday, we naturally were given turkey. They even had some officer cutting this big birthday cake with a sword. I knew this was a big deal back in the States, but I didn't think they'd do it in Korea.

Our tour of duty in Korea was for one year. My first and last meals in Korea were on the Corps's birthday, which was a great way to come and go.

In November of '51 the 1st Division was on the line near the east coast of Korea. In March they moved the whole division over to the west coast near Panmunjom. Don't ask me why, but on the east coast they called it the Minnesota Line and on the west coast it was the Jamestown Line.

So the first thing they issued me was the shoepacs. We used to call them the Mickey Mouse boots. They were a disaster when the winter came. You'd be running up and down those hills and your feet would sweat. Then when you'd stop, your feet would freeze.

Later on, the flak jackets appeared. I was one of the first guys in Korea to get one. The Top [master sergeant] suggested that someone shoot an M-1 into my jacket to see if they were any good. The only problem was he wanted me to be wearing it. Well, I told him to fuck off. He just laughed.

The Top and I had a strange relationship. His name was Master Sergeant Griffin. He was a regular Marine, and he felt I should also make a career of the Corps. I didn't. But he kept trying to toughen me up. You were supposed to get an R-and-R leave to Japan, but he never gave me mine. Outside of a few trips to Seoul, I stayed on the line for the whole year I was in Korea.

He was always on my ass for something. When I was on the guns, I would be two miles or so behind the MLR [main line of resistance]. One of our problems here was the prostitutes. You had to have been in Korea to realize what a hard land it was during the war. These people would do anything for food. These girls—and most of them were girls, not women—would come right into our area. They'd display their wares and try and entice the troops. We had to constantly be hustling them out. Most of us were horny as hell. It wasn't easy. The Top would always make sure I'd get this detail.

It was like that all the time. If a shitty detail came up, he'd always yell for Santella. He gave me a beaut one day. First he called me over.

"Santella, see that woman over there? Get her the hell outta here! You know these people. She might have a grenade up her ass."

I looked over at this woman; she was at least two football fields away. She must have been two hundred years old.

So I walked over to her.

"Come on, lady, you gotta get out of here."

She's rocking back and forth. "Shoot me, shoot me," she said in broken English. She looked like an old American Indian woman singing her death song.

"Goddamn you, lady, there ain't no way I'm going to shoot you."

I tried to pick her up, and the sweater she was wearing came apart in my hands. She was so wretched I couldn't stand it. I went back to the sergeant.

"Top, get two gooks to take her out of there, I can't do it."

That was one of the horror stories of the war. Those civilians were so poor. The few times I went to Seoul, it was dreadful. Open sewage, people living in huts. All of them scratching to stay alive.

The city was one big hovel. Someone told me it had been a great town before the war, but not when I saw it. The only halfway decent places were the bars and the cathouses. And they weren't exactly New Orleans.

Sometimes the Marines didn't help any. The gooks used to have honeywagons trying to pick up all the turds. The smell was unbelievable. One of our guys got all tanked up and heaved a hand grenade in the middle of the load. Christ, there was shit flying everywhere. What a mess!

Well, our job on the west front was to straighten out the line. I was a cannoneer and a forward observer. I'd usually go up in front of the MLR and phone back the coordinates so they'd know where to fire.

Sometimes I'd relay this information to battleships off the coast. They'd open up with their big guns. Christ, were they accurate, sometimes even more so than our own 155s. Other times I'd call in the Marine Air Corps. They'd also do a great job.

Of course, the Communists weren't sleeping. When we were in eastern Korea they hit us with 76 pack howitzers [mm guns]. They'd throw a barrage at the Marines, then move their guns as quickly as possible. Then they'd come at us again. They were very well trained and good.

When we got to the west they had bigger stuff, 106s or 107s. We were entrenched not only close to the peace talks but right near the road to Seoul. I guess both sides wanted to look good in that area.

Another one of our jobs was to try and make the gooks attack. We knew we could blow a hole in their ranks when they did. We'd make a lot of noise, drive our trucks all around, march away in field-marching order, you know, try and get them to think we'd pulled out. Christ, we marched up and down those hills until our feet killed us. The enemy fell for this once or twice, but they only sent out a probing squad.

Well, we got to the west coast in the spring of '52. That's when the real combat started. I can remember one of our observing planes being shot down, I think it was a Piper. The pilot was still alive, between the two lines. We opened up with every gun we had, trying to cover the guy as he tried to reach our MLR. It was like a football game, both sides trying to score a touchdown. Thank God he made it!

It was in Korea where I had my first experience with drugs. If there was any of that stuff in Connecticut in '50, I never saw it.

Well, there was this guy in our outfit from the Bronx. His name was Hughes. One time when we were off the lines, the two of us started drinking gin. We've got a buzz on when he says, "Let's go see the doc." Hell, I'm ready for anything, you know how it is. So we go over to sick bay.

"Doc," this guy says, "give me a shot."

"I can't, we need it for the wounded."

"Oh, come on, I need one badly."

"No, now get out of here."

So we go back to our drinking. I don't remember where we got that gin, maybe it was panther piss, but the next thing I know it's morning and I'm lying in a ditch by the side of the road. The only thing I can remember is Hughes asking the doc for a shot. I've got an incredible hangover—haven't had any gin since. But my curiosity got the better of me. I went to see the doc.

"Tell me one thing," I asked him, "what did Hughes mean when he asked you to give him a shot?"

"Narcotics, he wanted some dope. Well, fuck him, we need that stuff to help the guys they bring in who are in great pain."

I'd heard the Chinese would give it to their troops when they'd attack us, but I didn't know any of our guys used it.

Shortly afterwards, the gooks mounted a good-sized night attack. I think we were supporting the 5th Marines at the time. Christ, they're singing in that weird tone of theirs, ding, dong, wang. You know, it sounds like nothing you've ever heard. Well, I figured they must be hopped up. I felt that way the rest of the time I was in Korea.

Now for the sad part. About five years after I'd gotten home, I had to go to the Bronx. I thought I'd look up Hughes. I wish I hadn't. Both he and his mother were high on something. It wasn't liquor. They didn't make any sense at all. I got the hell out of their apartment as quickly as possible.

At any rate, I did spend most of my time either up front as an observer or back of the lines on our guns. I decided it was time for me to get another stripe. I'd been a PFC since I finished boot camp. I went to see the Top about it.

"*Corporal?*" he yelled. "You want to make corporal? Santella, I'm going to make you the best Marine in the Corps. You're a thirty-year man, I can tell. Now get the hell out of here!"

Jeez, talk about a love-hate relationship. The Top had at least twenty years in then. The sonofabitch wanted to make me his clone.

One thing I'll say about him, though, he was a real Marine! Just the opposite from another sergeant we had. This other guy was all spit and polish, always checking the guns. Christ, he'd make us clean everything, all that shit. But when the chips were down, he was nowhere to be found.

Top, on the other hand, was another breed of cat. He was always on my ass. But as I look back, most of it made sense.

And when we'd get some incoming, he was superb.

"Get your helmets on," he'd yell. "Get down in that hole. Stay cool. And don't come out until I say so. I'll know when the gooks are finished."

I still hated the sonofabitch, or thought I did, anyway.

At any rate, sometimes we'd get the word for direct fire. The Chinese had this one gun they'd drilled into the mountain. They'd quickly bring it up, fire a few rounds, then take it down. That sonofabitch must have been stuck a hell of a long way into that mountain, because we couldn't get it. We even tried VT shells, trying to bounce them into the hole. I don't think we ever did get that sucker.

Another time we'd been in this gully, executing direct fire. Hell, we'd been firing all day. We were still there well after night had fallen.

Okay. Do you know what rockets do at night? Well, all of a sudden our Marines started to let go with these rockets. Zoom, they make this funny sound. We tried to get through to them to tell them where we were, but something was screwed up. And these rockets are beginning to drop real close.

"That's it," Top hollers out, "CSMO!" [Close-station march order.] We got out of there as fast as we could. None of us got hit, but that's one of the unknown tragedies of war—the people who get killed by friendly fire.

At any rate, I received combat pay for twelve solid months and was under fire a minimum of six times each of these months. I was never hit, but I surely had some close calls.

One night I was lying in my sleeping bag, cursing out the Top. I'd been given hard duty every night for about a week. Some shells started to land over to our left. I didn't pay much attention to them until the Top came by.

"Santella," he yells, "get out of the bag and get down in this hole. That fire will be in our area any minute now."

So I'm still cursing him, but I jump into this ditch. He was right. That night my sleeping bag was riddled with shrapnel. Here is some of it, I've kept it for a souvenir.

My worst moment, however, came one night when we were at Marilyn Monroe. We called it that because these two hills were sticking up next to each other like two tits.

There were four of us, a lieutenant, a wireman, a radio operator, and myself. I was the forward observer. What looked like a platoon, maybe two, of Chinese came roaring over this hill. We were supposed to be guarded by eight or nine Marines who were set up in front of us.

Christ, they had a hell of a firefight with the gooks, but they couldn't stop them. They were overrun. I think they were all captured or killed.

Anyway, we're in this bunker, not making a sound. I don't think the chinks knew we were there. They went right past us. We waited quite a while, then radioed back for permission to get the hell out of there. We got it and the lieutenant told us to blow up all our equipment and take off. He started running, but it didn't take me long to run past him. Three of us got back to our lines, but the fourth, either the radio operator or the wireman, didn't make it. The Top spotted me.

"Santella, get over here on this sandbag detail." Oh, he was a sweetheart!

A week or so later, things had quieted down. I had about a month left before it would be sayonara for me. I was relaxing one afternoon when I heard the Top talking to another sergeant. Top was about to leave for the States. The other sergeant was congratulating him.

"Yeah," said the Top, "I've finished my year, but you know, there's one thing that bothers me."

"What's that?"

"It's Santella. He's a good Marine, but he's too reckless. He's got a month left. I'm afraid he'll get killed without me to look after him."

Can you beat that?

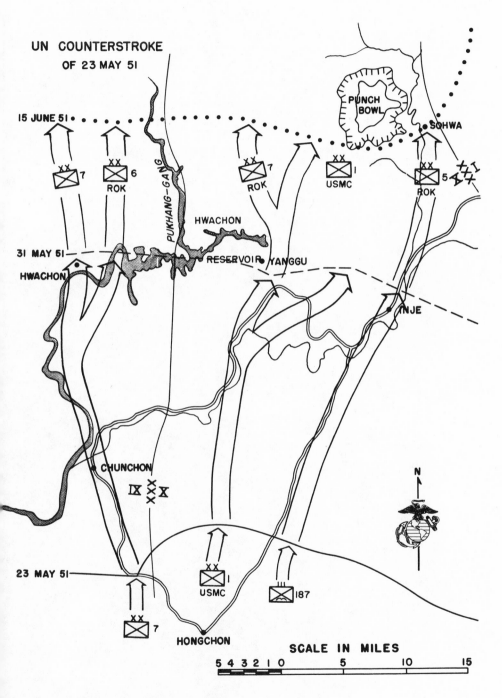

UN COUNTERSTROKE
OF 23 MAY 51

15 JUNE 51

PUNCH BOWL

SOHWA

7

6
ROK

PUKHANG-GANG

7
ROK

1
USMC

5
ROK

HWACHON

31 MAY 51

HWACHON

RESERVOIR YANGGU

INJE

CHUNCHON

IX

23 MAY 51

1
USMC

187

N

7

HONGCHON

SCALE IN MILES

5 4 3 2 1 0   5   10   15

e Punchbowl area. They didn't serve punch.

Arden Grover and
the Punchbowl

"Ask anyone who was with the 5th Marines in the summer
of '51. He'll tell you about Luke the Gook's Castle; it was
near the Punchbowl."

Arden Grover had gone into the Army Air Corps in late 1944.
He was about to get his wings when the war ended.

After his separation from the Air Corps, he'd entered Kenyon
College at Gambier, Ohio. He decided to join the Marine's Platoon
Leaders Program. This way he could get a USMCR commission. If
war broke out again, he was not going to sit on the sidelines.

And, indeed, war did break out in Korea. Arden thought he
would be called up immediately, but the months rolled by and he
still had not heard anything. He was beginning to think the Corps
had forgotten him. When he heard that a Marine general named
Merwin Silverthorn was going to address a group in Minneapolis, he
decided to attend. The thrust of Silverthorn's speech was an attempt
to get new Marine officers.

"We've already called up all our reserve officers," said Silverthorn.

Grover waited until the speech was over. Then he confronted
the general.

"Sir," he said, "here's one reserve officer you have missed."

"Well, son, we're not perfect. Give me the details; we need
young officers."

As Grover tells it. "I returned to my home in Duluth and
waited. The general must have worked fast, because about a week
later I received my orders telling me to report to Quantico on January 3, 1951. This meant I'd have plenty of time for the Christmas
parties before my departure.

"Hell, what a time I had! By the end of December I was completely exhausted. I felt awful. I went to our family doctor to find out what was wrong. He examined me.

"'Arden, my boy, you've just been kicking the gong around too much. Go home for a couple of days, then fly to Quantico. You'll be all right.'

"So that's how I arrived at Quantico, half hung over but on time."

The Corps was working fast with its young officers. By May, Grover was at Wonju in South Korea. He joined 1/3/5 as a platoon leader. They were headed toward the Punchbowl.

"I had a buddy with me named Steve Judson," Grover remembers. "He'd been with me since Quantico. We'd had one hell of a liberty together during the few days we'd spent in Japan on our way to Korea.

"Well, when we reached the front lines, we received a real pep talk from the colonel of the 5th, a Marine by the name of Dick Hayward. We were all real gung-ho. Remember, we didn't know what combat was all about. We could hear the artillery all night, which was quite disturbing.

"The next day, trucks took us to the front and immediately we were in combat. But the toughest thing I had to face was the news I received.

"I had been separated from Steve Judson for the first time since I'd been on active duty. Steve had been assigned to a rifle company of the 1st Marines. My God, he'd only been on the lines a matter of hours when he was killed.

"Talk about stark reality! Just a few months before, I'd had that Christmas bash in Duluth. I'd been an usher at a wedding and must have gone to six or seven parties.

"Now I was in a rifle company about to assault the gooks, and I get the word that a very close friend of mine had been killed. It surely made me realize that these were two different worlds.

"There was another Marine who'd also been in our class at Quantico. His name was Fagan. He lost a leg that very first day. Judson was from Vermont, but I can't remember where Fagan was from. But those first two weeks or so were just about as bad as anything I saw in Korea. We had started from a place called Inje and had moved north."

The dominant physical feature of the 5th Marine drive was a

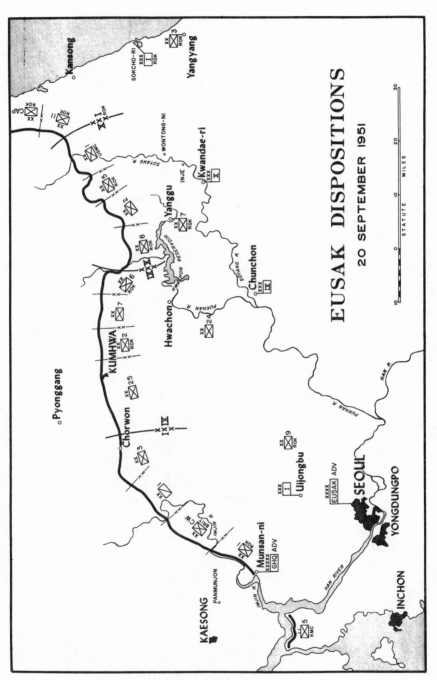

EUSAK Dispositions—the last Marine offensive.

place called the Punchbowl. This was a large area near the 38th Parallel. It was a huge bowl, a large, circular depression about three miles wide at the bottom and six at the top. The 5th Marines were approaching it from its lower lip.

Over on its left were Bloody Ridge and Heartbreak Ridge. The overall area was to see tremendous fighting well into the fall of '51. When the 2nd Division, U.S. Army, the French Battalion, and various ROK units succeeded in taking Bloody Ridge, they found that the North Koreans had fortified Heartbreak Ridge. They had to start all over again. As stated before, Korea was a war of hills.

Well, General Van Fleet had assigned the taking of the northeast rim of the Punchbowl to the 1st Marine Division. They got a lucky break. Their forceful assault caught the North Koreans in the process of relieving their troops, a very dangerous time for a unit under attack. The Marines suffered many casualties, but they did succeed in capturing the northeast rim.

The fighting continued well into the winter. No one is more vulnerable to the enemy's fire during such a period than second lieutenants. Grover was no exception.

"I was hit in the inside part of my thigh by shrapnel from a mortar shell," he recalls. "I was about to drive some wounded Marines back to an aid station at the time. It didn't hurt much, and even though I was bleeding profusely, I took them down. Then I collapsed.

"While I was driving, I'd look down at my crotch. I kept saying to myself, 'No, no, please not my family jewels.'

"Well, I eventually got home, went into business, and got married. I've fathered four children, so I guess my jewels came out of it all right."

Richard Newman:
The Kid from
St. Louis Faces His
Moment of Truth

Dick Newman is a perfect example of a young man that the U.S. Marines straightened out, but he paid an awesome price for it.

Born to a comfortable family in St. Louis, Missouri, he was, in his own words, a bit of a ne'er-do-well until he joined the Marine Corps.

"The main reason I went into the Corps was the draft," Dick remembers. "It was breathing down my neck. I can't say I was ever very gung-ho, but that part of my life means a hell of a lot more to me now than it did while I was on active duty."

Newman's moment of truth came at one of the thousands of Korean hills. Dick cannot even remember its name or number, nor does he remember the mortar shell that devastated his left leg, necessitating its amputation at the knee a few days later.

"I thought my life was over," he told me. "Then I realized I was lucky to be alive."

From then on, Dick fought his disability. He ended up graduating from the University of Pennsylvania and built himself an outstanding business career. He recently retired from the huge Buckingham Company, importers of liquor, where he was president and CEO. He now works for an executive search company in New York City and lives in suburban Chappaqua, New York, with his wife of twenty-five years.

PFC RICHARD NEWMAN
1st Recon Company, 1st Marine Division

Shortly after we arrived at Parris Island, our DI called us into formation.

"Listen, you idiots, one of you clowns has the crabs. Never mind who. Just remember, one of the stalwarts of Platoon 70 has some visitors in his crotch.

"So what am I going to do about it? I am going to take you down to the delouser and each one of you is going to get his balls sprayed. And that's the way it's going to be for the next ten weeks. If one of you screws up, everyone is going to pay the price. Forget that individualist bullshit. You jerks are going to learn to act as a team at Parris Island, so you better learn that *right now*! Might save your life if you get to Korea."

Wow! That's what he said and that is what he meant. If someone was out of step, the whole platoon had an extra hour of drill; if someone had dirty skivvies, we all had to break out the wash buckets. Sounds primitive as hell, but it worked.

Here was this DI, he had no college degree, but he was a bona fide psychologist. When Platoon 70 left that hole known as Parris Island, we were a team. With all its chickenshit, Parris Island was an excellent recruit depot.

Oh yes, by the way, we never did find out who had the crabs. Maybe no one. Who cares?

During the Korean War, a Marine stateside did not have to wear his uniform off the base. But I surely wore mine when I went home to St. Louis after boot camp. I wanted everyone to know I was a Marine. That is what Parris Island did for me, crabs or no crabs.

And something like Parris Island was just what I needed at that period in my life. I am from St. Louis, Missouri. My family was what we used to call "comfortable," but I had been in and out of trouble, nothing serious, but I'd accomplished very little ın my young life.

I'd had a bad scene with one of St. Louis's beauties, worked on a sheep farm in South Dakota and at Famous Barr, a department store in St. Louis, and finally as a shipping clerk for twenty-five dollars a week. To put it bluntly, I was a bit of a bum. When I tell my children this, they find it hard to believe, but it's true.

Then I met a guy from Belleville, Illinois, right across the river from St. Louis. The Korean War, or "police action" as Truman called it, was on. We were both draft bait. We decided to join the Marines before the Army got us. It seemed the macho thing to do, and I was macho as hell in those days. I'd seen just about every movie that had come up on the Marines. It was the outfit for me.

When I told my dad about my decision, he just shook his head.

"Son, as you know, I went to France in 1917 as an ambulance driver. I was only seventeen at the time, but I surely grew up in a hurry. War is nothing like the movies." He was right, but there was no stopping me.

Well, after my boot camp furlough, I reported to Camp Lejeune in North Carolina. Here I became a member of the Recon Company of the 2nd Division, and here the drudgery started. I hated it. We went on maneuvers, practiced landings—hell, I must have landed on Virginia Beach forty times—everything that would bore you to death. I kept putting in requests to go overseas, but was turned down. At twenty years of age I just didn't stop to realize the Corps had to have a division on the East Coast in case an emergency developed in Europe.

Then I got the brilliant idea to write my congressman and state my plight. That was it. In a few weeks I was out on the West Coast, headed for Korea. It was in the summer of '52.

But before I went over, sixteen of us in the same replacement draft decided to have a party. One of us registered at the best suite they had in some hotel in San Diego. All of us stayed in the suite. We hung a banner out one of the windows. It said, "Welcome. Big Party. Come On Up as Long as You Are a Female!"

Christ, what a ball! It lasted all night. You would be amazed how many broads got curious and came up. Talk about revelry, there were no holds barred. I think at one time we had a hundred people in that suite. There was plenty of booze. Our group left for Korea in style, and it's a good thing we did, because our troop ship was a real mess.

First of all, there were 5,000 troops on board. Our racks were stacked five deep. The lucky guys had the top sack. When we hit rough weather, the Marines with the more squeamish stomachs started to puke.

Well, the more they puked, the worse the stink, and the stink would make more guys puke. It was a treadmill going nowhere.

And with that many troops aboard, you could hardly turn around without bumping into somebody. We could go out on deck during the daytime, but not at night.

It was summer and it could get hot as hell. You had to stand in line to get a saltwater shower. It was one crummy trip. When we reached Japan, most of us were ready to go gaga.

The first thing I wanted to do after we landed in Japan was get a decent shower. I stood under that spray for about a half hour. After that, I went looking for female companionship. This was not hard to find in Japan at that time. After all, I didn't know when my next opportunity would arise. I hasten to point out that I was then a bachelor.

So I quickly arranged a love tryst with one of Japan's darlings and gave it my all. It was delightful. I was getting ready to hurry back to the ship when I ran into a real Japanese beauty, and I mean a knockout. I could quickly see we were going to get along famously. Tired or not, this was too good an opportunity to pass up. I knew I wouldn't be back to the ship on time, but so be it. What could they do, shoot me? I didn't think so.

The whole thing was like a dream. She even gave me a bottle of Canadian Club, which she wouldn't let me pay for. When I was absolutely exhausted, I gave her every cent I had and hustled back to the ship. I had about half a bottle of Canadian Club left, which I stuck inside my jacket.

I reached the ship shortly before it sailed, which was a lucky break for me. If I had missed it, I could have ended up in Portsmouth Prison.

When I boarded ship, the first one to spot me was the officer of the day. He didn't seem to care that I was several hours late. He did look suspiciously at the bulge in my jacket.

"Got any liquor?" he asked. "No sir," I answered.

Then he took his swagger stick and hit my jacket.

"Hand it over, Marine," he said.

That was the end of my Canadian Club. I didn't see him throw it overboard. I think the sonofabitch drank it himself.

The ship then took off for Korea. We landed at Inchon. We were disembarked very quickly and I was immediately sent to the 1st Division's Recon Company up at the front. Here I met a great group of Marines. It was different from the recon group I'd been in back in the States—far less formal.

Take the officers—they never wore their insignias. Everyone, officers and enlisted, was known by his first name. This was a very pleasant surprise. I'm sure you've heard rumors of the fragging that went on in Vietnam. Well, we would never have had any of the crap in our outfit; our officers were just like the rest of us.

Our weapons were superb. We had our M-1s, but we also had an abundance of automatic weapons. We had plenty of BARs, Thompsons, and grease guns. I asked one of our sergeants why we had all the firepower. He laughed. "You'll find out!" he answered.

Well, just before I'd joined Recon, I'd noticed a drip from my penis. Ah, my God, I thought, one of the girls in Japan had given me a dose. The minute I arrived at Recon, I went over to sick bay.

"Doc," I said to one of the corpsmen, "I think I've got the clap."

"Well, well," he answered, "let's find out."

He then took a smear and stuck it under a microscope.

"I'm happy to tell you," he said, "that you don't have gonorrhea. What you have is a strain. Don't be so ambitious next time."

So I joined my new company with a dripping pecker.

I've told you the officers did not wear their rank. I found out this was because we were always running into snipers. When we went on patrol, we would usually go very close to the Chinese lines. If any of those gooks would spot a rank on a collar, they'd zero right in on the guy. As for the relaxed camaraderie our officers had with the men, they just seemed to feel it was a better way to run the company. They were right.

We had discipline, all right, especially out on patrol, but it was not of the "by the book" kind. Hell, our officers knew the men weren't getting a liquor ration. They'd *share* their ration with us.

As for combat, there was never any of that crap of telling the men what to do and then sitting back on their asses while we did it. They'd do anything we would, and then some. I cannot overemphasize how well I think everything worked in our company!

Anyway, shortly after I arrived, we went into action. I was told to go and pick any weapon I wanted. I chose a grease gun. When we ran into some Chinese, I got so scared I peed my pants, but I didn't bug out. I stayed and did the best job I could. I never really stopped being scared until after I was hit.

This brings me around to a pet theory of mine about why the Marines always seem to do a damn good job. Before we went into combat, we were always being told we would do a good job because we wouldn't want to let our Corps down. Well, that is part of it. But I think it was more that you did not want to let your buddies down. How could you face them if you bugged out? Oh, there were plenty of times when I wondered what the hell I was doing there, but I never considered taking off.

Take Christmas Eve, 1952. We were out on one of our nightly patrols. The gooks had their loudspeakers going full blast. They were telling us it wasn't our war, all the fat capitalists were back home sleeping with our girlfriends and wives, that the folks in the States didn't even know there was a war on—all that crap they were always throwing at us.

Then they'd play Christmas songs and tell us we'd all be going home in burial bags and would never again have a Christmas dinner with our family.

In the meantime we are getting closer and closer to the Chinese lines. Then, wham, they opened up on us. We all went down, but the guy on my left and the guy on my right were both hit. I can first remember being grateful that it wasn't me. You always felt that way. Then I started firing my grease gun. I sure as hell couldn't let those two guys down, could I?

And, by the way, neither one of those Marines was killed. They had their tickets home.

Actually, that was a typical patrol. We were constantly going into no-man's-land and constantly taking casualties. As I recall, Recon Company had about 60 percent casualties while I was with them. Most were wounded but several were killed.

Recon was all volunteers. You could go to another outfit if you so desired. Many of our men were hard and fast anticommunists. There were all kinds. We had several refugees from central Europe who had come to America after the Communists took over their native countries. We had Japanese and Chinese—you name it and we had it.

We did have one great thing about us, this was our living condi-

tions when we weren't on patrol. Our quarters were well behind the
MLR. We ate well, slept well, and partied well.

If we knew we weren't going out for a couple of days, we'd ar-
range a little gathering. One way or another we'd get some beer or
liquor and tie one on. There was even a rumor going around that
some of the men would smuggle in some women, but heaven forbid.
It would be real relaxed and would include the officer.

There was one first lieutenant who arrived shortly after I did.
He wanted more inspections, felt we should not have our wingdings
and should police the area. We were all horrified, including our captain. The new officer was soon transferred out of Recon. As one of my
mates put it, "Good riddance!"

Well, we never knew when we'd get word to saddle up, which
meant we were going out. And, as my father had told me, it wasn't like
the movies. The next time you see a war film, notice how bunched up
the men get. This was a no-no. One Chinese burp gun could get too
many Marines that way.

And the noise—I don't think you can really capture it on film.
Once the firing would start, it would be deafening. You are trying to
stay alive, but you're not dwelling on it. Most of your actions are
reflexive.

It happens so fast you lose your perception of time. No matter
how long it lasts, it's impossible to judge correctly the time that has
elapsed during a firefight.

When you truly would get scared was when the mortars started.
I'm sure you've heard that Marine Corps legend about Lou Diamond
putting a mortar shell down the stack of a destroyer off Guadalcanal.
Well, these Chinese were just as good as Diamond. If they were
firing at a moving vehicle, they would track it. It might take four or
five shells, but the chances are they'd get it. They could do the same
with men. My God, they were deadly!

So, on January 15, 1953, I started out on my last patrol. I never
found out why, but we were at full strength. We even had the cooks,
bakers, clerks—everyone who could walk. We were going out in a
skirmish line, which is something we rarely did, and we were going
out in the daylight, something we had never done since I had joined
the company over four months earlier.

Sensing that something must be up, the Chinese were quickly
reinforcing their position, and that's when our air power came into

play. I had never seen them in action. They were magnificent. Our pilots were bombing and strafing those gooks like there was no tomorrow.

By this time we were only a couple hundred yards from the Chinese, and it was then that our pilots started in with the napalm. If you've never seen a napalm attack, you never want to. It was brutal!

We had now moved close to a mile from our own MLR. Things were really heating up. Air attack or no air attack, the Chinese still had one hell of a lot of firepower. We were pinned down in a ravine when someone yelled out, "Okay, we're going up that hill!"

I didn't necessarily want to go along with him, but if that's what he wanted, that's what he was going to get.

So we started out. I was carrying a BAR. I remember that clearly, because it was the only time I carried one while in Korea. I could actually see the gooks on the top of the hill, looking down on us.

I was carrying my weapon in the cradle of my arm. No tripod. I was firing it as I went forward. Then the gooks opened up with those damn mortars.

Well, they say you never hear the one that hits you, and it's true. The next thing I knew, I was in a field hospital behind the lines.

A few months later I met a buddy in the Oak Knoll Naval Hospital in Oakland, California. He had been clobbered by a land mine after I'd been hit. He told me what had happened.

You see, there was a Marine in our outfit named Leo Succhi. He was a Polish kid from Detroit. I am Jewish and it always seemed to me that Leo didn't care for Jews. We were always arguing and had almost come to blows a number of times.

And who do you think it was who probably saved my life? Succhi, of course! Some of these cooks and bakers who were out with us for the first time were supposed to act as stretcher bearers. Succhi saw me go down. He yelled for some of them to come get me, but they wanted no part of leaving the ravine. So Succhi pointed his Thompson at them.

"You'd better get up here and pick up Newman!" he yelled. "If you don't, I'm going to open up on you!"

That was it. A couple of them ran up the hill and dragged me back to the ravine. Then four of them stuck me on a stretcher and carried me back a mile or so to the field hospital. I never saw Succhi again, but, Leo, *shalom*.

Well, when I woke up in the field hospital, there was a priest chanting Latin by my sack. I was quite groggy, but I remember saying to him, "Father, what are you doing?"

"You're badly hurt, son. I'm giving you the last rites."

"But I'm Jewish!"

"Oh, you've lost your dog tags, son. We had no way of knowing your religion. We saw the name Newman on the back of your jacket. That could be anything. I didn't want to take any chances."

While he was saying that, I couldn't help but think about the joke concerning giving chicken soup to the dead guy. That one that ends up with the Jewish mother saying, "So, it couldn't hurt."

Anyway, it gave me a chuckle, and chuckles were to be few and far between for me over the next few months.

As I began to look around, I noticed that I had a cast going up my entire leg and another one on my arm. I was in a great deal of pain. They kept giving me morphine, and my mind would wander in and out of consciousness. You lose track of reality.

For instance, I had grown a beautiful mustache while with Recon. A small piece of shrapnel had landed in my upper lip. They had to shave my mustache before taking it out. So here am I, lying on my back, I don't know the extent of my injuries, they are giving me morphine for the tremendous pain, and I'm pissed off because they have shaved off my mustache. That was the last thing I can remember before I went into a state of shock.

Next, they flew me to the hospital ship *Constellation*. I had lost all sense of time. I can't tell you how long it took to get there. Everything is a blur. I can vaguely remember two doctors talking. One was using the words *gangrene* and *operate*. The next thing I knew, I was coming out of the anesthesia they'd given me. I was in traction, but I sensed something was wrong. Those same two doctors were staring down at me. Then I looked at my leg.

My God, it wasn't there!

I cannot describe the utter terror that overcame me. I tried to get up and take a poke at the nearest doctor, but I fell back and blacked out again.

When I next came to, I was in officers' country. I guess they thought I might kick off, and it would be bad for morale if I died in the ward. A corpsman was sitting by my sack. He'd been there twenty-four hours.

Now let me clear one thing up. Many people think you have an amputation and that is it. Baloney! I was one very sick Marine for at least a week. There had been a hell of a shock to my system. Such a setback can destroy you. My will to live was down around zero.

Then they started to work on me. They told me that my arm had also been badly mashed, but they were sure they could save it, that plenty of guys were worse off than me, that they could do wonders for me in the way of an artificial limb—things like that. It would be a long time before I could accept my loss, but I think my return to reality started right there on the *Constellation*.

From the hospital ship I was flown to Japan, where I spent a week or two, then on to the Oak Knoll Naval Hospital in Oakland, California. Here I came under the care of an old-line Navy doctor named Conte. It was one of the luckiest breaks of my life.

Conte was a marvel. Not only was he a great orthopedic surgeon, but he could convince you that things were not as bad as you imagined. For instance, he came over to me one day when I was really in the dumps.

"What's the matter with you, Newman?" he asked.

"Sir, I was just thinking about my life. What woman is going to want a man with one leg?"

"Don't worry, son," he answered. "Anyone hung the way you are isn't going to have any problems in that direction." I broke up.

There wasn't much laughter, though, mainly hard work and a determination not to let myself become a cripple for the rest of my days.

They operated on me again, squaring away the stump. They called it a recision. Then they started to fit me for an artificial leg. Conte didn't believe in letting you sit around. He kept everything moving. He understood the folly of letting a man who'd lost a limb just ferment.

A great help on my mental problem was the ward where they sent me. Everyone in it was an amputee. Most of them had passed through that period of terror that always comes when you realize part of your body is gone forever. They were too busy trying to adjust to their own situations to sit around and pine. That did wonders for me.

Then I met an operating-room nurse. She was a real classy lady.

She showed me that one leg was going to be no problem as far as the fairer sex was concerned. We got along famously.

The big question was, what would I do next? I quickly decided to go back to school. Let's face it, it's hard as hell to get anywhere without an education. As a disabled veteran, I would qualify for Public Law 16. That would take care of my tuition, and my disability would handle my living expenses. I was set.

There is a lot more to life than an education, though. There is the determination to overcome the obstacles that come up. I can thank the Marine Corps for teaching me that. However, I paid one hell of high price for that lesson! You might say I paid my dues.

James Brady
and the Eastern
Front

Where's our battalion?
It's hanging on the old barbed wire.
I seen 'em I seen 'em,
Hanging on the old barbed wire.

—British song from World War I

By November of 1951 the 1st Marine Division had moved from
Pusan back into North Korea, on the far east coast, near the Sea of
Japan. It was here on the ninth of November that the 11th Marines
fired a huge artillery barrage at the North Koreans. This was followed by 50,000 leaflets telling the North Koreans to come on over
the next day, surrender and help the Marines celebrate the Marine
Corps birthday. Twenty-two North Koreans obliged. It is not known
if this was in answer to the leaflets or the barrage.

And it was here, during the Thanksgiving weekend, that James
Brady joined D/2/7 on the front lines. A brand new second lieutenant, Brady and several other young officers had been flown from California. The attrition of second lieutenants in the 1st Marine Division
meant that the rifle companies of the 1st were always in need of
officers.

"We were flown to Korea," remembers Brady, "down near
Pusan. We were quickly hustled into a smaller plane and flown up
near the 38th Parallel. Next we were loaded aboard trucks and taken
to within a mile or two of the front. As I remember we covered the
rest of the journey on foot. What impressed me the most was the
rapidity of the whole thing. It seemed like one minute we were having a drink at the officers' club in Camp Pendleton and the next
thing we knew we were facing the North Koreans."

The first thing that struck Brady was the similarity between the front lines and New England.

"I'd done a good deal of skiing," he said. "This place looked just like Vermont. There was a lot of snow on the ground and a lot of pine trees. There were very steep ridge lines with little frozen streams in every cut. Many of the hills were quite high. I'd say where we were was about 700 meters up. You could see the Sea of Japan in the distance. There was one U.S. cruiser sitting at a calm in the water. I remember thinking how cold that water looked."

Another thing that Brady remembered was the World War I atmosphere that surrounded D Company's area.

"There were trenches and bunkers," he said, "just like France. We had an elaborate setup of barbed wire in front of us. In the early morning when the mist would lift, one could easily turn the clock back to 1918 and visualize the Kaiser's soldiers coming over, with their spiked helmets glaring at us. We'd be firing at them over the sandbags that we had erected at the bunker line.

"Our captain was an outstanding young Marine from Rhode Island. You could tell that he had natural leadership qualifications. His name was John Chaffee, the same Chaffee who was later Secretary of the Navy and is now a senator from Rhode Island. He was one hell of a company commander in 1951.

"When we arrived at D Company's CP, we were told to take it easy for the first five days and just observe. Then we'd be given our commands. So, that's just what we started to do, Mac Allen, who had come over with me, and myself.

"Mac had been an enlisted Marine at the end of World War II. When the war ended, he had graduated from V.M.I. and had gone to graduate school at Harvard. Now he was back in the Corps as a second lieutenant."

These two young officers never did get those five days to adjust to their new situation. The second night they were there all hell broke out.

"It started with a North Korean mortar barrage," remembered Brady. "It seemed to go on forever, but it probably lasted ten to twelve minutes. When it was over someone yelled out, "Here they come!" I later was told that was how they did it, first the barrage, then the assault.

"Everyone started to fire. I had a carbine; I was later to get a

.45, but first I had a carbine. I do think it was our machine guns that caused most of the carnage though, but whatever, we did shoot the hell out of them. Somehow one of them did get through. He was actually on the top of one of our bunkers and was about to drop a hand grenade down one of our tin chimneys when someone shot him.

"As dawn started to break through, I looked out at the wire in front of our immediate position. There were four or five North Koreans' bodies hanging on the wire. It made me think of those World War I movies I had seen when I was a kid in the 1930s. You know, *All Quiet on the Western Front* and *The Road to Glory*, films like that. They always had bodies hanging on the wire.

"There was also a trail of blood, headed away from the wire. This meant that at least one of them had been seriously wounded. The blood on the snow looked like lacquer, the kind I used to put on my skis.

"These bodies were the first dead men I had ever seen, outside of elderly relatives who'd been worked on by the undertaker. They looked completely different from the dead Koreans. The bodies on the wire looked like empty clothes. It was weird.

"Anyway, the Marines started out after the retreating Koreans. While I was somewhat of an extra wheel, I went along. Going down that hill was rough going because of the deep snow. When we got to the bottom, we were in a valley called the Sayang-Gang.

"We kept this up for about an hour when we came to a clump of blood. Obviously one of the wounded had stopped here to defecate. The stool was crawling with body worms.

"'Holy Christ,' I said to myself, 'What are we doing?' Here we were chasing a badly wounded man through the snow. He had stopped to take a shit and he obviously was sick other than his wound. What a wretched creature he must have been. I'm as gung-ho as the next guy, but I really began to wish he'd get away, and he did."

This was a typical action on the eastern front. Mainly small actions but constant. Brady did not see any Chinese until the spring of '52, when the whole division moved across Korea to the western front. Here he faced the CCF. I asked him to draw a comparison between the two, the North Koreans and the Chinese.

"They were quite different," he told me. "The Chinese were

more like a professional army while the North Koreans were not as organized. I always felt that if you were hopelessly trapped, you could surrender to the Chinese. The North Koreans were more apt to kill you.

"Remember, on the east coast we were well into North Korea. Those guys were actually fighting an invading force. And, they were mean sonsofbitches. They were great with mortars but didn't have nearly as much artillery as the Chinese. It was on the west coast where we ran into the heavy stuff.

"I can recall one Chinese who we had killed," Brady continued. "He had his service record in his pocket. He'd gone into the Chinese army to fight the Japanese in 1937. When that war ended, he fought the Communists. After the Nationalists were defeated, he went over to the CCF. In other words he was truly a professional soldier. And he was only a PFC. The CCF was loaded with men like that. The NKPA was not.

"One more thing. The North Koreans I saw were much harder to capture than the Chinese. I guess you could say the NKPA were mainly fanatics and the CCP were not. That's how I found them anyway."

Brady spent the winter of '51–'52 on the east coast and moved over to the west coast with the 1st Division. He actually fought in two different campaigns, one against the North Koreans and another against the Chinese.

In the summer of '52 he received some good news. Along with five other officers in his company, he was upped a grade. Before getting his silver bars they had to pass a physical. They went to a hospital ship off Inchon.

"This wiseass Naval doctor examined us," said Brady. "Then he shook his head. 'Sorry, men,' he said, 'I can't pass you. You all have high blood pressure.'

"Well, what the hell did he expect? Constant combat and all that starchy food. Of course our blood pressure was up.

"Then our captain, a Marine named Logan, spoke up. 'Does that mean we can go home?'

"That was it, he passed us all and we went back to the front."

Ross Dwyer and the South Korean Marines

"While you are in Oceanside, you should try to see Major General Ross Dwyer. Ross was not only in Korea, but he served for several months with the South Korean Marines. He can tell you all about those troops."

The man who told me this was Ray Murray. I then called Ross and set up a meeting for the next day. It turned out to be both informative and entertaining.

Ross is another of the three-war (World War II, Korea, and Vietnam) retired Marine generals, living between Los Angeles and San Diego.

Living is comfortable for these men. While they do dwell greatly on the years from Pearl Harbor to the American pull-out from Vietnam, they frequently combine these thoughts with hope for the future. They certainly do not live in the past.

"We didn't learn our lesson from Korea," says Dwyer, "or we wouldn't have gone to Vietnam. You shouldn't ask American kids to put their lives on the line unless you are going all out. Let us hope there is not another war, but if there is, let's not try to fight it with one arm behind our back."

MAJOR ROSS DWYER
1st Marine Division

The Chinese were always trying to keep the pressure up. Sometimes they would go all out like they did at Bunker Hill, but they never seemed to go any further than our outposts. I always felt they could have done a lot better if they'd avoided the outposts and gone straight for our main line of resistance. We were spread rather thinly; they could have punched big holes all along our line.

But that's how it was while I was in Korea in '52 and '53. The peace talks seemed to be going nowhere and we were holding the line, constantly suffering casualties.

Well, I guess I always knew I'd be a Marine. I was born in Honolulu. My dad was working for the Commercial Pacific Cable Company. They had stations in San Francisco, Honolulu, Manila, Shanghai, Midway, and Guam. While our family spent most of our time in San Francisco and Honolulu, we did visit Guam on several occasions. As a youngster I got to know many of the men in the Marine detachment on that island, even had some pictures taken of me with Marine headgear on. This can greatly impress a young kid.

Anyway, in 1938 I entered Stanford University. During my junior year this young Marine lieutenant drove up to Stanford in a Buick convertible with the top down. He was wearing his dress blues. He was looking for recruits for the Platoon Leaders Class. He painted a great picture, including tennis and golf. The class consisted of two summers at Quantico, Virginia. You would obtain a Marine commission upon college graduation. It sounded great to me, so I joined up.

Then came Pearl Harbor. My father was in Shanghai at the time, and was easily captured. He wasn't exchanged until 1944, when the Swedish liner *Gripsholm* brought a boatload of Americans back to the States.

In the meantime I'd been lucky enough to get a regular commission in the Corps. I was sent to Marine Sea School at the Norfolk Navy Yard in Portsmouth, Virginia, then commanded by Long John Henley, a gruff old-timer.

Next I went aboard the USS *South Dakota*, a battleship. After service in the Atlantic, we went to the Pacific. The other battleship in our division was the USS *Alabama*. That's the ship where Bob Feller, the great pitcher, was a gunnery officer.

We were involved in a flock of campaigns, took a bad pasting off Saipan. I came back to the States in late '44. I was set to go back to the Pacific as a tank officer when the war ended.

Well, when the Korean War started, I was a major in the 2nd Battalion of the 8th Marines at Camp Lejeune. And there I stayed. As a regular officer, I was very anxious to get to Korea, but I understood the reasons for keeping a Marine division on the east coast. Washington had no way of knowing which way the Soviets would jump. Greece and the Middle East were trouble spots. Who knew what could break out there? Besides, we had to have a place to separate the reserve units.

You see, we'd had a real problem at the beginning of the war. We'd immediately sent a reserve company from Arizona to Korea. They'd been badly shot up at Seoul and at the Chosin. This meant we'd zapped a whole community in Arizona. We were now trying not to have all the men in a reserve unit go to Korea in the same outfit.

We did have a hard core of outstanding officers at Camp Lejeune, some of whom never did get to Korea. Jim Masters was the regimental commander, a fine Marine. Tony Walker was another. He was also in the 2nd Battalion of the 8th. Tony had picked up the nickname "Cold Steel" in World War II. He was the most unlikely Yale graduate who ever came down the pike.

Well, we trained this unit for three months. They were in top shape. Naturally I thought I'd be going to Korea with them, but it wasn't to be. Just about all of 2/8 went to Korea in the same replacement draft, but I stayed behind. I can still hear the sound of the train as it pulled out of Jacksonville.

Instead of Korea, I ended up being sent to Corps headquarters at Washington, D.C. I was still a captain, which was beginning to frustrate the hell out of me. For the next year or so, I guess I was a pain in the neck to headquarters. Then I was promoted to major and received my orders for Korea at practically the same time. I landed at Inchon in September of '52, almost exactly two years after our original amphibious landing.

First we went to Ascom—or, as the troops called it, Ashcan—City. Here I was amazed at the size of the military installation we had there. It was huge. Then I took a train to the front and reported in. I think General Selden was still the commanding officer of the 1st Division, but shortly after I arrived, Al Pollock took over. I don't know if Pollock was in France in '18, but he was of that vintage. He'd been an outstanding officer in World War II.

At any rate, the timing of my arrival was bad. I ended up the executive officer of the Marine liaison group with the Korean Marines. Most of the time they were on the left flank of the line. It wasn't what I wanted.

Well, the first thing they did was give me an orientation tour of the 1st Division's line, starting with the 7th Marines on the right flank. This line was about thirty-five miles long, which is a lot of territory for one division—even a reinforced division such as ours—to handle.

The head of our advisory group was a Marine named Lieutenant Colonel Bob Thompson. I knew Bob well, had been in a car pool with him when we both were stationed in Washington. A fine Marine.

The Korean Marine colonel was named Kim Suk Bum. He'd been trained in the Japanese Army and was a very tough individual. He ran a taut ship and was very aggressive.

Well, if you spent any time with those Korean Marines, you had to admire them greatly. What they may have lacked in military knowledge they made up for in guts and discipline.

That discipline, though, could pose a problem. As an American I soon learned to keep quiet about it.

Early in my service there I had an occasion to hold an inspection of the troops. They were getting ready for a visit from Lem Shepherd, the Marine Commandant.

I pointed out that one of these men needed a shave. Just like that, there was a sergeant with a razor giving the guy a dry shave. The man stood stiffly at attention during the whole thing. I complained about another [Korean] Marine and the sergeant came over and knocked the guy down. Their idea of summary discipline was summary, believe me.

From then on I said nothing but words like *excellent* and *splendid*. I didn't want some poor guy's death on my conscience.

They had another little trick that was quite effective. The Koreans were wild drivers. They were always getting ticketed by the

MPs. When this would happen, the officer in charge would really do a job on the driver.

They had a stockade behind the lines. They'd put this guy in it and make him squat on his hands and knees for forty-eight hours. There was a sign hung around his neck saying that he had brought disgrace upon the Korean Marine Regiment.

Well, you know Lem Shepherd. He's a man who can command the respect of his troops and still be a gentleman. When he did come, he kept in mind what would happen if he found fault with any of the troops.

There was one thing that happened, though, that we all got a big kick out of. One of the Korean officers made a flowery speech welcoming Shepherd. His English was quite good. You could see he was proud as a peacock of his ability to speak English. After he finished, one of our young lieutenants repeated the speech to the troops in flawless Korean. This took a bit of the wind out of the Korean officer's sails.

And, incidentally, all the American Marine lieutenants attached to the Marine Advisory Group were regular officers. They were top men.

The big test for the Korean Marines came on October 10. You had these outposts in front of the MLR up and down the line. One of these was near the Sanchon River. I forgot how far in front of the MLR this one was, but it was a long way. It was here that the Chinese launched a major attack on the tenth of October. These Korean Marines did a tremendous job in holding them off. They were helped greatly by some Charlie rockets we had behind their lines.

In the meantime we had an American soldier who was acting as a radio interpreter. He understood Chinese. He'd give us a blow-by-blow translation of what the Chinese were saying. They were giving this Chinese officer hell for not advancing any faster. His advance was being held up by the fire from the outpost.

Then our rockets opened up. There was a long pause on the radio. Then it came through that the Chinese officer had been killed by the rockets and that our rocket barrage had pretty well used up his troops.

We were rather sure that the outpost had held, but we wanted to know what shape they were in. So the next morning I started out for the post. It was a long walk through Indian country. As I approached, this young Korean Marine was telling me by sign language to be very careful.

When I got there, it was a mess—empty shells, used cartridge belts, dead bodies—but they had held. I was proud as hell of them. They were brave fighters, fighting for their homeland. When I was first assigned to them, I had been disappointed, but I very quickly became quite attached to them.

Across from our lines there was a little mountain called Tae Dak San. I was told it meant "big hill." The Korean Marine colonel started calling me Tae Dak San because of my size. This would be considered an honor in Korea.

My tour with the Koreans was marred by a tragic loss. Bob Thompson was killed by a helicopter blade in a fluke accident. As I said, I'd gotten to know him quite well in Washington. Writing the letter to his wife was a very sad ordeal.

At any rate, in the winter of '52–'53, the legendary Lew Walt came to Korea. I was about to leave the advisory group and was going to be assigned to the 7th Marines. Walt was going to take over as colonel of the 5th Marines.

So Walt showed up first at the headquarters of the Korean Marine Advisory Group.

"Where is the commanding officer?" he said to me.

"Probably held up by a jeep or helicopter, Colonel."

"Major, when I'm told I am going to have a tour by an area's commanding officer, that's what I expect!"

"I guess in his absence I'm the commanding officer."

"Let's get going, then.'

So we started off. I am sure you know that Lew was a no-nonsense-type guy. This was going to be no picnic. We didn't have an itinerary, I'd have to ad lib all the way. I'd just have to stay cool.

Talk about Murphy's Law. Wow! Everything that could go wrong did. I made no excuses for anything, just went right along doing the best job I could. When we were through, Colonel Walt gave me a stern look.

"Major, how long have you to go with the Advisory Group?"

"Not long at all, Colonel. I'm about to leave for one of our regiments."

"I see. Well, carry on." Then he quite brusquely left.

It had been a long, hard, cold day.

The next morning I got a phone call. I thought I was in hot water.

"Major, report in to the 5th Marine Regiment at once. You are to be the operations officer under Colonel Walt." *C'est la guerre.*

The 5th was in reserve at the time. I went to work right away. My biggest problem was a bad cold I couldn't shake. It kept getting worse. Finally, I just couldn't get out of my cot. I'd gotten quite feverish and had dozed off. When I woke up, there is Colonel Walt, standing over me.

"Get ready, Major. There will be a helicopter here shortly. You're going to the hospital."

I had pneumonia, but you have no idea what four or five days with good food, clean sheets, and medication can do for you. In a week or so I was back with the 5th Marines.

The 5th soon took over the right flank of the Marine line. In front of us were Reno, Carson, and Vegas. These outposts were about 1,200 meters out.

We were under orders not to attempt any aggressive action of company strength or above without checking it first with General Taylor's 8th Army headquarters. Taylor had taken over from James Van Fleet when Van Fleet resigned. This was quite frustrating for a Marine regiment.

We did follow a very active night-probing routine. This at least kept us aware of what the Chinese were doing. All our movements were of limited objectives but were quite aggressive. Any regiment under the command of Lew Walt would have to be aggressive. Tactically, we were not in the best of positions. The terrain along the whole battle line favored the Chinese because they had the high ground and could look down on us. Besides, the line we were holding was altogether too long. We couldn't possibly properly man it. We made the most of what we had, though. A battalion would have as many as eighty machine guns for covering fire.

Then we had our helicopters. They were great for stringing wire, medical evacuation, observation, and supplies. We always felt we were way ahead of our Army in the use of helicopters.

At any rate, the Chinese were not under the restrictions we were, concerning large assaults, and on March 23 [1953] they started a major attack. First they hit the 1st Marines on Hill 229 on our left.

They had Bunker Hill in front of them. But it wasn't long before the Chinese artillery was hitting us also.

Next they went after our outposts, Carson, Reno, and Vegas. Those poor guys caught hell. Vegas was in deep trouble. Carson held, but we lost contact with Reno. We had to counterattack and stabilize the outposts. We also reinforced them. The action took from three to four days.

A short time afterwards, the 5th was relieved and went into reserve. Ed Wheeler, our executive officer, had to go back and see General Taylor. The 8th Army wanted huge amounts of paperwork about the action. It was a pain in the neck for Wheeler, but he did it.

After this, Lew Walt was promoted to brigadier general and went to act as Al Pollock's G-3 at Division Headquarters. He took me, Joe Platt, and Oscar Peatross with him.

At about this same time the whole 1st Marine Division was relieved from the front. It had been there a hell of a long time.

The outfit coming in was the U.S. Army's 25th Infantry Division, headed up by a major general named "Hanging Sam" Williams. When their advance officers came in to be briefed, they were very secretive. They even wore bags over their heads. By God, the Chinese weren't going to know who was coming in.

Then, just as our whole division was pulling out, the Chinese loudspeaker started to blare.

"Goodbye, U.S. Marines, welcome to the 25th Infantry Division of the U.S. Army."

I wonder how old "Hanging Sam" felt about that.

Well, at 1st Division headquarters we had Bill Bruce as chief of staff. With Al Pollock as commanding general and Walt and Bruce there also, I think we had as good a leadership team as you could find anywhere in the Corps.

General Pollock was reporting to Bruce Clark, an Army general and a fine soldier. He was the commander of I Corps, 8th Army.

While we were in reserve, there was a deep penetration of the right flank of the MLR. I spent a lot of my time helping to plan the counterattack in case the Chinese broke through. They didn't.

For the rest of the time I was in Korea, we were constantly under instructions to keep our casualties at a minimum. They didn't want any more burial bags. Well, neither did we. But to stay put while the enemy is still being aggressive is not the way Marines fight a war. At any rate, I think we did a darn good job.

Sometime late in the spring I was ordered back to the States. I missed those last few months of the war, when the Chinese really poured it on.

When I got back to Washington, I was appointed aide to Admiral Arthur Radford, the Chairman of the Joint Chiefs of Staff.

They took my leave away and said I was to report immediately. I first went to see Colonel Brute Krulak. Brute inspected me, then took me in to see the Commandant, Lem Shepherd. The general gave me a pep talk, told me what a great job I'd done in Korea, then he smiled.

"Ross," he said, "I just know you'll take good care of my good friend Reddy at the Joint Chiefs."

Now for one more item. Many years after the Korean War, I was at a high-level meeting in Washington. It was a reception for the South Korean Minister of Defense. He walked into the main room, looked at me, and smiled.

"Hello, Tae Dak San."

It was my old friend Colonel Kim Suk Bum, the onetime CO of the Korean Marines.

The Big Move

The 1st Marine Division spent the winter of 1951–52 on the eastern end of the front. In an attempt to make living conditions as pleasant as possible, they had cut down hundreds of trees to help make their bunkers. They were in a heavily mountainous area, facing mainly North Koreans.

Then, in the late winter, General Van Fleet visited their front to give the Marines new orders. The whole front was going to be changed around. The Marines were going to leave the east coast and go all the way over to the west coast, near Panmunjom and the Imjin River. There they would relieve the 1st ROK Division. Counting the South Korean Marine regiment, this meant moving about 26,000 troops.

"This prevented many logistic problems beyond belief," I was told by Brigadier General Gordon Gayle, then a lieutenant colonel and the G-3 of the 1st Marine Division.

"First there were the logs for our bunkers," Gayle said. "It was against the law to cut down trees where we were going, so we had to take down the logs we'd cut down on the east coast and pack them up. This was a small matter compared to the thousands of tons of military equipment we had to move, but it's one that always gives me a laugh."

The equipment Gayle was talking about was mind-boggling. Artillery, tanks, weapons, everything they had was to be moved. The really heavy equipment, such as tanks, was put aboard ship and sent around the end of the peninsula. The rest of the material was moved by trucks, hundreds of them. Just try to imagine moving a whole fighting division, with everything they're going to need, into a defensive position.

"Another problem," said Gayle, "was the command structure. We did not want our men under South Korean command at any time. This meant a hell of a juggling act.

"The first regiment we sent was the South Korean Marines. They went under the command of the ROK regiment we were to relieve. Then we moved a [U.S.] Marine regiment over, keeping another regiment on the east coast and the third in reserve.

"When we did send the 1st, 5th, and 7th Marines over, General Selden quickly flew over to take command," said Gayle. "Once he got there, he was naturally the boss.

"One of the toughest jobs we had," continued Gayle, "was moving the 1st Armored Amphibian Battalion over. They went aboard LSTs, crewed by Japanese. The weather was bad, squally and foggy. The ships had to be blacked out. It was quite a trip, but the whole division finally arrived, and there we'd sit until the end of the war. We did get a surprise shortly after we had settled in, and that was how the ROK fought the war.

"First it was their officers. Hell, most of them spent the nights in the rear echelon. This was not the way the Marines did things, particularly when we were facing the Chinese, and that's all we saw on the western end of the line.

"Then there was the so-called unwritten truth. It was like the quiet sectors of World War I. You don't fire on us and we won't fire on you. But could you really trust those birds?

"Anyway, we were used to combat, that's what we were there for, and no sooner had we arrived than our 11th Marines quickly let the Chinese know how it was going to be."

Ted Williams:
The Kid from
Left Field

About once a decade the baseball world has a personality who is bigger than life. Such a person is Ted Williams. Whatever Teddy Ballgame did was news and still is. To New England baseball figures, there is only one Number Nine.

For reasons known only to themselves, there was a small clique of Boston baseball writers who chose to persecute Williams. They're all dead now, and mentioning their names would be meaningless. Suffice it to say that one of these scribes failed to acknowledge that Ted even belonged on a ballot that ranked from 1 through 10 the Most Valuable Players in the American League for 1947. In 1947, Ted won the American League's Triple Crown.* If that writer had voted him tenth, Williams would have tied for the MVP Award in '47.

Ted will be sixty-nine on his next birthday. Each spring he spends a month or so working with the Boston Red Sox minor league players in Winter Haven, Florida. Because he undoubtedly knows more about hitting a baseball coming at the batter at ninety miles an hour from a distance of about fifty-seven feet than anyone else on earth, he has an attentive audience.

His love of baseball and his other great passion, fishing, are well

*To do this, a player must lead his league in batting, home runs, and runs batted in. Ted is the only American Leaguer to have won the Triple Crown twice.

known. What is not generally known is the great affection he holds for the U.S. Marines with whom he served in Korea in 1953. Let him tell you about it.

CAPTAIN THEODORE S. WILLIAMS
U.S. Marine Air Corps

It's a funny thing, but, as the years go by, I think you appreciate more and more what a great thing it was to be a U.S. Marine. I certainly can't say that I was happy every minute I was on active duty. I sure as hell wasn't on cloud nine when I crash-landed my F-9 jet that the Chinese had shot full of holes, or when I was sick as a dog with my respiratory problems in Korea. But I don't dwell on those things now. I did what I was supposed to do and that's that.

All right, back to July of 1950. I was having a great year with the Boston Red Sox. We'd lost out to the Yankees on the last day of the season the year before, and I'd missed out on my third Triple Crown by one base hit. I felt both these things could be changed in '50. Then came disaster.

It happened in the first inning of the All Star Game at Comiskey Park in Chicago. Ralph Kiner hit a shot that I caught while banging into the left-field wall. While making the catch, I broke my right elbow. It would never really be the same for years.

That injury was much more on my mind than the war that had broken out in Korea the month before. I was in the Marine Reserves. They told me when I was separated after World War II that unless we got into another war I wouldn't be called back, and I certainly didn't believe that what was going on in Korea would have them call back a thirty-two-year-old pilot, but it sure as hell was a war.

At the beginning of 1952, I got the word that I was to be recalled to active duty. I was going to be thirty-four years of age that August.

Now, I've never said it quite this way before, but I felt it was definitely unfair. I thought they must have been really hard up for pilots, but I decided I wasn't going to do any bellyaching about it. Surely someone else would figure out they could fight that war without me. I kept saying it couldn't happen, but it did. The end result had me back in the Corps. I got to fly jets. I had some experience in combat. I met the greatest bunch of guys I've ever known. There is something you get in combat that you get nowhere else. There is a camaraderie that is unique. You can find out just what a guy has and what he does not have.

In Korea we had men in our squadron like Major Harrington, Mitchell, and John Glenn. These guys were all gung-ho regulars. Hell, they all wanted to win the Medal of Honor. They taught a reserve like me what the Corps really means. They had Captain T. S. Williams thinking like them. It was quite an experience.

Well, when I first went back into the Corps, I was sent to Willow Grove, Pennsylvania. There I met my old friend Bill Churchman, who'd just returned from Korea. He gave me the word.

"Ted," he told me, "try to get into jets. If you go to Korea, and you will, it's plain arithmetic. You'll probably make a lot of bombing raids in support of the ground troops. If you are in a Corsair, you'll go down at 400 miles per hour and come up at about the same. If you are in a jet, you'll make your run at 500 and come out at 500. The Corsair is a great plane, but the jets will give you more speed when the gooks are firing at you."

That made a lot of sense to me, so I put in for jets. The major told me he couldn't promise anything, but he'd see what he could do and, by God, he did. My next stop was Cherry Point, where I was to learn how to fly jets, which, I'm happy to tell you, I picked up quite easily.

Now, you might recall that Jerry Coleman, the Yankee second baseman, was also called back by the Marines at about the same time. He's the guy whose banjo hit had ended up costing us the pennant in '49.

Well, Jerry, a hell of a nice guy, flew Corsairs in Korea. I heard that on one of his first missions the plane ahead of him had been blown apart by the Chinese. Jerry also made it back to the States and resumed his baseball career, but he had one hell of an initiation to combat in Korea.

So, as I said, the F-9 jet was not too difficult to learn to fly, even though I was a little leery of it at first because of an incident that had happened at Willow Grove just before I'd left for Cherry Point. An F-9 had exploded when landing. It was a hell of a mess.

When it happened, I was relaxing in my sack. I heard the sir-

ens, and having always been a fire-alarm buff, I jumped into my car
and raced over to see what was going on.

Christ, it was awful! At first they couldn't find the pilot. Then a
Marine pulled out a foot. It was still in the pilot's boot. That guy was
spread all over the place. I guess that was the only thing wrong about
those jets. You were going so damn fast that if you got in a jam, it was
hard to get out of trouble due to the speed of the plane.

After Cherry Point, I was sent to the winter training operation
the Corps had in the Sierra Mountains. That's where my respiratory
problems started in earnest. They were nothing new. All during my
baseball career, and still today, I have to be very careful about catching cold. If I do come down with a virus, it is extremely difficult for
me to shake it. It can linger for weeks. It can also develop into pneumonia.

At any rate, the virus I'd picked up in those damn mountains
was still with me when my group arrived in Japan. We were there
two or three days. The rest of the pilots went out to enjoy the bright
lights of Tokyo, but not T. S. Williams. I sacked in the entire time
we were there, but it did no good. When we arrived in Pohang, I
still had the cold. I was to spend the next five months in Korea, fly
thirty-nine missions, make a crash landing, and I was never healthy.

In Korea I was attached to K-3. It was an F-9 base. The F-86's
were over near Inchon. They were just about as good as any jet fighters we had. They'd fly above us when we'd go on our bombing runs.
Every now and then they'd run into some enemy jets, but I can't
remember them having any dogfights. I asked one of the pilots who'd
seen a Chinese jet what they were like.

"Oh, Christ," he told me, "all they'd do was zoom us. They'd
get the hell out of there before we could get a shot off. We were
dying to tangle with one of 'em, but it was impossible."

Our job was to support the ground-pounders on the front lines.
We'd dive down on the Chinese, drop our load, and get the hell out
of there as fast as we could.

Like all the pilots, I carried a revolver on these missions in case
we were shot down. What the hell good that peashooter was going to
be, only God knows. Mine was never loaded. I'd decided that if I
was forced to parachute out behind the Chinese lines, I was going to
float down with my hands up in the air.

"I'm Captain T. S. Williams," I was going to tell the gooks, "and I don't know a fuckin' thing."

Normally we'd face nothing more powerful than a 40 mm. They'd save the 90s for the heavy bombers. We were supposed to go in rather low for accuracy, which would expose us to the Chinese machine guns. We did. It was no picnic.

One mission I remember vividly happened just before I went to the hospital. It was led by our general, Ben Robertshaw. He'd been one of the top bomber pilots the Corps had in the fighting down in the Solomon Islands during World War II.

Coincidentally, I'd seen him play football when I was a kid in San Diego. He was playing for either the Marine Corps or the Naval Air Corps, can't remember which, but I do remember he was the star of the game.

At any rate, there were so many planes involved in this raid, it seemed to take us forever to get the show on the road. We finally got over the target, dropped our load, and came out. Jeez, then Robertshaw decided he wanted to find out how much damage we'd done, so back we go to the target.

By this time we're getting pretty low on fuel. We've got to get back to Pohang with what we've got left. The general takes us up to about 38,000 feet. At that high altitude we could conserve some fuel.

But when he gets back to our airstrip, he goes directly down, so we all followed suit. Christ, that drop killed my ears. Now I not only have my respiratory problem, but my ears are in lousy shape.

Another time I went off on what we called an early-early. On these flights you'd get over the target just as dawn was breaking. John Glenn was our leader that day.

Hell, you'd think the Chinese knew we were coming. They're filling the air with all kinds of flak. You could see those 40s bursting everywhere. Amazingly, no one was hit, but we sure took a lot of shit on that raid.

A word about John Glenn. That guy was just about as close to being a natural leader as anyone I've ever known. Just a superb person! He sent me a letter several years ago, telling me he'd been chosen to represent the Marine Corps in the space program. I wish I'd kept it. I may not agree with his politics, but I sure admire him as a man.

So that's the way it went. We did go after a bridge or two, and I remember once going after a factory where the North Koreans were making hand grenades, but our main job was close air support of the ground troops. Whenever we'd get a call from the rifle companies, we'd be alerted. The caller would give us the word: "There're some gooks down here, right over a knoll. We can't get at 'em."

We'd send a spotter plane over. He'd shoot off a flare and get back to us. "That's a little short. Blast 'em over that ridge."

We'd go over, climb to about 15,000 feet, make our run, and vamoose. I don't think it was possible for a pilot not to have a queasy stomach when he was making his run, but that's war, I guess.

I'd always feel like hell when we got back to base. I'd usually check sick bay to see if I was as bad as I felt. About halfway through my stay in Korea, I felt miserable. I asked the doctor to check my chest. He did and just shook his head.

"Ted," he said, "this is ridiculous. You've got pneumonia. I'm sending you to a hospital ship immediately."

The next thing I knew, I was on a helicopter headed for a ship off Inchon, and there I spent the next three weeks. At first I felt so shitty I didn't care if I lived or died. Then I started to get my strength back. It wasn't long before they had me back at Pohang, ready to go out on missions again. A week or two after I got back, I came very close to getting killed. I was a long way from Fenway Park in Boston.

The raid was a big one. We were told there could be as many as 10,000 Chinese encamped behind their lines. As always, they'd be camouflaged damn well. Those bastards could hide in a bathtub. This meant we'd be dropping "daisy cutters," a very potent antipersonnel bomb.

It didn't take us long to reach our target. As we were going down, I was startled to see the guy ahead of me starting to jinx [zigzag]. You weren't supposed to do that until you were coming out of your dive. I'm going straight for the target so naturally I'm closing in on him.

So I have to start jinxing while I'm looking for a feasible target. We were told to drop our bombs from 2,000 feet, but we never did. We'd usually go lower than that, and this time I'd gone a lot lower.

I released my bombs, and as I did, it seemed that every fuckin' gook in Korea opened up on me. Machine guns, burp guns, even rifles, you name it, they were all zeroing in on me and they all didn't miss.

Jeez, my stick is shaking, my fire warning light, my dual warning light, my hydraulic lighting, every goddamn light in my cockpit is lit. My stick is shaking like hell, which tells me I've got a hydraulic leak.

So, goddammit, I began to climb. My plane is starting to smoke. Another pilot, Lieutenant Larry Hawkins, pulls up near me. I get on the radio, but it isn't working. I'd been hit in the accessory section. I was lucky the engine was working.

Anyway, he followed me up and we started for home. Thank God his radio was working. He alerted the fields that I was in real trouble.

We quickly got behind our lines and Larry is trying to talk to me with motions. I later found out he was telling me to bail out, but that was one thing I always dreaded. I am just a fraction under the height limit for a pilot, and I was always afraid I might not make it out of the small cockpit.

So, it took us about fifteen minutes to spot one of our fields. I think it was K-13. Now it's time for me to land. The fire is getting worse. I tried to put my wheels down when—boom!—an explosion occurs. It blows off one of my wheels and it was only by the grace of God it didn't blow off one of the wings.

Then I went in. I could see two fire engines waiting for me. I hit the ground flush and started to skid. Christ, I must have skidded close to a mile. There were a group of Marines standing on the other end of the runway. They sure as hell scattered.

I kept pumping the brakes, but of course they weren't working. I'm yelling out loud, "When is this fuckin' plane going to stop? Stop, you bastard, stop!"

It finally did stop, right near the end of the runway. Two Marines appeared out of nowhere to help me out of the cockpit. The plane is burning just about everywhere but the cockpit. When I touched ground, I threw my fuckin' flight helmet down. Christ, was I mad! I'd been scared, but now I was just mad, mad at the whole world. I get that way. Back in the States when I was at the plate, I was always aware how much that baseball would hurt if it hit you. Hell, it could kill you. But when the pitcher threw one at me, then I'd get angry, forget everything except that I wanted to knock the hell out of the ball. I think most ballplayers feel that way.

That's the way I felt when I realized how badly my plane was shot up. At first I was scared to death, petrified. Was this going to be it for me? Then I said to myself, "The hell with these gooks. I'm not going to let them kill me." Maybe that's why I was able to land, that and the fact the F-9 was one hell of an airplane.

Well, I stayed angry for a day or two. Everything seemed to bother me at the same time. I always felt the Marine Corps came out second best when it came to getting equipment. The government certainly didn't pamper us when it came to gear. Take the sack I had in Korea. I mean, this was one horseshit bed, must have been built for a midget. The springs on it were from a jet tire. When you're really angry, it's the little things that drive you batty.

The day after my crash landing I was scheduled to go up on another mission. My cold was still with me, and the pain in my ears when I would fly was almost unbearable, but I went up. I later heard the doctor raised hell about it. You were supposed to have a day or two off after a crash landing.

I kept flying until June. Then, once again, the doctor stepped in: "We're going to send you to Tokyo. We don't have the equipment to treat those ears of yours here."

I got to Tokyo only to find out they didn't have it there, either. So I was off to Honolulu. This was the end of the line. The doctors there said I definitely shouldn't be flying in combat. Besides, the war was almost over. They could end it without me.

So I came back to the States, threw out the first ball at the All Star Game in Cincinnati, and resumed my major league career. I came to the plate 110 times the last part of the 1953 season, and got on base fifty-six of them. This wasn't bad for a guy who was flying in combat at the beginning of that season. Joe Cronin said I'd set back spring training fifty years.

Well, all this happened thirty-four years ago. People will tell me what a shame it was I had to go back in the service a second time, but now I'm kinda glad I did. I wish my health had been better, but I couldn't help that. A hell of a lot of fliers did a great deal more than I did over there, but I did my best. Besides, I am a U.S. Marine and I'll be one till I die.

The Reserves

"I was drinking beer with Richie Murtaugh at Angie's Blue Moon bar in New London [Connecticut]. We were both students at the Fort Trumbull branch of the University of Connecticut. Murtaugh had been in the Corps during World War II.

"Anyway, Rich came up with a brilliant idea. 'Let's go join the Marine Corps Reserves,' he said. 'The Corps has these outstanding khaki pants. They'll go great with a sports coat in the summer.' That was it. And we got the khaki pants.

"A year or so later we both left New London. Murtaugh got himself a spot commission in the Army, and I went home to West Hartford, Connecticut. I'd forgotten all about the Corps, but they hadn't forgotten about me. No sir!

"Well, you could have knocked me over with a feather when I was called up for the Korean police action. I never did get to Korea, spent most of my time at Camp Pendleton. I came out as a sergeant. I returned to UConn, this time at Storrs, the main branch, and graduated.

"That's all a hell of a long time ago. But I could have easily gone to Korea and been killed. All that over a pair of khaki pants."

This was told me by one Dudley Donnelly. He was undoubtedly an extreme case. However, very few of those in the reserves expected to end up in Korea, particularly those who had been in the Pacific in World War II.

Take Bob Houston of Kansas, a World War II Marine. He was at college in July of '50. He was reading the daily paper when he got a jolt.

266

"I was thinking of going to the movies, so I decided to check the paper to see what flicks were playing. I saw this notice about Truman calling up the Marine Reserves. I turned the page. Then, wham, it hit me. Hell, *I* was in the Marine Corps Reserves. I immediately called my mother to see if anything had arrived from the Corps addressed to me. Mother was in tears.

"'Yes, Bob,' she sobbed, 'you've been recalled to active duty.'

"'Mom,' I said, 'you write on that telegram "deceased," and send it back.'

"Then I thought awhile.

"'No, don't do that, Mom. I'll report, but it won't amount to much.'

"So I reported, on August 1. A week or so later we got the word we would be going overseas on August 10.

"Well, what the hell was this? I couldn't believe it. My father and mother were separated at this time. Dad was living in Washington, D.C. I called him on the phone. 'Dad,' I said, 'I'm on my way.'

"'Where to?'

"'Korea!'

"'Korea? You're still in college.'

"'No, they've called me up.'

"'Well, they can't do that.'

"'Dad, they've done it!'

"And I was right. There was a change in my status, though. Instead of tanks, where I was in World War II, I was stuck in the Marine Air Corps over at Osan in South Korea. I was in K-13 as a mechanic."

Then there's Roy Wilson of Louisville, Kentucky. A few years after he'd been discharged from World War II, he realized he missed the Corps. He decided at least to join the reserves. When he was called up, he actually welcomed it.

"I was single at the time; it seemed like a good thing to do. I never realized how it would affect my life.

"When we mustered in at Louisville, I felt sorry for the mother of one of the eighteen-year-old kids called up. He was anxious as hell to go, but his mother—I knew the family—wanted no part of it.

"'Roy, you take care of Bobby, do you hear?'

"Of course, Bob was mortified beyond belief. I assured her I would, then I winked at Bob.

"We got to Pendleton and were immediately given a very thorough physical. I was with Bobby when he got the bad news.

"'Son,' the doctor said, 'you are on active duty for thirty days. On the thirty-first day you're going home.' Hell, the kid had a punctured eardrum. Now it was his turn to cry, but he was sent home to mama.

"The rest of us headed for Korea. I was ordered to join the 1st Tank Battalion at the Reservoir, but I only got as far as Koto-ri. From there on, we helped cover the division on the way down to Hungnam. When we got to the sea, we stood guard, keeping the Chinese at bay. From what I saw, those frozen gooks were in no hurry to bother us.

"Next we went back to South Korea to regroup, then started the trip back up for the spring offensive of '51.

"Somewhere in central Korea, near the Hwachon Reservoir, I came down with a sore throat. Our corpsman seemed puzzled.

"'You've got more than a sore throat. I'm sending you back to Battalion.'

"Here it was the same story. Now they sent me to the hospital ship *Repose*. At this point I was getting concerned. Hell, I was only twenty-five years old. What in hell did I have?

"Our corpsman from the Louisville reserve unit was on the *Repose*, so I asked him, 'What's up?'

"'Beats me, Roy. All I know is they're really worried about you.'

"Then I got the word from the top surgeon on the *Repose*.

"'Wilson, I'm afraid you have a cancerous tumor on your thyroid gland. We're flying you back to the St. Albans Naval Hospital on Long Island. One of the very best surgeons we can get is going to operate on you.'

"Well, obviously they got it all. And while I was there, I met a beautiful nurse from Minnesota. I married her and she's still my wife. I might say that my going to Korea ended up with one of those bad news/good news stories."

The Korean War ended up being the last time the Marine Corps Reserves had a general call-up. It had been massive. There are those who feel that the reasons they were not called up for Vietnam were political. Maybe so. But without them in Korea, the role of the Corps in that conflict would have been considerably smaller.

Dick Munro:
When the CEO
Went to War

Dick Munro is currently the chief executive officer of Time, Inc., one of the world's most powerful publishing empires. That seems quite a feat when one considers that thirty-five years ago he was a ground-pounder with F/2/5th Marines, facing the Chinese on the Jamestown Line.

When talking with this former corporal, it becomes patently evident that he was just one of the troops, perhaps a bit more educated—he had finished one term at Colgate—but indeed, just another Marine on the lines. His tour in Korea was not to be a long one. In a little over two months he was wounded three times. The third wound resulted in a lengthy hospital stay and the end of his days as an active Marine.

After his discharge from the Corps he returned to Colgate, finished his education, and was soon on his way toward his immensely successful career in the business world.

Married to the same woman for twenty-five years, Dick is the father of three sons. He lives in New Canaan, Connecticut, and travels forty miles daily to New York City, where the headquarters of Time, Inc., is located.

As he looks back on his days in Korea, he gives the Corps some of the credit for his success in business.

"I have a very warm feeling about my days in the Corps," says Dick. "Above all, I learned self-discipline. You can't succeed in business without it."

CORPORAL RICHARD MUNRO
F Company, 2nd Battalion, 5th Marines

In the fall of 1950 I was a freshman at Colgate University in Hamilton, New York. I really can't remember any warlike atmosphere on the campus except for everyone's concern about the draft. The word was that they were going to start taking the guys out of college and stick them in the Army.

Well, don't ask me why, but I didn't want to be drafted. So I went back to West Palm Beach, teamed up with a couple of guys I'd gone to high school with, and joined the Corps. I'd been born in Syracuse, New York, but my parents were divorced and my mother left for Florida. I used to spend the summers in Syracuse and the rest of the year in West Palm Beach.

I arrived in Parris Island in January of '51. My first reaction was simple: I thought I was in an insane asylum, these guys were all nuts. Most of my platoon was made up of guys from the rural South, and most of them had little education. I think these men were the ones the DIs worked over pretty good.

I remember one kid, must have been about seventeen, received a box of candy from home. The DI caught him eating the goodies. Hell, the DI made him keep eating the damn candy until he threw up. We had a lot of chickenshit like that, but no real physical abuse. Drill, yes, my God, yes, but little strenuous exercise.

I did see our DIs slap boots, but never any of those horror stories of really kicking the hell out of the recruits you read about.

But I'll never forget my DI. His name was Smitty, I think he was a sergeant. I can see him today as clearly as if it were yesterday. I'll never forget his face. If he was supposed to scare the crap out of you, well, he did a good job on me.

Where I really did a job was on the rifle range. They say the rifle instructors like to get a guy who has never fired a piece before. He won't have any bad habits to correct. I fit this pattern and I ended up firing expert, so I guess there is something to that theory. When I finished training, I was assigned to Parris Island as a rifle instructor.

I spent the next eighteen or nineteen months there, and it was good duty. I worked with every kind of recruit imaginable. There were kids from the mountains who had fired rifles all their lives. They'd been brought up using windage instead of sight leverage. Then I recall a platoon of Yalies who'd been in the Platoon Leaders Class. They were going to be second lieutenants, but first they had to go through Parris Island.

They had a policy then where if you had a minimum of time left on your cruise, you wouldn't be sent to Korea. As the months rolled on I became more and more convinced that I was not to leave Parris Island before my enlistment was up. Then one day I looked at the bulletin board. There it was: Munro—Camp Pendleton.

It was a bit of a shock. Korea was almost never mentioned by the rifle instructors. I cannot remember any Korean veterans getting sent back to Parris Island. Hell, I'd practically forgotten there was a war going on, but the Corps hadn't forgotten me. I may have been a member of the Parris Island rifle team, but this made no difference. I was now to find out what the Marine Corps was all about.

At any rate, I had been reading the papers every day. Korea was not often front-page news. It was nothing like Vietnam, where the war came into your living room every night. But I had read enough to know it was a country I had no interest in visiting. However, you're in the Corps and they tell you to go, you go. I was soon aboard a troopship headed for Japan. And what a fiasco this trip turned into!

A day or two after we left San Diego we ran into some rough weather. I've never been seasick in my life, but I might have been just about the only Marine on that ship who can say that. It was vomit city! People all around me were throwing up all the time. We were stacked five or more racks on top of each other. It seems to me that many of the Marines spent half the trip leaning over the rail of the ship, puking their guts out. You didn't want to go above decks because if the wind was going in the wrong direction, you'd get puked on.

However, it was much worse below decks. You'd have a guy in one of the upper sacks let go, and it was a disaster. I didn't get that stink out of my nose until we landed.

Well, we first landed in Japan and very quickly took off again, this time for Inchon. Here we got a welcoming speech from some officer.

"Sorry," he said, "we haven't got much of a war for you, but hang around for a while, it'll get better."

This guy was fuckin' crazy! What did he think we wanted, the war to heat up? I looked over at a buddy I'd made on the troopship. He was as amazed as I was. We just shrugged our shoulders and smiled.

Next we received another talk by a sergeant.

"Okay," he said, "you're going to run into a lot of civilians. Be sure and be very careful about the kids. Everyone likes kids. But some of these little bastards can be full of baloney about how bad we are. They may not realize what they're doing, but they might try and stick a hand grenade up your ass. If you have to, shoot them, better them than you."

Now, I'd like to get one thing straight. You know all the publicity about My Lai in Vietnam. Well, I never saw anything in Korea vaguely resembling that incident, nor did I hear any talk about such an atrocity. Korea was not Vietnam.

Anyway, we were soon headed for the lines. I can't remember if we went by rail or by trucks, maybe both, but we got there. It couldn't have been too many miles, but, you know, I was there for about two months and I never knew just where we were. All I know is, we were in a trench facing the Chinese. They had loudspeakers that were always telling us how bad the capitalists were, and how we were the lackeys of the big fat bosses back in the States. We used to like to hear them, it gave us a laugh.

There was another thing they did that didn't give anyone a laugh. A Marine told me to look through one of our periscopes that was centered in on the Chinese, and what a shock I got.

These gooks had put several stakes in the ground with human heads on the tops of them. We'd been told that we were facing Manchurians, and I guess that's an old Manchurian custom. I thought this was a bit gruesome, but I had to admit, it sure made me realize we were at war.

Normally, the days weren't bad. We'd either sack in or lounge around, shooting the breeze or bitching about something. They'd get hot food up to us most days, and damn good food, I might add. It was kind of a surrealistic life. You felt you were detached from the world. Just you and your platoon, or company, living on another planet.

Day or night, however, there'd always be the chance that they'd "walk the trenches" with their mortars. And they were good, my God, they were good! I'd be terrified. You'd just cringe and hope. When I got into a real heavy firefight later on, things just happened so fast you didn't have time to think, but it wasn't that way with their mortars. I'd just keep saying, "Not me, not me." It was horrifying.

I wasn't there very long before it *was* me. I got a small piece of shrapnel in my backside. It was only a surface wound. I figured I'd have someone flick it out and put a bandage on it. Then I got the word.

"No shit, Dick," a buddy told me, "go back down and get a stitch or two on it. That way you'll get a Purple Heart. If you get three of them, they'll send you home." That sounded pretty good to me.

As a matter of fact, I even thought of sticking a piece of shrapnel in me. I think everyone did. But I never got serious about it, nor did I know anyone who did.

Now for the big event of each twenty-four hours—the patrol. We had them every night, and it seems to me I was on most of them.

First an officer would ask for volunteers to take the point. These officers, incidentally, were usually two or three years older than I. When I was back in the States, I more or less didn't care too much for officers. It was different on the lines.

You see, we had the feeling that we were all in the same thing together. We lived in such close proximity that we got to know each other quite well. Besides, Fox Company seemed to have real good ones.

Well, when they'd ask for volunteers to take the point, they'd always get them. I've never been able to figure this out. To be the first guy out in the pitch dark, all alone, well, you had to be more gung-ho than Dick Munro. I'd go out every time I was wanted, but *ask* for the point? Not me.

Anyway, we'd go out and roam around. We knew the Chinese were doing the same thing. The word was to try and nab one of them. That was a big deal. Don't kill them, capture them. The guy who could do this would get a week's R-and-R.

We had been told to keep our nostrils clear. These chinks were fed garlic every day. If you smelled garlic, you were to drop down. On all the patrols I had gone out on up until my last one, I never saw a Chinese.

Another thing we were told was how good the gooks were. Remember, they'd been fighting most of their lives. First it was the Japanese. The Communists' Eight Route Army really fought against the Japs. Then it was Chiang Kai-shek's army. Hell, these Chinese had been at war for years. They were real professional.

Anyway, as good as the Chinese were, life on the lines wasn't always bad. If we weren't getting any incoming from their mortars, things could be quite pleasant. I think this was greatly due to the men I was with. I was only in Fox Company two months or so, and I can't remember any of the names, but I'd certainly like to see some of those guys today. A few of them were real comedians, and others thought they were John Wayne. These were the guys who'd always take the point.

Well, the patrols remained constant. I remember being told by one of the short-timers always to remain on the alert out there, no matter how many patrols you'd gone on without seeing any gooks.

"Your time will come," he said, "it always does."

He was right. I think it was late in March. We'd gone out into what I guess you can call no-man's-land. It was a foggy night, with a mist coming in. One of our guys on the point showed up, making a motion for us to drop down. We'd been as quiet as possible; talking was strictly taboo when you were out there.

The next thing I knew, I could see these figures coming out of the fog. My God, they looked huge! It was one hell of an eerie scene.

We had a lieutenant with us who'd been on the lines about as long as I had. Maybe if he'd been through some firefights, he would have known enough to let them get closer. However, they were close enough so we could smell the garlic.

Communications between our lieutenant and the rest of us were not good because you can't say a word. Maybe he gave the word to fire, or maybe some trigger-happy Marine just let go, who knows, but it started and all hell broke loose.

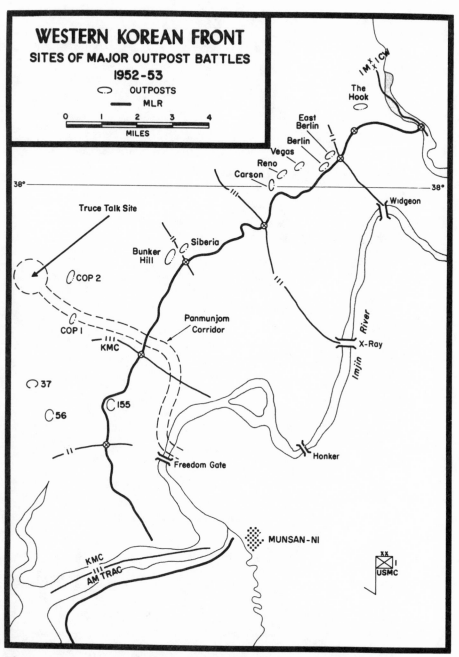

The western front—World War I all over again.

I had my M-1, and as soon as I heard the first shot, I opened up, as did the rest of our platoon. It never entered my mind that I was shooting at human beings. I was on somewhat of a high, just blazing away.

The Chinese immediately dropped down and, of course, they also started firing. I'm aiming at their flashes. Then I also realized, shit, they're firing at my flashes. I'd been kneeling, but I quickly went into the prone position.

Then they came at us.

Now comes the weird part. One of them stuck a bayonet in my leg and I don't even remember it happening. He must have come at me from the side. I don't know if he was shot by one of our people or if he kept going. I was on such a high I didn't know what had happened until I saw the blood.

The whole thing was like a zoo. It was dark, and as they mingled in with us, you couldn't tell who was whom. Maybe it was a Marine who stuck the bayonet in my leg by mistake. Who knows?

Anyway, all of a sudden the Chinese just seemed to evaporate. All was quiet for a while, then a firefight started again, but not as fierce as before. Then came the grenade, and I had an instant of horror.

I saw it hit and I knew I was going to get at least part of the blast. It lifted me up in the air but, thank God, my feet took most of the shrapnel. If it had been my head, I would have been killed. As it was, I had a concussion.

It was my feet, though, that were hit badly. They seemed to be shattered and were bleeding profusely. As the shock of being hit started to wear off, I realized what tremendous pain I was in.

By this time the Chinese seemed to have disappeared completely. All I could hear was some of the other wounded moaning, and I'm sure I was also yelling. A corpsman came over and started dragging me back to our lines. He gave me a shot of morphine that did deaden the pain.

When he got me back to the bunker, he started to work on my feet. One of our guys was watching him.

"Oh Christ," he said, "look at Dick's feet!"

"Oh shit," I said to myself, "I'm going to lose my feet!"

Next, a helicopter came down, just like they do in "M*A*S*H," and loaded up our wounded. There were two of us who didn't get inside. They strapped us to the outside and loaded us up with blankets. I'll say one thing for the morphine, it really worked. I can't remember any further excruciating pain. What I do remember is the dark winter night and feeling how weird it was to be flying over central Korea like that.

We got to an aid station and out came the M*A*S*H people on the double. That was when I found out that one guy had died in the helicopter during the flight.

They worked on my feet for a few days, then flew me over to the hospital in Japan. And it was in Japan where I was really exposed to the horrors of war.

I was in an orthopedic ward with all the amputees, guys with one leg or no legs at all. Most of these Marines had been athletic types just a short time ago. Now they were going to be cripples for the rest of their lives. Many of them were also experiencing a great deal of pain.

The doctors' jobs were not easy. They had to be half medical men and half psychologists. The last thing these guys needed was sympathy. The sooner they faced up to their predicaments, the better off they'd be.

So the doctors would try and make a joke out of it. They used to call the guys with no legs "Shorty."

Then they'd say to someone who had a left leg only, "What you want to do is find a guy with just a right leg, the two of you can buy your shoes together."

Sounds cruel, but it worked.

Another important thing was this Catholic chaplain we had. He was like the one we'd had on the lines. Hell, he looked like he'd played football for Notre Dame. He'd always come up to you with kind of a gruff greeting.

"And how the hell are you today?" he'd say.

I'm a Protestant, but I must admit those Catholic chaplains seemed to fit right in with the men. Great guys and fearless.*

Well, I was eventually sent back to the States. They always send you to the naval hospital nearest your home. I ended up at Jacksonville Naval Hospital in northern Florida. I spent some time there and was discharged. I quickly returned to Colgate, finished my education, and went to work.

---

*Chesty Puller, an Episcopalian, said the same thing in his book.

I've had various jobs at Time, Inc., including a ten-year stint as publisher of *Sports Illustrated*.

Now I am the CEO, and I really think I can give part of the credit for my good fortune to the Corps. My experience as a Marine was a very positive thing. As an enlisted man I learned real self-discipline. I actually think a guy in the ranks has to learn this more than an officer. It has been immensely important to me in my business career.

Celebrities

The World War II Marine and his kid brother, the Korean War Marine, had many similarities, not the least of these was the awareness of celebrities. Marines will always talk of actors, ballplayers, fighters—you name it. And the Marine who can boast of a personal encounter with any well-known personality will always hold the center of attraction, at least until his story can be topped.

One Marine told me of sitting in the front row at a show put on by a well-known Hollywood sex symbol.

"I was in the front row," he told me, "when out she comes, looking like a million dollars. She comes to the edge of the stage and leans over to talk to me. Christ, her two boobs are practically hanging out! I figured she must really like me, because she knows I'm looking right at those watermelons she's throwing around and she has this big smile on her face with the most beautiful set of teeth you've ever seen lighting up the place.

"Jeez, then she goes on to the next guy and does the same thing. Before she was through, she worked over the whole row.

"Okay, now this is the truth. The guy next to me was killed a month or two later at an outpost called Vegas. I think it was damn nice of that beauty to show him her knockers. Might have been the last pair he ever saw."

It wasn't only the beautiful stars that impressed the troops. It was also the male stars and the athletes. One stood out above all the others. It was John Wayne, the Duke himself.

Ironically, Wayne was never in combat. As a matter of fact, he was never in the service, nor was he one of the stars who spent a great deal of time entertaining the troops. But he was Sergeant Striker in *The Sands of Iwo Jima*.* There was a Sergeant Striker in every young Marine's life. He was tremendously easy to relate to. Wayne will always be Sergeant Striker to the Marine Corps, a bit of an idol.

I could find no record of Wayne going to Korea, but many others did. Jack Benny was there with his whole crew. Even the aging "Mammy" singer of another generation, Al Jolson, made the trip. He was a big hit. He put all he had into what turned out to be his last big show. Jolson died of exhaustion shortly after he returned home.

Then, of course, there was the tireless Bob Hope. As a matter of fact, the Marines went to Wonsan fully expecting to land under fire. This didn't happen. The night before they went in, Bob Hope and Jerry Colonna put on a show for the troops already there.

One Marine told me his fondest memory of his Marine days was a liberty where he'd tied in with Robert Mitchum while still in California. Another Korean War Marine still talks about going through boot camp during World War II with Jonathan Winters. To a third, it was being in a sick bay with Ted Williams.

There was a problem, though, when the USO shows would come visit the men. While many of these troupes would not have headliners with them, they all had very attractive young budding stars. This could create great envy between the ranks and the officers.

A onetime young second lieutenant told me, "I had a PFC in my platoon that I used to joke a lot with. After we'd seen one of those shows, he came over to me with a leering smile on his face.

"'Which one of the dolls did you get?' he asked.

"'Which one did I get?' I answered. 'They are for majors or above. Maybe a captain if he looks like Tyrone Powers. But I wouldn't advise that you ask the same question of the colonel.'"

Finally, there is the story of Marilyn Monroe's trip to Korea. There probably was not a single Marine who had not seen Marilyn's famous calendar. The thought of seeing that calendar come to life was most appealing. They all wanted to see the ill-fated bombshell, and many of them did.

---

*They should remake that movie, with the real language of war, à la *Platoon*. It would be great.

Marilyn put on one hell of a show, and the applause was deafening. Mass personal acclamation was somewhat new to Miss Monroe. She thrived on it. When she returned to the States, she told her current heartthrob how great the cheers had been.

"Wow," she said, "it was wonderful! You've never heard such cheering."

Joe DiMaggio just smiled.

"Oh yes, I have," he said.

Jack Orth:
The New England
Yankee

There were thousands of American youngsters who grew up on Hollywood's version of World War II. Brian Donlevy, machine-gunning hordes of onrushing Japanese and gallantly fading out to certain death as the film ends, made one hell of an impression on an eleven-year-old boy.

Of course, the film wasn't quite true to fact. The stand at Wake Island depicted in the movie was truly one of the most heroic such fights of World War II. However, the major, played by Donlevy, spent the rest of the war in a Japanese prison camp, as did most of his troops. But it was all quite heady to young Jack Orth. When the Korean War broke out, he quickly left school to enlist in the Corps.

Then came almost two years when Orth seemed to spend his time everywhere but in Korea. There was plenty of war left, though, and Jack finally got to Korea. On the lines for the better part of a year, he was hit three times before he got home to Newton Center, Massachusetts.

Today, at fifty-five years of age, he lives in Plymouth, Massachusetts, the heart of New England. He very successfully sells advertising in trade publications. But when he looks back over the years to his days in Korea, he is once again on the lines facing the Chinese.

"That was really something!" he'll say.

CORPORAL JACK ORTH
H Company, 3rd Battalion, 7th Marines

That's right, I was hit for the third time about two weeks before the war ended. I have always gotten a big kick out of those people who think the fighting practically stopped once the peace talks started at Panmunjom. Baloney! We were taking casualties every day. So were the U.S. Army, the Turks, the Princess Pats, the South Koreans—all the United Nations forces. And also the Chinese and the North Koreans—everyone who was on the lines.

As a matter of fact, some of the worst fighting of the war occurred the month before the Armistice was signed.

Well, let's go back to December of 1941. I was living in Newton Center, Massachusetts, right outside of Boston. I think I was in the fourth or fifth grade. Each Sunday we'd have a big dinner around one o'clock. That is what my family was doing when we heard the news about the Japanese bombing of Pearl Harbor. Everyone was in a state of shock. Can you imagine how exciting this was to a ten-year-old kid? At that age you really cannot conceive of what death really is. The war became a big game.

I can remember this pal I had who had some toy soldiers. I'd go over to his house and we'd play war. We'd stand his soldiers up and one by one we'd knock them down. The ones we'd push over were the ones who'd been killed. We didn't think about what it meant to have hot metal tearing into flesh. They were dead, that's all. As I said, war was a game.

We'd stopped playing games by the summer of '45, but I must confess that when the war did end, I felt I'd been cheated. So did a lot of other guys I knew. When the Korean War came, I felt I was lucky. Now I could go to war. I must have been nuts.

There was a time when I did have second thoughts, though. I had a friend named Waldo Jones, a couple of years older than I. Waldo was in the Marines when the war broke out.

Jeez, he was called up in July, quickly went to Korea, and was just as quickly killed. No toy soldier, someone I knew, killed, just like that!

But it didn't stop me. By November of '50 I was down at Parris

Island, a spot that can take an eighteen-year-old kid and bring him into the real world in a big hurry.

After several weeks of all that drilling, hikes under full marching order, and just plain chickenshit, I was pretty well fed up. Above all, it was the never-leaving-your-platoon crap that was driving me nuts.

Then one day this chaplain came into our barracks to make an announcement.

"Would any of you men like to be baptized?" he said.

Wow! Get away from these hairy assholes I had been living with for a few hours. It sounded great.

"Yes sir," I said, "I would. I've been meditating on that for several weeks. I need religious help."

Then my buddy, George—we called him "Greek"—also piped up.

"Same here, sir," he said.

So for the next three or four hours we were away from the platoon. It was great.

Then this chaplain sends a baptismal certificate to my mother, telling her I was now a member of the Baptist Church. Oh Christ, did Mother hit the roof!

You see, we're an old New England family. My mother was a serious, churchgoing Congregationalist, the religion of the early settlers. I'd been baptized shortly after I was born. I had a hard time explaining my sudden conversion to the Baptist Church.

At this time one of our DIs was named Dugus. He was a World War II guy called up for the Korean War. He was from Attleboro, Massachusetts, where he'd been a policeman. The minute he found out I was from Newton, I was in trouble.

"Oh," he said, "we have a mama's boy from snooty Newton. Well, isn't that peachy! We're going to make a Marine out of you. So forget all that country club shit. You're all mine now, Orth, and you better shape up."

He was really just a lot of talk, though. I took to military life pretty well, even shot a high expert on the rifle range. This above all gets respect at Parris Island. When it was all over, Dugus rated me right up there.

After Parris Island I was sent to the 6th Marines at Camp Lejeune. Here I received intensified training as a scout. I also ran into an officer, a great officer, I may add, also from the Boston area, only he was just the opposite from my friend from Attleboro. This guy was from Wellesley, which is a lot like Newton Center.

His name was Peter Kimball. He had a Bronze Star from World War II. He was also a reservist. I remember one little talk he had with us.

"Look," he said, "I've been called up for this thing, which means I had to leave my home and job. But while I'm here, I am going to do everything I can to get you ready for combat in Korea. It might help you get back to your families when it's over."

And he did. He knew all about combat and he taught us everything he knew. His wife and two children were also at Lejeune. I used to go over to his quarters and baby-sit for him when he'd take his wife out. It could really piss you off if some officers asked you to do this, but not Kimball. I was glad to do it. Besides, it meant a little extra beer money.

In the meantime I was doing everything but going to Korea. I even had one of those six-month Med cruises where we practiced amphibious landings all over the Mediterranean. I kept bugging the sergeant major to see if I could get to Korea, without any luck. Finally I got called to his office.

"Okay, Orth," he said, "we're putting you in the next replacement draft. But don't blame me if after you are there for a while you realize what a dungheap that place is. Good luck, you'll need it!"

So the draft went out to Camp Pendleton, and what did we do there? We trained for another ten weeks, that's what. By this time I had to be the best fuckin' trained Marine in the history of the Corps. We finally went aboard ship and set out for Korea, where we landed in January of '53, more than two years after I had joined the Corps.

We went ashore at Inchon and quickly boarded a train for the front. Christ, it was right out of World War I. The only difference was there were no cheering people waving flags as we boarded, just a few pathetic-looking kids in rags, trying to sell us chewing gum and booze. One of them was yelling, "Sheba, Sheba," which we later found out meant broads. How he figured we were going to work it while we were on the troop train I never did find out.

The train was a real relic. It made that one from Yemassee to Port Royal in South Carolina look like the *20th Century Limited*.

And cold, good God, it was cold! Remember, this was the dead of winter. We froze our asses off. There was no head on the train.

This meant we'd have periodic stops on the way to relieve ourselves. It was so bad we were actually glad to reach the front, even though we could hear gunfire.

When we got there I was assigned to H&S Company, 3rd Battalion, 7th Marines. My first job was to interrogate the men when they came off patrol. We were up near the 38th Parallel, but I cannot remember exactly where it was.

I was a corporal at the time, even though I had left Lejeune a buck sergeant. I'd been so bored with all that training at Pendleton that when I tied in with this good-looking doll in Los Angeles, I stayed over the hill for a week. When I came back to camp, they took away one of my stripes.

Okay. The reason I was told to do the interrogating was due to my spec number. I had been made a scout at Lejeune, a job that falls under intelligence. The minute they saw that number they gave me the job, which was fine with me, but I felt I could do much better if I actually went out with the troops.

Well, you know the Corps—if it's not by the book, you don't do it. And the book says the interrogator does not go on patrol. I kept pestering the hell out of them. Finally they threw up their hands and sent me to H Company as a rifleman. They were glad to get rid of me.

No one paid much attention to me that first day I joined my new company. They were too excited about the news they'd just received. It seemed that a while back they'd been told to take a hill called the Hook. They had a Texas lieutenant named O'Brien, whose platoon was slated to spearhead the drive.

Jeez, on the way up, five gooks jumped out of nowhere and went for O'Brien. The guy must have had tremendous reflexes, because he dropped all five. He was also wounded, but did this stop him? Hell, no! He continued to lead his platoon. He must have been a hell of an officer.

Well, the day I arrived, they'd just found out O'Brien had been awarded the Medal of Honor. He was very popular, and his men were really living it up. O'Brien's wound had healed and he was back with How Company, but they were rushing him to Inchon that night. They didn't want to have a Medal of Honor man get killed before he got his award.

As it turned out, the way the men felt about O'Brien was the way they felt about most of their officers. They had a captain named McCullough, whom everyone liked. He was another great guy.

But to me the real outstanding Marine in H Company was our gunnery sergeant, Gunny Parks.

Do you remember John Wayne as Sergeant Striker in *The Sands of Iwo Jima?* Well, Parks was that and more so. The term *leadership* is bandied around a hell of a lot, but let's face it, there are very few natural leaders. When you do have one, combat will usually show you his ability. Parks had it in spades.

I can remember one time toward the end of the war that will show you what I mean. We were going up to the MLR, and after that to our two outposts out in front of the main trench. They were called Berlin and East Berlin. There was this long, hilly dirt road to the trench.

Hell, as we started to approach our line, we began to get a lot of incoming fire. Most of us started to jump into whatever holes we could find. Not the Gunny. He keeps calmly walking up the road.

"Come on, you assholes," he yells, "this is nothing. Let's get up this fuckin' hill!"

Do you know, we got back on the road. No one was hit as we moved into position.

With the Gunny, it was like he didn't give a shit. We all felt the sonofabitch was bulletproof.

What we were doing in '53 was the last of the World War I type of trench warfare. It was right out of *Journey's End*. Most of the incoming would come at night. If it got bad there, you'd always have Parks, the real cool Parks, going around and checking each guy.

"How yuh doing, Orth?" he'd say. "This isn't bad tonight, just sit on your ass and wait it out."

We weren't sure we believed him. Guys would sometimes get hit. But just having the Gunny there helped a lot. There wasn't any way you could pull the wool over his eyes, though, no way at all. We weren't supposed to have any booze on the lines, but most of us tried to get some. We didn't think the Gunny knew anything about it, but of course he did. He came over to me one day and gave me the word.

"Okay, Orth, where's the beer?"

"What beer?"

"Look, Orth, if anyone has any beer, it's you. Where is it?"

I figured what the hell, if he looked for it, he'd find it, and he might really be pissed off at me. So I broke out my beer. The Gunny grabs one, sits down, and starts to drink it.

"Okay, asshole," he says, "do you think this fuckin' war will ever end?"

You see, if the Gunny called you an asshole, that meant everything was all right. When he just said, "Hey, you!" then watch out.

Well, we sure as hell didn't just sit there and take the shelling. We were always sending out patrols, which sometimes meant a lark, but sometimes meant casualties.

Every now and then the Chinese would try something. I can vividly remember the first time they attacked us in force, because it seemed so incongruous to me, really eerie, out of another world.

We had just relieved a platoon at an outpost called Vegas. It must have been at least four or five hundred yards in front of the MLR, maybe a half-mile. It had the highest elevation for miles around. You had a tremendous view. It also had the reputation of taking the most incoming on the MLR. It had to be relieved every three or four days. You knew it was a bad spot, because not only the Gunny but the captain went with us.

Plus, the men we relieved looked like zombies. Most of them had that vacant stare you get from constant shelling. Christ, they were a mess!

Okay. It must have happened the second night we were there. Someone yelled that he could see lights in the distance. It was the Chinese, all right; many of them were carrying torches.

We immediately gave the alert and phoned our artillery. The Chinese had to cross over a valley, then come up the hill to get at us. Our artillery had it all planned. If the gooks pulled an attack, they could catch them in the valley, particularly with those rocket launchers they had on the back of jeeps.

The Chinese kept getting closer. With all the torches they were carrying, lighting up the valley, you could see them darn well. They were screaming at this point, that high-pitched screaming of theirs.

Now here is where it gets real weird. There were hundreds of these Chinese. We were just a platoon, maybe fifty Marines, stuck out in a very vulnerable position. If these gooks get at us, we're going to have a very hard time staying alive, much less holding our position.

And what am I thinking of? I'm thinking about how much this lit-up evening scene reminds me of some night baseball games I had seen at Fenway Park in the summer of '52.

Then our artillery started the outgoing. Our people were well behind our lines so we could watch those rockets all the way.

My God, what slaughter! It was hard to realize those were human beings being blown to pieces down there. They reminded me of those toy soldiers I'd played with during World War II. They just kept coming and our artillery kept firing. It finally ended. God knows how many the Chinese lost, but they never got to us.

The next day I was out at the point of Vegas with a Marine called Reilly. We were manning a Browning .50-caliber machine gun. We were bullshitting about something when a shell landed right near us. It killed poor Reilly and the concussion knocked me cold. I came to a short time later, but I was bleeding through my nose and I had one hell of a headache.

They took me back of the lines, where I rested for about a week. I seemed all right, but, my God, those headaches were driving me nuts. I was hit two other times, in my left thigh and my back, but it was that concussion that stayed with me.

Regardless of the headaches, I went back to the lines and that in-and-out routine. Our company would spend about thirty days on the lines, then go in reserve for a while. Of those thirty days, each man would spend four or five days at the outpost. This was the most exposed duty we had, so they tried to have each man spend equal time there.

The main event was the patrols going out each night. We'd try to ambush the Chinese and they'd try to do the same to us. It was a deadly game.

There was one of these patrols that I can especially remember, maybe because I received the Bronze Star out of it and I wasn't on the patrol.

The night before, I had taken a patrol out, but nothing had happened. It was raining like hell and you could hardly see your hand in front of you. The next night it was raining just as hard, but the night patrol had to go out. The poor bastards stumbled into a mine field. Back on the lines we could actually hear the guys screaming. They were all friends of mine. So a sergeant named Rankin and myself started out to see if we could help. We had to be very careful because there was no way of knowing if all the mines had gone off or not.

When we reached our buddies, I picked up a guy named Harris who was a very close friend of mine. He was a black kid from Chicago whom we called Beebop. He was badly hurt, but I thought he'd make it and he did. I carried Beebop back to our lines and they quickly got him to a field hospital.

Of the twelve guys on the patrol, six died and six made it. They were all hit. Rankin ended up with the Silver Star and I got the Bronze Star. Rankin was a sergeant and I was a PFC. Rank does have its privileges.

We had left two or three of our dead in no-man's-land, which is strictly taboo as far as the Corps is concerned. The next night I went out again.

In the meantime the rain had continued and it was pitch dark. I managed to find one body and headed back for the MLR. Somewhere along the way I lost my footing. As I fell, I dropped the body into a shell hole that was filled with rainwater.

Do you remember doing the dead man's float when you were a kid? That's what this poor guy was doing. Right there in the shell hole. I was wet, tired, and just plain miserable. As I looked down at the corpse, I cursed all wars and the men who start them.

That all happened up near East Berlin. Shortly afterward we were relieved. A few days later the company that relieved us was hit by a massive Chinese attack. They ended up losing a whole slew of Marines and being driven from the position.

So we have to retake it. The word goes out that we were going to charge up the hill in broad daylight. Oh my God, I thought, we'll be slaughtered. Have you ever seen that Australian film *Gallipoli*? Well, I was sitting in my den the other night, watching it on the tube. At the end of the movie the Anzacs charge against the Turkish machine guns and are decimated. I had tears in my eyes as I watched it. That's exactly what would have happened to us if we'd charged in daylight.

Nevertheless, when the time came we were ready. Our artillery was to give them hell, then we were going in. Everyone was scared shitless, but we were going in.

Then the word came down. We weren't to go against them in daylight. Even Gunny Parks was happy. "I told you, I told you," he kept saying. "Even those jerks back at headquarters ain't that stupid."

Hell, the next night we sent a reinforced patrol out who retook the place with no trouble. The Chinese had been manning it with ten men. But ten men with automatic weapons can shoot the hell out of a charging group in daylight.

Well, that's how it went. We were always relieving some outfit or being relieved. Sometimes the other outfit would be Marines and sometimes someone else. It was anyone's guess who they would be.

I remember taking over a position one time from the Turks. They were wild men. We'd heard they would cut off the ears of the gooks and carry them on a string. Very tough birds.

We would also frequently work with the U.S. Army. They were good troops, but they did things a little differently from the Marines. Here's what I mean.

I went out on a patrol one night with an Army unit. I was the only Marine on the patrol. It was headed up by an Army master sergeant. His job was to take us to different areas and phone in what we'd seen. We got to the first area and he reported in.

"We are at Number One and no Chinese," he said.

Then we all lay down. A little while later he reported in again.

"We are at Number Two and have seen no Chinese."

We didn't move. A while later:

"We are at Number Three and have seen no Chinese!"

Well, what the hell is he doing? I went over to him.

"Sergeant, what the hell is this?"

"Look, jarhead," he answered, "when you're with your people, do it your way. When you are with us, do it my way. We don't want to fuck around with those people over there, not unless it's necessary."*

I had to admit he had a point, but I'd never seen it happen in our outfit.

While all this was going on, the scuttlebutt of an armistice was rampant, but no one bothered to tell the Chinese. They seemed to intensify their shelling and attacks up and down the line. It was during one of these attacks that I was once again wounded.

---

*In his excellent book *The Last Parallel*, Martin Russ tells of a Marine corporal doing the same thing on a patrol in Korea.

At the time it happened, we were getting ready to be relieved by the 5th Marines. The Chinese thought differently. Christ, those bastards were everywhere. Guys were being blown away right and left. I was helping a wounded buddy named Stan down a slope so he could be evacuated. Stan was from Pittsburgh. He had been wounded in the neck. I didn't think he was going to make it, but he fooled us. I used to hear from him every now and again. He still lives near Pittsburgh.

Well, as I got him to a corpsman, my old friend the Gunny nabbed me. "Orth, take these stretcher bearers back up the hill and bring some more wounded down here."

The bearers were South Koreans and I don't think they wanted any part of it, but they were game. They just shrugged their shoulders and started off.

We got about halfway up the hill when a mortar shell landed right in the middle of us. It killed the bearers, but, thanks to my flak jacket, only wounded me. That jacket, though, looked like a piece of Swiss cheese. My left leg was bleeding like hell, but I was still able to make it down the slope, where I met the Gunny.

"Hit again, Orth," he said. "We better get your ass out of here before you get killed."

He called over a tank from C Company and helped me get into it. "Take this guy to the aid station," he said to the driver. "He gets wounded too many times."

Then he turned to me.

"Orth, give me your Camels; there's plenty of those where you're going."

Can you believe that? Here is Parks in the middle of a firefight, and he's worrying about cigarettes.

That was the end of Korea for me. It was also the last time I saw Gunnery Sergeant Parks. It was June of 1953, a few weeks before it all ended.

Well, that's close to thirty-five years ago now. As a friend of mine said to me a while back, "Jack, you're on the second nine." Gunny Parks must be in his mid-sixties if he's still alive. Maybe some summer afternoon I'll walk into a bar for a cool one and someone will call my name.

"Orth, you asshole," he'll say, "been wounded lately?"

Here and There

The Gentleman Marine

When the Marines were given the word to get a brigade to Pusan as quickly as possible, the command was given to a veteran Marine officer named Edward Craig. According to everyone I talked with, Craig was a superb Marine. Perhaps Lem Shepherd put it best:

"Eddie Craig did a great job with the Brigade. When they arrived, they sent him over to the Naktong, where they were assigned to an Army division, I think it was the 25th.

"They went right into combat, stopped the North Koreans in their tracks, successfully counterattacked, and were withdrawn. Then the Army took over. The Communists hit the soldiers with everything they had and retook all the ground the Marines had paid dearly to capture. The Army general had to go to Craig with hat in hand. 'General,' he said, 'I'm mortified. We've lost what you just captured. I must ask you to have your brigade come back to the Naktong and do it over again. My men have been fighting for several weeks. They're pretty used up.'

"Well, Eddie was not only a damn good general, but he was also a gentleman. He had no desire to kick the general when he was down, figuratively speaking, that is. He put a hand on the Army general's shoulder. 'General,' he said, 'it could have happened to us if we'd stayed. Of course we'll return. That's what we're here for, to fight Communists!'

"And they did return and they retook the area. That's the type of man Edward Craig is."

I did not have the heart to point out to General Shepherd that the Marines who were in that brigade were normally not as charitable as Craig was to the Army.

The Candidate

"I had started my OCS at Quantico in July of '52," remembers Bill Montgomery, today the CEO of the Xerox Credit Company. "Adlai Stevenson III was in my class. Going to the slop chute was strictly taboo at the time, but they did let us break the rule one time during our training. This was during the Democratic National Convention. The whole class was allowed to watch Adlai's father being nominated for the presidency.

"What a break! None of us had even smelled any beer for at least four or five weeks. I guess we overdid it a bit. No one said anything, though, not until 0400 the next morning. Then came the reckoning.

"'Hit the deck!' our sergeant yelled. 'Everyone outside for physical drill under arms. We've got to get rid of all that brew you gentlemen consumed last evening.'

"Oh, that guy really worked our asses off!"

By September the presidential race was in high gear. The Republicans had nominated General of the Armies Dwight D. Eisenhower for the top spot. His son John had already been in Korea, which was a real plus for the general, as the war was a top priority in the election. The peace talks had gone on for over a year, and the American people were getting bone-weary of the war. The presidential campaign was going against Stevenson, so when he was invited to speak at his son's commissioning, he jumped at it.

"I remember the ceremony," says Montgomery. "It was down at the main side of Quantico. The TV cameras were there, along with several reporters. It wasn't billed as a campaign speech, but it was certainly good PR for a guy running for the White House.

"It didn't do any good, though," Montgomery continued, "Stevenson lost the election. I guess the American people really didn't want to elect a man who had his picture taken showing a big hole in the sole of one of his shoes."

The Shot Heard 'Round the World

"It was around the first of October, 1951," recalls Joe McDermott. "Most of the Inchon landing Marines had gone home, but I was still in Korea. So were Spider Martin and Walter Cole. We were just about the last of the original group to go back to the States when we left the next month.

"Anyway, I had been raised in Manhattan and I hated the Brooklyn Dodgers. Cole and I had borrowed Tommy Consolo's radio and were listening to the final playoff game between the Dodgers and the New York Giants on the armed forces network. The Dodgers seemed to have it locked up when the Giants started to rally. Brooklyn brought in Ralph Branca to pitch, and Bobby Thomson hit one out of the Polo Grounds to win it for the Giants. It was the shot heard 'round the world.

"Holy Christ, I couldn't believe it. I shot off my M-1 and started to cheer like hell. I think Cole thought I was nuts. It was one time in Korea when I was completely happy, war or no war."

Picking Up the Brass

Ed Simmons is a Marine brigadier general (ret.). He is now in charge of the Corps History and Museum Division. He has fond memories of a famous Marine character.

"Joe Fisher is one of the better known Marine Corps characters of recent times," he told me. "He was a platoon sergeant at Iwo, stayed in the Corps and got a commission. When we formed up for Korea, he was given Item Company of the 1st Marines by direct orders of Chesty Puller.

"Bull, as he was known, was a great Marine and he was also quite an actor. He had grown a handlebar mustache and looked like a real hellbent-for-election leatherneck. He wore a BAR belt, instead of a pack, where he'd keep his toilet articles and anything else he needed. He also carried an M-1 rifle.

"There was a slight problem when he assembled Item Company's lieutenants. Joe was still a first lieutenant, so naturally all of his officers had to be junior to Joe. But it worked out all right. I know his executive officer, Charlie Mattox, was killed at the Chosin and three of his other officers were wounded.

"Well, after we took Inchon, we moved on Seoul. It was a hill-to-hill operation on a daily basis.

"I had Weapons Company 3/1 at the time. Our job was to fire in support of the 3rd Battalion's companies as they'd attack the hills. We came to one of them that had been pulverized by the 11th Artillery guns. I was convinced there were no North Koreans left there, but not Fisher, he was raring to go.

"He grabbed his M-1 and started firing it from his hip.

"'Let's go get 'em, men,' he yelled."

His gunnery sergeant disagreed.

"No, skipper, you go get 'em; I'll stay here and pick up the brass!"

A New Expression

In *Semper Fi, Mac*, I have a section where I explained the many uses by the World War II Marine of the expression *fuckin' A*. A Korean War Marine, Joe DeMarco, remembered that section well. Joe had been a radio man at the Chosin Reservoir.

"There was one that we used in Korea that you forgot," he told me. "It was *fuckin' A, dot dash*."

Thank you, Joe.

The 6th Division Meeting

Sal Cavallaro had already spent several months in hospitals. His face was still a mess. He was hoping for something to relieve his boredom.

"I was lying in my sack when this pompous-looking Marine captain came by. He had 'rear-echelon pogue' written all over him. You know the look. The kinda guy who would be in charge of a mess kit repair unit.

"He stopped at my sack.

"'Marine,' he said, 'are you ready to get your Purple Heart from General Shepherd?'

"'Certainly,' I answered, 'it will be good to see the general again.'

"'*What*? Do *you* know the general?'

"'Hell, yes. I was with the general on Okinawa and at Tsingtao. We were both with the 6th Division.'

"'Oh, the 6th Division, that's all the general talks about. You'd think the 6th Division won the war.'

"'It did!'"

A short time later, General Shepherd came over to Sal's sack. When he found out that Cavallaro had been in the 6th Division, his eyes lit up.

"'No kidding,' he said, 'you were one of my boys in '45. Well, what a job you men did!'"

The two men, the general and the corporal, spent the next ten minutes talking about the 6th.

The next day the captain returned to the hospital. He presented Sal with an autographed copy of a book on the 6th Division.

"'The general wanted you to have this,' he said.

"He is one hell of an officer, that General Shepherd!"

Corporal Rudy Miller
Communications
2nd Battalion, 7th Marines

"My enlistment was up. I'd gone into the Corps in July of '47. It had been just what I'd hoped it would be. I'd been with the 9th Marines on Guam, spent close to a year in China, and had come back to Camp Lejeune.

"Now it was July of '50. I'd been processed for discharge and was to leave for White Plains, New York, the next day.

"That night a staff sergeant came in to the casual squad room where I'd just hit the sack.

"'Turn to, Miller,' he bellowed. "You're going back to your unit.'

"'Not me, I'm out tomorrow, I'm going home.'

"'Baloney, all discharges have been canceled. You're still in the

Corps, convenience of the government, they call it. You're probably going to Korea.'"

Corporal Miller got home, all right. Six months later, after he'd been hit in both legs with a Chinese mortar shell at the Chosin.

In July of 1950, Miller had never heard of the Chosin Reservoir.

Brigadier General Gordon Gayle Remembers

"When General Gerry Thomas was CO of the 1st Division, he had issued orders for his regimental commanders to wear white scarves. He also wore a white scarf. He then told his divisional staff officers to wear red scarves. His purpose was clear. He wanted the troops to know that the staff officers would also go up to the front.

And with Thomas this was mandatory. All staff officers had to visit the MLR frequently, even go out to the outposts. Thomas had been an enlisted man in World War I. He didn't want the staff spending all their time back of the lines, as many had done during the First War.

"Well, when I was G-3 for Thomas, and Jim Tinsley was his G-2, we were walking up to the MLR. We were two or three hundred yards away when a truckload of Marines went by. They knew who we were by our scarves. One of them waved at us.

"'Oh, get up closer, Colonel, it's *real* exciting!'

"The other Marines broke up. So did we."

The Gamy Side

"Of course I had to pay. The bullshit of beautiful nurses falling in love with enlisted men was only for Hollywood. Twenty-five dollars, but it was worth every penny. That couldn't get you Powerful Katrinka today, but this was 1952. It was a pretty good hunk of change then.

"She had this corpsman working with her. He got me aside one night and asked me if I was interested. When he told me who it would be, interested, I'll say I was interested. She was a real good-looking redhead, a lieutenant.

"I was told to meet her at a certain elevator. It was real early in the morning, maybe 0200. I got in the elevator and there she was, with a big smile on her face. All she was wearing was a kimono. There was this cot there, with scrubbed white sheets, in the elevator.

"Holy Christ, for a guy who'd just spent six months on the line listening to those hairy-ass guys farting before breakfast, well, this was heaven.

"It was all over in about sixty seconds. We then got off the elevator. She talked with me for about five minutes, told me she was from the state of Washington and was saving up her money for when she got out of the Navy. Then she kissed me on the cheek and left.

"I went back to the ward, jumped into my sack. Jeez, I just thought of the nurse for five minutes and got a hard-on. She was a real redhead."

(Name of contributor withheld by request.)

General Pollock Gets the Word

"I had just had what felt like a ton of shrapnel taken out of my back in the operating room of the hospital ship *Repose*. I was lying in my sack when Major General Pollock walked in. I think he'd just been relieved as commanding general of our division.

"Well, the general is going up and down the ward, shaking everyone's hand, thanking all the wounded guys and giving them a little pep talk. You could see he was moved by the whole thing. He came to a young Marine who had lost an eye.

"'Don't worry, son, we'll have you patched up and back on the line in no time.'

"The kid looked up at the general.

"'In a pig's ass you will!'

"Dead silence.

"Then Pollock, who'd seen enough combat to last a lifetime, doubled up with laughter.

"'Attaboy, son, you're all Marine!' he said."

The Chinese Hordes

The American newspapers were always printing such headlines as THE HORDES OF CHINESE RED. As the war dragged on, massed Chinese troops became quite rare, but the headlines persisted. The Marines even had a joke about these headlines:

1ST MARINE: Hey, Mac, my girlfriend's letters are always telling me to watch out for the Chinese hordes.

2ND MARINE: Izzat so?

(Two minute pause.)

1ST MARINE: Mac, how many hordes in a platoon?

Who Goes There?

As the war progressed, the black Marine became more and more a part of the fighting force. Men in combat are always looking for a much-needed laugh. There were many jokes that developed over integration. Here's one of them:

A black Marine was separated from his platoon while on patrol. He tried desperately to get back to his lines. When he got close, a Marine yelled out, "Who goes there?"

"PFC William Brown."

"What's the password?"

"Don't know no password."

"Well, you *better* know one, or I'm going to open fire."

Dead silence. Then: "Hey, man, you ever seen a black Chinaman?"

Truman's Police Action

The Marines—and, I assume, the Army as well—did not care for the term "police action." It smacked too much of the local gendarme giving out speeding tickets. One Marine put it this way:

"If this is a police action, why don't we get J. Edgar Hoover to

send over his G-men? They can cuff these bastards and throw them
in the hoosegow. Then we can go home."

Who Won the War?

A World War II Marine met a Marine veteran of the Korean
War. Their conversation went like this:

WORLD WAR II MARINE: You guys had a rough time. So did we,
but at least we won our war.

KOREAN WAR MARINE: No, you didn't. We won our war. You
lost yours.

WORLD WAR II MARINE: The hell you say. The Japanese surren-
dered on the *Missouri*. All you got was an armistice.

KOREAN WAR MARINE: Izzat so? Well, look at Hitachi, Canon,
Honda, Mitsubishi, Toyota, any number of Jap companies. Hell, the
Nips own half of Hawaii. They buy more American companies each
year. If Kim had signed a surrender on the *Missouri*, he'd now own a
brownstone on Fifth Avenue. You'd have the Bank of Pyongyang
right next door. We'd be taking summer vacations on the lovely Yalu
and ski trips to that winter wonderland, the Chosin. But do we? No.
North Korea is broke. Japan could end up being the richest nation in
the world. You won your war? Bullshit! We won our war. You lost
World War II.

(Thanks to Spider Martin.)

George Broadhead: The Kid from Ebbets Field

"Sure, I was raised in Brooklyn. My dad took me to Ebbets Field to see my first major league ball game when I was eight years old. Those were the great years of Dixie Walker, Pee Wee Reese, Pete Reiser, Whit Wyatt, and Kirby Higbe, or, as they called him in Flatbush, "Koiby." It was just before Roger Kahn's *Boys of Summer*.

"I'd always thought that if I had a son, how great it would be to take him to Ebbets for his first game. But that fat-ass O'Malley took care of that!"

George's feelings about Walter O'Malley, the owner of the Dodgers, were shared by the three other Marines I talked to who had gone into the Corps from Brooklyn. They're still unhappy about their Dodgers moving to Los Angeles.

A strong family man, George's biggest problem today, however, is getting to see his three children. His former wife moved to Seattle, Washington, after their divorce. Since he is the New York manager of advertising sales for Newhouse Newspapers, this means one hell of a trip. When he talks about his situation, he shakes his head and laughs.

"This is bad enough. But during the divorce she told the judge that I scared her because the Marines had turned me into a trained killer. Hell, I've never personally owned a firearm in my life.

"On the other hand, when I got married, my wife owned both a pistol and a shotgun. The judge was a woman. I honestly feel she sided with my wife. What are you going to do?"

Of particular interest is his run-in with a homosexual before going overseas. The year 1951 was long before gay rights had become a way of life in Brooklyn. Stories such as George's were quite common in World War II and the Korean War.

George was seriously wounded on the last day of the war. He was awarded the Silver Star for bravery on that day.

CORPORAL GEORGE BROADHEAD
H Company, 3rd Battalion, 1st Marines

I had gone into the Corps in May of '51. I wanted badly to get to Korea, but the months kept going by and I was still in the States. Finally, in August of '52, I was ordered out to Camp Pendleton. This could mean only one thing—Korea.

A buddy of mine, Al Cicola, was in the same replacement draft. We figured we'd fly out to the Coast and take three days to see Hollywood. We'd been going to the movies for years, but had never been in the film capital of the world.

When we arrived, I called a guy named Dick Prebor. I'd known Dick for years. He was a very successful music arranger. He was glad to hear from me.

"I'm having a few friends over for cocktails," he said. "Why don't you stop by?"

This sounded great, so we took him up on his invitation. We're having a bang-up time when another one of the guests came over to us.

"Do you two Marines have a place to stay tonight?"

"I don't know. I better check with Al."

It seemed like a good deal, but this guy seemed a little goosy to me. I got Dick aside, told him about the invitation. "But, Dick," I added, "is this guy a queer?"

Dick laughed. "As a three-dollar bill. But he's just built one of the most beautiful homes in Hollywood. He knows you're a friend of mine. I don't think he'll try anything. Go along with it. It'll be an experience."

A few minutes later the guy came over to me again.

"Well, George, am I going to have the pleasure of your company?" He's got this sick little smile on his face.

"Sure. Dick says you have a beautiful new home, plenty of room. Thank you."

"Well, let's go, it's getting late."

Jeez, he whisked us out of there in no time at all.

We're driving along Sunset Boulevard in this guy's Lincoln Continental with the top down. He's playing the big shot, pointing out the sights to a couple of young Marines from Brooklyn.

"There's Schwab's Pharmacy, where Lana Turner was discovered. There's Grauman's Chinese Theater." You know, things like that. If he wanted to impress us, he was succeeding. Then we got to his place.

Wow! what a spread! It was built hanging out over a cliff. There're a lot of them like that now, but there weren't many in those days. It seemed like the whole front of the place was made of glass. It was quite a pad.

He's still playing the big shot, though.

"Oh, by the way," he said, "my next-door neighbor is Hopalong Cassidy. But don't go over in the morning and bother him. My guests are always doing that. He gives me hell about it."

Well, we went inside and he took us on a Cook's tour. My God, it was incredible. He'd spent some time with the U.S. Navy in China right after the war, and he'd been big in the black market over there. He had all this Chinese stuff that had to be worth a fortune.

He's also got this tremendous telescope that had come off a Japanese battleship. Don't know how the hell he'd gotten that baby.

"See that red light in the distance?" he said to me. It must have been ten or so miles away.

"Look at it through the telescope."

Jeez, it was a Coca-Cola sign. I could read it like it was across the street.

Next he showed us his bar. It looked like something out of a high-class nightclub. We had another drink or two, then we got the word.

"Gentlemen," he said, "time to hit the sack. I'll show you where we're going to sleep."

He opened this door and there's these two twin beds. I figure they're for Al and me. I was wrong.

"George," he said, "this is where we are going to sleep. My houseboy will fix up something for Al in the other room."

Oh-oh, now I know I am in deep shit! This bird wants his pound of flesh. I figure I better play it cool. So I quickly got out of my uniform and jumped into my rack, pulling the covers over me.

"Aren't you going to take a shower?" he asks.

I thought awhile and said to myself, "Why not, I'm supposed to be a Marine." If this guy tries anything, I'll set him straight. So I go into the bathroom, which just happens *not* to have a door. He's got the mirrors set up so he can see everything.

Well, the hell with him. I took off my skivvies and jumped in the shower.

Holy shit! The bottom of the shower is all foam-rubber tits, with the nipples and everything. We had a guy in our replacement draft who was always talking about walking across a field of nothing but tits. I thought of him and started to laugh. Then my host started to giggle.

"I thought you'd like my shower mat," he yelled.

Anyway, I finished my shower and returned to my rack. He turned out the lights. Then this weird red light went on from the ceiling. This guy was really something!

It wasn't funny, though, when he tried to get into bed with me. I had to give him the word.

"I don't fool around with guys," I told him. "I like girls. Now get the hell back in the other bed!"

Now get this. This clown said *I* must be nuts. He whined some, but that was it.

The next morning he was quite polite but very curt.

"My houseboy will drive you to Hollywood and Vine." Then he shook my hand and giggled.

Now it's no longer the Lincoln. Now it's his 1938 Plymouth. The minute Al got in the car, he looked at me.

"For Christ's sakes, do you know that at 0300 that jerk came down to where I was sleeping and started to rub my legs. 'My,' he said, 'you have hairy legs!'

"'Yeah, I do,' I said, 'and if you don't stop playing with them, I'm going to break your jaw.'

"'Oh, don't get so huffy.'

"That was it. He left me alone. But did you know he was a fruitcake?"

I just laughed.

Well, when we got back to Pendleton, we told our story. The boys got a real charge out of it. The rest of the time we were together, someone was always yelling at Al, "My, you have hairy legs!"

But I'll tell you, when you look back thirty-five or so years, it's liberties like that one that can really give you a laugh.

Well, around the end of October we left for Korea. We were on a troopship, the USS *John Polk*.

Most of us aboard were Marines, but we also had several doggies on board. I remember that vividly, because they really gave us the business about the Corps's birthday.

It was on November 10. We were getting close to Japan when all of a sudden this announcement came over the loudspeaker.

"Now hear this, now hear this. All Marines lay below for the cutting of the cake and ice cream. Happy birthday."

The cutting of the cake and ice cream. Jeez, did those Army guys rib us about that one! They don't have traditions like that in the Army.

Shortly after the birthday, we landed in Japan. We were all given a day or so liberty, and by November of '52 the Japs were ready for the Yankee dollar. You could buy anything. It was interesting to watch the various forms of intoxication the troops would be in when they returned to the ship.

We quickly got to Korea. I was assigned to H/3 of the 1st Marines. Well, hell, my old buddy from Brooklyn, Willard T. O'Hara, was in How Company. I couldn't be happier.

The 3rd Battalion was in reserve when I joined it, due to go back in the lines the next day. The first thing I did was look up Will. When I found him, there he was, sitting on his bunk with a Black Watch cap on, drinking beer. We sat there for hours, drinking beer and bullshitting. I'd met Will through Joe Paterno's sister back in Brooklyn. We'd had some great times together.

Okay. When H went back up the next day, it was to Hill 119, on the west side of the Imjin River. The word I'd received was they didn't want the new men to do much the first few days, just observe. However, I was eager as hell. When this tech sergeant asked for volunteers, I was the first guy to say I'd go.

What he wanted was to run a telephone line from our hill over to the next one, also manned by Marines. So me and a Marine from Mississippi named C. W. Bird started out. It was raining like hell, a real shitty night. We had to stay above the trench line, not a good place to be.

We'd gone about halfway when the line snapped. The next thing I know, there are several gooks coming toward me. I don't know what to do. Should I shoot them? Or are they our gooks? Fortunately, I didn't fire. They were South Koreans, hauling up our ammunition supply. So much for my first night on the lines.

The next night they called for a clutch platoon. We're to support another platoon that is having a raid on the Chinese hill in front of us. We heard a lot of firing. Then our lieutenant gives us the word.

"Forget it, we're not going to be needed." That's it.

So I went over to the lieutenant.

"Sir, I've got a buddy out in an advanced bunker. Can I go visit him?"

"Why not? But I think you're nuts."

Out I go. It's dark as hell. I'm all alone. It's getting a little hairy. I got near the bunker where O'Hara is supposed to be. I called his name softly. No answer. So I called out again. Still no answer. Then I really let go.

"*Willard T. O'Hara!*"

"Knock it off, you asshole, get down here!"

I jumped into the bunker. There's my buddy, sitting down with all these Yobos, the South Koreans who would lug stuff for us. I'm surprised to see he's saying the rosary. What I didn't know was Will had been hit twice and a corpsman had died in his arms. Will had helped the poor guy say the Act of Contrition while he died.

"Jeez, George, what in hell are you doing here?"

"I thought I'd come out to see if you needed any help."

"Oh, for Christ's sake, George! This isn't a street fight back in the neighborhood. This is real war. You're going to get your ass shot off."

He was right. No more crazy stuff for me.

A day or two later I saw a sight that I'll never forget. It shows you how crazy things can get in combat. These two guys were coming down this hill. They were Hawkins, from South Carolina, and Mayberry, from Ohio. They were holding each other up. Both had been hit and were bleeding like stuck pigs. You could see the wounds were no joke but they weren't going to be fatal.

Jeez, these guys were singing the Marine Hymn at the top of

their lungs. Can you beat that? Maybe it was because they were probably going to be sent back to the States. It was quite a sight!

Well, that's the way it was—twenty-five or so days on the lines, back to reserve for a while, and then a return to the MLR.

I can remember one time when there was a shower set up a few hundred yards behind our line. It was great for a while, but then the chinks started to zero in on the guys going back to clean up. They hit two Marines. It became very dangerous to go back for a shower.

So we all made a bet to see who could go the longest without taking a shower. One by one we all gave up; shelling or no shelling, we made a beeline for the shower. Everyone, that is, but Jim Hilton. Oh no, not Hilton. He'd brush his teeth three or four times a day. But shower, not on your life!

Now Jim Hilton was the best combat Marine who ever walked the face of the earth. He was the biggest guy in the outfit, really tough. No one was going to try and make him hit that shower.

"Not me," he'd say. "I'm not afraid of the shelling." And he wasn't. "But I'll be a sonofabitch if I'm going to get my ass shot off just to get a shower."

When we went off the lines, he still had not showered. When he finally decided to break down, we all cheered. We even had a ceremony. Doc Dillion, our corpsman, got out his scissors and cut Hilton's longjohns off. Needless to say, Hilton won the bet hands down.

We had another guy in our squad named Marty Boyle, from Pringle, Pennsylvania. Marty was a great guy. Well, who shows up but the sergeant who had recruited Marty back in Pringle. Marty couldn't believe this.

"Oh Christ," he said to the guy, "do you remember me?"

"Sure, I recruited you back in Pennsylvania. How are you?"

"How am I? I've been freezing my nuts off. Running patrols. Getting my ass shot at. I was on Bunker Hill when it was real bad. And you want to know how it is, ya fuckhead, you?"

"Okay, buddy. I see what you mean. You've had enough. I'm going to get you transferred to a cushy job."

So the sergeant gets Marty transferred to supply. Good old Marty ends up in charge of the beer detail. You had to order the beer by the case. You'd pick it up when you went in reserve. One thing I can say, I never saw any beer up on the lines.

Well, in his new routine, Marty made sure his old squad had

plenty of beer. If a Marine had left for the States without picking up his beer, it seemed to end up with us. And once it almost ended up in disaster.

This night we were really burning down the barn. Marty had somehow thrown in an extra case. Everyone was singing and hollering, really having a sensational time. This tech sergeant, a guy we never saw on the lines, burst in on us.

"All right, you guys, knock it off. Lights out. Stop this racket!"

This really annoyed Hilton. Normally he was a quiet, unassuming guy, the kind who would always take the point on a patrol and keep his mouth shut. Not this time!

"No, Top. We get treated like men on the line. But guys like you treat us like babies when we're in reserve. Get the fuck out of our tent!"

The sergeant was livid.

"Oh, a wiseass! I'm going to write you up." And he did. Both Hilton and another guy.

A couple of days later, just before we were going back to the front, the two of them were up before Captain Carl Grey.

"Look, you two," said Grey, "go easy on the sergeant. He's been around a long time. Now go back to your unit. We're moving up." Grey was a great officer.

So, we went back in. Hill 229, Hedy, Reo, Carson, you name it, we were there. And on Hedy our squad lost some great guys.

One of them was named Ronald T. Ferguson. He was a BAR man and a good one. But you could just sense it, he was going to get hit.

We were on outpost, in front of the MLR. The Chinese decided to probe us. We were hit badly enough, but they were really after our MLR. Ronnie decided he better take the finger. We told him that would be suicide.

"Maybe so," he said, "but out there I can really rack those bastards up."

He was right. And he made it. But I remember O'Hara giving me the word.

"George, that Ferguson is a hell of a Marine. But he's going to get killed. We better get him out of here."

It was too late. The next day, Ferguson, Sergeant Smith, and Jerry Paxton must have thought we had taken the salt out of the

Chinese, because they were sitting outside of the outpost. Someone had gotten a package from home. They were splitting it up.

Well, Hedy was one outpost where you just couldn't sit outside. There was a disabled American tank in no-man's-land. The Chinese were always using it for snipers.

It wasn't the snipers that got them, though. Just two very well-placed mortar shells. It got all three.

Smith was also a good man. He'd spent most of his tour of duty behind the lines. He didn't have too much time left before he was to go home.

And Paxton was also tops. He was from West Virginia. I was showing a picture of our squad to another Marine back in Brooklyn after the war. His name was Jerry Stillman. He recognized Paxton.

"Jeez, George," he said, "that's Paxton. He went through boot camp with me. What's he doing these days?" I had to tell him that I saw Paxton get killed.

The real tragedy was Ferguson, though. He had a brother, a year or so younger than he was. His brother had also gone in the Marine Corps and was killed just before the war ended.

Ronnie's parents were divorced. I went to see his mother after the war. She was living in Huntington Beach, California. She told me that Ronnie was buried near her in California and that her other son was buried in East Liverpool, Ohio. The father took care of the son's grave in Ohio and she took care of Ronnie's.

I guess the pity of the whole thing was the waste. You had to be on your toes every minute, even if things seemed quiet.

By this time I'd made corporal. My main job was being a linesman. If the telephone lines between the hills would break, I'd go out and splice the lines. You had to do this at night or you would be a sitting duck.

Well, one night I was called into the CP by Lieutenant Brown, a very popular officer. Brown was a tremendous farter. If things would get real dull on the lines, he used to show us how he could light his farts. Truly amazing.

Anyway, Brown had some work for me. The line had broken somehow and I was to go out and splice it. This was no routine job. The chinks had been particularly active at this time.

I took off, trying to find the break. I was alone, and to tell you the truth I was nervous. There were a lot of fresh graves, which meant there had been a lot of shelling in the area. I found the break, fixed it, and started back.

Jeez, a mortar round dropped close enough to throw dirt all over me. Those Chinamen were deadly with their mortars. I was in real trouble. I spotted this bunker which I figured had some of our forward observers in it.

I jumped in, trying to remain calm.

"Hey," I said, "it's kinda cold out there. Got any hot chocolate?" Dead silence.

Then one of these FOs spoke up.

"Don't snow me, Broadhead. You just had the shit scared out of you out there."

I was really startled. Who was this guy? Then it dawned on me. It was Artie Cleary. I hadn't see him since I was twelve. He was the guy who was caught walking out of Sears, Roebuck, with a model airplane. Jeez, another guy from the neighborhood. Brooklyn was sure represented on the line.

I got back to the CP and asked if they were now getting through on the line. They were. And then I met our new captain, John Zulkofski, another great Marine.

"A little rough out there tonight, Corporal?" he said to me.

"Yeah, but nothing I can't handle."

Captain Grey, who was turning over his command to Zulkofski, then piped in.

"See what I mean, John? The fucking morale around here is great."

That's the way it was with our officers, just about all of them. Oh, when we'd get a new lieutenant, he'd frequently be an asshole for a while, then he'd realize that the troops knew a little more than he did about what was going on at the front, and he'd quiet down.

There was one time in particular when a new lieutenant was given the word, but good. I can't remember when it was, but here's what happened.

This new shavetail had just finished cleaning his .45. He started pointing it in different directions. His finger was outside the trigger guard. As he'd point it, he'd go "Bang." Finally Jim Hilton spoke up.

"Did you get him, Lieutenant?"

This pissed the lieutenant off.

He stared at Hilton.

"I *beg* your pardon."

"Look, Lieutenant, that's a .45-caliber pistol you're waving around. It can blow a man's head off."

"I'll have you know that I was on the pistol team at Annapolis."

We're trying not to laugh.

"Oh, that's good. Well, if you point it at me again, I'm going to shove it up your ass!"

"*You* are on report!"

The lieutenant the new man was replacing was a real Marine. He put his hand on the new guy's shoulder and took him aside. One of our guys could hear their conversation.

"Look," he said, "Hilton is only a PFC, but he's the best Marine in the platoon. Besides, if it gets around that you were pointing a .45 at him, you're going to be in deep trouble. Up here, we just let things like that stay within the platoon."

That was it.

Well, whenever you were on the lines, there was always the chance of getting shelled. You had to wear your flak jacket. They were great. Not only did they save lives, but they stopped many men from getting serious wounds.

We had this kid from Vermont who was really riddled with shrapnel. Without his jacket he would have definitely been killed. As it turned out, his wounds were minor. He did get a Heart, and a telegram went home to his parents. They were quite upset. I remember him saying he wished he didn't get the damn medal.

A month or so later I got hit for the first time. I was with a Marine named Kelly. He was from Boston. We were on the reverse side of this hill when a shell came over. It got us both but most of the shrapnel was absorbed by our jackets. Doc Dillion picked out the small pieces that were lodged in my leg and put bandages on the wounds. Then he started to write me up for a Heart.

"The hell with that," I said. "I don't want any telegram going home. If I am going to get a Heart, I want it to be a real wound." I think most of us felt that way. There were probably thousands of such wounds that were never reported throughout the entire American forces in Korea.

Some of the hills we would go to were a lot easier than others. Take 229, this was a quiet one. We called it Hill R-and-R. We'd spent about a month there and were scheduled to be relieved the next day. A sergeant from the Army's 25th Division had come up to see what it was like.

This guy was a short-timer. He'd already been wounded and was on edge. He'd been through some very heavy combat. It was my job to show him around.

"Sarge," I said to this guy, "this is an easy hill. You should be able to put your time in and go home. Your biggest problem will be the rats."

Just as I said this, we heard a couple of shells go off over to our left. You see, our trenches were not one continuous line across Korea. There would be spaces between the bunkers.

Well, I knew what those sounds were, but I couldn't tell the doggie. The one thing the men at the outpost didn't want was an officer checking on them. Every now and then they'd hurl a grenade or two and report rounds coming in. Naturally, the lieutenants were in no big hurry to dash through a rice paddy to get to the men if they were being shelled.

After a few minutes we heard three more rounds. This meant they were having a tough time convincing the officer to stay away. This must have done it, because we heard no more. But we had a hard job convincing the sergeant that 229 was an easy hill.

At about this time we got the word from headquarters to turn in our carbines. They said they were always jamming. Well, if you kept the carbines in a hot bunker, they would sweat, so to speak. Then, when you took them outside, they would freeze up. But if you kept them outside and didn't let them get hot, they never seemed to jam.

Besides, the carbine was easier to maneuver in the trenches than the M-1. So Captain Zulkofski told us not to turn them in, just keep them out of sight. He turned out to be a great captain, one of the best.

One time, when a group of us went down to take a shower, the captain forgot his towel. One of our guys ran out with it and gave it to him. He then put it around his neck. I spotted this. I knew he came from Long Island.

"So, Captain, we're going to Brighton Beach, maybe?"

He laughed. "Broadhead, where you from?"

"Brooklyn."

"Okay, you stay with me. You're a good man."

From then on I got along great with the captain.

Well, around the middle of June in '53, things started to heat up all along the line. Then I got the word that I was to be transferred to battalion headquarters. The hell with this. I wanted to stay with H Company. So I went to the captain.

"Captain," I said, "I've got a problem." We were in reserve, about to go to the lines. The officers had really tied one on the night before. Zulkofski was obviously hung over.

"Broadhead," he said, "as long as I'm alive you'll never have a problem. What is it?"

I told him about my transfer.

"Bullshit! You're my lineman." That was the end of it.

The next day, four of us were sent up to this forward bunker. We were to relieve the 7th Marines, who'd had a tremendous pasting. The ones who were left all had the Asiatic stare.

I've always felt the gooks knew for some time when they were going to sign the cease-fire. They were willing to lose thousands of more troops just to take all our high group.

Anyway, we went into this bunker.

"Don't stand that close to the entrance," this guy from the 7th Marines said to us. "We had two guys killed there about an hour ago." We moved.

The captain from the 7th was on the phone. "General, some men from the 1st Marines are here." Then he said, "Yes sir," and hung up.

"All right, which of you Marines are from the 1st?" No one said anything, so I said I was.

"You are to go down the hill and tell your battalion commander to stand by. There is no sense in bringing your men up here while all these artillery shells are coming in." And by this time it was really coming in. It was brutal. I stopped for a few minutes in the MLR. I have never seen since such casualties. Wounded and dead Marines were everywhere.

So I started down the hill with the artillery fire all around me, and who do I run into but Lieutenant Carlos Romano.

"George, how are you?" Jeez, you'd think we were standing on the corner of 42nd and Broadway.

"Sir, I've got to get word to the battalion telling them not to come as yet. There's too much shit flying around."

"Okay. I'll take care of my platoon. See you later."

Romano had this big mustache and chewed strong Italian tobacco. He was so popular with his troops that they all started chewing it. Quite a guy!

Well, I couldn't get to Ted Lutz. He had already taken his platoon into the lines. Eventually the whole 3rd Battalion moved in. The only thing left for the 7th was to gather up their dead and move out. It was pretty gruesome to watch those guys picking up the bodies of their buddies. Some of the corpses were in pieces. You were apt to step on a guy's foot in the trenches. Marines don't leave their dead for the rats. They got them all out.

This was on Hill 111. The other two companies of our 3rd Battalion, George and Item, were to our left on Hill 119. They had run into a hornets' nest. Both their skippers were hit. Battalion had to send a Major Robert Thurston up to merge the two companies into one command.

Thurston was very quiet, a G-3 type. Whenever you'd see him, you'd automatically throw him a salute.

Well, you know they say that some men are born to lead. Maybe so. But they are very rare. Thurston was one of these men. He seemed to be everywhere at once. The two companies had suffered about 50 percent casualties. A buddy of mine in Item Company told me about it after the war:

"That fucker was doing it all. Pulling the men together, shooting, killing, running all over the place. I can't remember how many times we repulsed those chinks. I do know that whenever they tried to overrun us, Thurston would always be in the thick of it."

Thurston was finally wounded; I think he eventually lost an arm or maybe a leg. Whatever, he became a legend in our battalion. We all felt he would get the Medal of Honor. When he ended up with just the Silver Star, we were pissed off. Hell, the guy was a one-man army!

That's the way it was the last month of the war. Constant probing and shelling by the Chinese. The American casualties were extremely heavy up and down the line. My time to be hit came shortly after midnight on July 27.

The Chinese fire was extremely heavy that night. I remember one of our guys had pulled the pin on a grenade and was about to throw it when he got hit and dropped the grenade. Horace Drake picked it up and threw it out. It had no sooner left his hand when it went off. It came back on him and messed up his face pretty badly, but did not kill him. I saw him in Tennessee after the war. They had done a great job on his face.

In the meantime our command post had lost communications with one of our platoons, about 700 yards away.

"Skipper," I said, "I can fix that fucker. I'll go out."

"Oh, for Christ sakes, Broadhead, I don't want you getting your ass blown off!"

"It won't happen. I can do it quickly. I've had a lot of practice."

So I took off. Halfway there, I saw these two Chinamen digging in. I was in a hurry, so I circumvented them.

Then I got it! The blast picked me up and threw me down. This time, without my vest, I would certainly have been killed. But my thighs and legs were really clobbered. I could still run, though, so I kept going. I found the break, spliced it, and headed back.

Oh shit! Just before I got back, a shell tore it apart.

"Great job, Broadhead, but we lost it again," I was told.

"Skipper, I'm going back. I'm going to fix that sonofabitch or die trying."

So out I went again. I found the break, fixed it, and headed back.

The skipper just laughed. "Broadhead, you're one gutsy sonofabitch! I'm going to put you in for the Navy Cross."

Later that day, the war ended.

I did get the Silver Star, which was a lot more than many guys got who'd done some very brave things.

Jim Hilton ended up with a Letter of Commendation. If you read the fuckin' thing, you would think he should have been given the bloody Medal of Honor. He now works in Washington, D.C., where he's an electrical wizard for the government. He's also a karate expert. I feel sorry for any mugger who picks out Jim for a target.

I've tried to keep track of a lot of the guys I was in the Corps with. Al Cicola is a lawyer out on Long Island. He does quite well.

The skipper, John Zulkofski, passed on a few years ago. John had built up quite a real-estate business. His wife now runs it. They had six kids.

Marty Boyle, the guy who got us the extra beer, is out in Arizona. I think he works with handicapped kids. And Willard T.

O'Hara ended up a college professor out on the West Coast. He married one of his students.

But of all the things that happened to me in Korea, the one that has stuck with me the most was watching Ferguson, Smith, and Paxton blown away in March of '53. I write a lot of poetry. One spring I penned the following:

> *In March when spring should come,*
> *But never does for some,*
> *I think of you and die. . . .*

In Memorium

Beverly, Massachusetts, is about thirty miles north of Boston. It is a beautiful town, particularly in the early fall, when the first signs of its brilliant foliage are beginning to appear. The crispness of its September weather and the brightness of its sunshine put one in mind of a Norman Rockwell painting.

In late September of 1986, the town was decked out in its festive best. A local holiday had been declared, for on this day the memory of one of her sons, Corporal Joseph Vittori, was to be honored. Vittori had been killed in action thirty-five years before, during the last Marine offensive of the Korean War. He was posthumously awarded the Congressional Medal of Honor in 1952.

I first heard about Corporal Vittori and the coming ceremony from Colonel Brooke Nihart (USMC ret.), deputy director for Marine Museums. Brooke had been Joe's battalion commander in September of '51.

He phoned me in June of '86.

"Henry," he said, "they are going to name a park after Joe Vittori up in Beverly, Massachusetts. Joe was a BAR man in F/2/1 during our fight for Hill 749. I've been asked to speak during the ceremony. Are you interested?"

"You bet I am. Name the day. I'll be there."

I was delighted to accept. Nihart is not only one of my favorite people, but he was one hell of a Marine. He served in the Pacific during World War II, and was awarded the Navy Cross during the same Korean action in which Vittori won the Medal of Honor.

Besides, I was thrilled to think a New England town would remember the heroic deeds of a young Marine during the Korean War at this late date.

I arrived in Beverly just as the ceremony started, on September 20. It was being held at the Italian-American War Veterans Hall. There were several speakers. One was Colonel Nihart. He talked about Joe and the night he had been killed. He pointed out that Joe's BAR had been greatly responsible for breaking up several Chinese counterattacks on Hill 749. Nihart did an excellent job, no flowery baloney, just an excellent job.

Next came the parade. It was a typical American affair, more a pleasant stroll through the center of town than a military march. There was a good deal of hand-clapping as a platoon or so of Marine Korean War veterans marched by. They were out of step. Thirty-five years is a long time. The young men who had fought in Korea were now pushing sixty.

After the parade, everyone went to a small but well-kept park that housed a Little League baseball field. There were more speeches as they dedicated the park to Joe. It was here that I got a chance to talk to several of Joe's buddies.

One of them was named Bill Wickers. He had known Vittori since their days at Brown Grammar School. Bill had also been a Marine, serving with H/3/1 at the Chosin Reservoir. To Bill, Joe was, above all, a great human being.

"He was about six feet, built like a piece of iron," Bill remembered, "loved sports, particularly football. Joe had gotten strong working on his dad's farm. But he also had a great sense of humor. I remember one morning when I was over at the farm. Joey was milking the cows.

"'Bill,' he said, 'did ya ever see the five-pointed star on a cow's tit?'

"'No,' I answered, 'didn't know they had one.'

"'Lean over, ya gotta look real close.'

"So I stuck my face down near the teat. Wham, Joey squeezed and I got about a half a quart of milk in my face. He was always doing things like that."

We were soon joined by two or three other friends of Joe. They painted a great picture of him, but it soon became evident that Joe Vittori had been no goody-goody.

"Don't get us wrong," one said. "Joe could drink his beer with the best of 'em." The others responded with laughter.

"Yeah, and he'd chase a little tail like the rest of us." More laughter and nodding of heads in agreement.

Someone started a story about Joe's swimming a river in the eternal quest of all young Marines, but he was quickly told to knock it off. Joe had heard there was something to be had on the other side.

"No details, no details," another friend of Joe's said, and that was it.

I had already gotten what I needed anyway. In many ways, Joe was no different from his fellow Marines, except in battle. The story of Joe in combat at Hill 749 was told to me by Colonel Nihart.

"When I took over the battalion [in August 1951]," the colonel said, "I asked who were the real producers, the ones you could always count on if things got rough. They told me about Joe.

"'Vittori,' they said, 'is one of the best BAR men in the Corps. He's recently returned from the hospital, went there to get a wound patched up. We wanted to make him a fire team leader, but he'd have no part of it. He wanted his BAR back. We told him okay. So he went looking for his BAR.

"'It seemed the Marine we'd given it to had let it go to hell. There was rust in the barrel, grit all over it. It was a mess. Joe took one look at it and blew his stack. He cold-cocked the guy and took back his BAR. That's the kinda of guy Vittori is.'

"That was enough for me," said Nihart. "I knew Fox Company had one hell of a BAR man.

"About a month later we went on the attack. We were headed for Hill 749. The North Koreans were fighting for every foot of ground. It was brutal.

"We finally took the place and set up our defense on a ridgeline several hundred yards forward of 749. We knew the NKPA were going to try and take the hill back.

"Our main defense was two light machine guns, fairly close together, backed up by two heavy machine guns. We had our riflemen all around them.

"That's where Joe comes in. His BAR was to see that no Koreans would sneak up and heave a hand grenade at the machine guns. Joe could move around easily with the BAR and let go a burst if he saw anything moving near the guns. Those machine guns could lay down a field of fire that could keep the mass of the enemy away, but you had to keep a sharp eye out for those who broke through. It would only take one or two of them to put those guns out of action.

"Joe seemed to be everywhere at once all night long, popping out of this hole and that hole. He went back for more ammunition under tremendous fire several times. He seemed to lead a charmed life. As Joe moved from place to place, he'd tell other Marines where they were needed. If there was ever a natural leader, it was Joe.

"The sad part is that he was killed just before the last assault was repulsed. A few more minutes and he would have been home scot-free.

"The next morning, Joe's name was on everybody's lips. The story of what he'd done was making the rounds.

"'Did you hear what Vittori did last night?' one Marine told me. 'When some North Koreans broke through over on the left, he grabbed a couple of our guys and threw those gooks the hell out of there.'

"I went over to his body," continued Nihart, "and about ten yards forward of Joe there was a dead North Korean sergeant. The fellow had a pistol in one hand and a hand grenade in the other. He'd obviously been hit by a BAR. Joe must have got him just as he was going to throw a grenade at our machine gunners.

"As I went to pick up the pistol the dead sergeant had in his hand, I heard this guy yell at me, 'No, no, Colonel, booby trap, booby trap!'

"Well, how in the hell could anyone booby-trap a body that close to our lines, with the amount of lead that had been flying around?

"I picked up the guy's pistol and stuck it in my pack.

"Now, did you ever see those pistols they'd use in burlesque shows? The comic would pull the trigger and a cloth would stick out of the barrel with BANG written on it? Well, the dead guy's pistol had a little North Korean flag hanging from its barrel, only it didn't say BANG. It shot real bullets. I have the pistol here at our museum."

Jake Petronzio joined us at this point. Jake was a sergeant during the Korean War. He stayed in the Corps after the war ended, got a commission, and retired as a captain ten years ago. Jake was in charge of the ceremony. He was nodding his head in agreement.

"That's right, Colonel," he said, "I saw that sergeant. Most of his squad had been cut down around him. Joe must have died hard."

"He surely did. Of course, I put him up for the Medal of Honor. No one earned that medal more than Joe did.

"There were others, though. A man named Corporal Blassingame. He was a big, good-looking Marine, a section leader on the heavy machine guns, the Browning water-cooled, Model 1917. Blassingame kept those guns going all night. He did a great job.

"A day or two later we got the word from the 8th Army to put a man up for the Army's DSC. I put forward the name of Blassingame. I don't know if he ever got the medal. He should have, and I hope he did."

Well, we ended up back at the Italian-American Club, where we were given a luncheon and a beer or two. There was more talk about Joe. As I left the club, I tried to put together what I had heard.

Most Marines, frightened or not, usually act well in combat, well but certainly not heroically. There are the rare exceptions, men who seem to thrive in a battle. They are the take-charge guys, the men who, even in the organized—or disorganized—mayhem of a firefight, always seem to know what they are doing. They are frequently killed, and most of the time their deeds go unsung. But in Vittori's case this was impossible. Too many Marines knew what he was doing. He played a very big part in holding Hill 749, and everyone seemed to have known that he had done this.

Brooke Nihart is another one of these men. He is actually very modest and quite scholarly. I knew him for six or seven years before I found out about his Navy Cross, and that he had been in command of 2/1 at 749 for the three days in September of 1951 when it was a raging inferno. It was his daughter, Kathy, who told me about it. The colonel made all the right moves. I am sure that if 749 had fallen, Nihart would not be with us today.

The Drive Home

It is about 200 miles from Beverly to southern Connecticut. I spent the entire drive dwelling on the Korean War Marines. It was a thoughtful three or four hours.

I thought of what bad shape their Corps had been in when the war started and how quickly they had put together a brigade for Pusan and a division for Inchon. Then, when they thought the war was over, they were sent to Hungnam, in North Korea, to start their march to the Chosin Reservoir and the subsequent retreat back to the sea—a retreat under which living conditions were inconceivably harsh.

From Hungnam it was back to Pusan, where they would have to start all over again, and they did just that. Now names such as Wonju, the Punchbowl, Luke the Gook's Castle, and Horseshoe Ridge became part of Marine Corps lore. There was another Chinese offensive, which was stopped cold, and the long, drawn-out peace talks started.

A year after Inchon, the last Marine Corps offensive began, but it soon ground to a halt. There was another winter in Korea as the war of movement turned into a war of positioning.

The following spring, the entire 1st Marine Division was moved from the east coast over to the west coast, to the gates of Seoul. Here they would sit under World War I conditions. This was the stagnant period of the Korean War, the period of nightly patrolling, ingoing and outgoing shelling, and always the weekly casualty lists.

The Armistice was finally signed, and the killing stopped. The United Nations had not succeeded in uniting the two Koreas, but that was not what they had gone there to do. They had gone there to throw the North Koreans out of South Korea, and in this they were completely successful. It was the United Nations' finest hour.

And what of the United States Marine Corps? What did it gain for the loss of a man such as Joe Vittori and its thousands of other casualties, in addition to the time-honored phrase, "job well done"?

Well, one never hears Harry Truman's term "the Navy's police force" any longer. The Marine Commandant is a full member of the Joint Chiefs of Staff. The Corps has three full divisions and a fourth in active reserve. It has 200,000 men on active duty, which, according to its former Commandant, General P.X. Kelly, makes it larger than the British Army. It may have paid a dreadful price, but it is now a vital part of its country's defense, and will remain so for a long, long time.

Finis

Jerry Hotchkiss (G/3/1) was a young second lieutenant on the lines when the fighting stopped. Six months or so later he was sent home. There was a middle-aged woman sitting next to Jerry on the airplane that took him from San Francisco to New York. She introduced herself and started a conversation.

"Going home?" she asked.

"Yes, I am."

"Where are you coming from?"

"Korea."

"Korea? Do we still have troops there?"

Hotchkiss laughed as he told me this.

"I wonder what she thinks now—if she's still alive, that is. Here it is, thirty-five years later, and we *still* have troops there."

Index